BILL TAN

AN ORDINARY OLYMPIAN

BUT WHAT A LIFE

Printed by Leiston Press

Bill Tancred

An Ordinary Olympian But What A Life

British Library Cataloguing in Publication Data

A catalogue record for this book is available from the British Library.

ISBN 978-1-911311-13-3

(Cover by Getty Images)

Printed by Leiston Press, Masterlord Ind Est,

Leiston, Suffolk IP16 4JD

01728 833003

www.leistonpress.com

To Angela, Nicola, Andrea and Joanna and to the rest of my family, my friends and the athletics public who have supported me throughout the journey of life – Thank you.

Special thanks to my daughter Nicola who has worked tirelessly in the production of this book.

Photographs

While every effort has been made to trace and acknowledge all copyright holders, I would like to apologise should there be any errors or omissions.

Bill Tancred

William Raymond `Bill` Tancred (born 6 August 1942) is a leading sports administrator, academic and former international athlete. He competed at the 1968 and 1972 Summer Olympics in the discus and won bronze and silver medals in successive Commonwealth Games from 1970 to 1974. He was the British National discus champion on seven occasions and held the British record for 25 years his personal best being 64.94m in 1974. On competitive retirement, he became coach to the British Amateur Athletics Board and to the International Amateur Athletics Federation.

Bill Tancred was born in Quetta, Baluchistan, India and grew up in Felixstowe and Ipswich before retiring to Felixstowe in 2014.

He was a former regular soldier with the Ist East Anglian regiment and the Royal Army Physical Training Corps. After military service in Aden and at the Royal Military Academy, Sandhurst he attended Loughborough College and the University including West Virginia University, USA the latter on a NATO Fellowship. As an academic he has taught in schools, polytechnics and universities and among his many positions was for a long time the Director of Physical Education and Sport at Sheffield University as well as being Professor of Sports Studies at Buckinghamshire Chilterns University College and the Director of Sport at University Campus Suffolk.

Bill is published author having written a number of books as well as many articles in journals and newspapers. He has also presented papers at conferences in subjects relating to human sports performance, health related fitness and coaching.

During his career he has served on numerous sports committees to include the Olympians, England Athletics (East) Council, Healthy Ambitions Suffolk, Chair of Suffolk Sport and the Chair to the International Athletes` Club. Currently he is Patron to Inspire Suffolk, President of Suffolk Sport and Visiting Professor of Sports and Exercise Science at the University of Suffolk.

CONTENTS

1. MY EARLY DAYS LIVING IN INDIA

I was born on the 6 August 1942 in Quetta, Baluchistan in British India before independence partitioned the subcontinent into India and Pakistan. My parents christened me William Raymond Tancred and I took the forename from my mother's father, Major William Donovan who had served in the Indian Army Service Corps.

When I was born, my father Adrian was serving in the Baluchistan Police and it was in Quetta that my mother Elsie met and married my father. I was the eldest sibling followed my sister Maureen, brothers Geoffrey and Peter. Anita, another sister, was born in Ipswich, Suffolk in the early sixties.

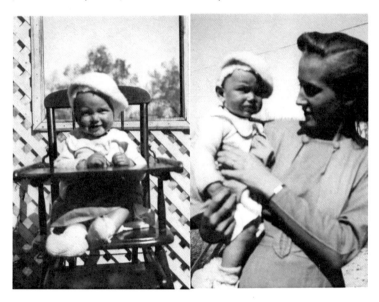

6 months old William   My mother and I in Quetta

Fashioned by a disciplined Police life similar to the Army, my father was a disciplinarian. He had no time for `lazy` individuals and acted with authority. A man of quicksilver moods, he could be charming and combustible within seconds like turning on and off a switch. Tall, good looking with a Clark Gable persona he could charm most people. What he had in abundance was confidence. He would often say to me `failure is not in the family motto`! I absorbed a great many of his values and his ambition for me.

My mother on the other hand was a warm, maternal and calm character, who

1

could be dependably optimistic in difficult situations. She had a philosophy believing things would work out in the end, so told us not to worry. On the other hand, my father would shake his head in disbelief!

It was my father who introduced me to taking up sport as he himself was a good all-round sportsman. His first love was athletics particularly the decathlon in which the discus and javelin were his stronger events. He also excelled as a good club hockey player and boxed occasionally in minor competitions.

My little Indian friends after a game of gilli-danda- the balloon is for the best player!

My first introduction to sport was playing a game with my little Indian boyfriends called gilli-danda. The game itself is played with two sticks: a large one called danda, which is used to hit a smaller one the gilli, which was chiselled to a point at both ends. The game is closely related to cricket and no wonder that India and Pakistan have good international cricket teams, because it developed wonderful hand-eye coordination. We would also have contests to see how far we could throw a cricket ball and I always managed to beat my friends, including the older boys. Such an early introduction to throwing would prove to be most beneficial to me in my athletics career in England.

Brother Geoff, myself with Indian seller of fruit.

We lived in Gymkhana Road in Quetta next to the racecourse. I would go there at every opportunity as it was exhilarating to watch the jockeys with their wonderful coloured tunics and beautiful horses getting ready to race. Although not old enough to gamble, I would often mix with the punters and note their faces in times of winning and losing. It was a great education for I have never gambled large amounts of money in all my life. However, going to the races was full of excitement, colour and had a special atmosphere.

A hunting party with my father at the back with his hat on, Mum is in the middle with me and my sister Maureen, in the front.

On days when there was no racing, I would spend time with the other Indian boys playing on the railway lines. We would see all the steam trains go by and try to identify all the different types using these lines. However, on occasions we would place coins on the railway lines to see them being squashed when the trains went over them. There would be absolute delight amongst us in seeing the coins crushed to powder! What If my parents knew? Such danger, but it was very exciting to say the least.

Playing outdoors was a way of life for me as in addition to the above, we would climb trees, watch different types of birds such as black kites, white eyed buzzards and vultures. However, I do remember on one day whilst playing outdoors, I was bitten by a dog on my calf and was bandaged up by a play mate`s mother. On returning home my parents on seeing my bleeding leg and poor bandage application, insisted a hospital visit was urgent. Furthermore, in the district there was an outbreak of rabies and on reporting to my father that the dog in question was wild looking and had red eyes, this incident had to be taken seriously. Luckily all was well but I was `grounded` for a few days to help the leg to heal.

By playing with my Indian friends, it enabled me to become proficient in speaking excellent Urdo, so much so that I could understand every word that my parents were saying although they thought it was a secret code between the two of them! Looking back it is a shame that by coming to England, I did not continue to speak this language on a regular basis and over time, forgot most of the words.

Brothers` Geoff, Peter and sister Maureen, with myself at the back with Mum and Dad, prior to leaving India to the UK in 1949. Dad is looking rather stern.

4

In 1947, India wanted their Independence and politically, it was becoming a bit of a `hotbed`. My father being in the Baluchistan Police was concerned for the family's safety, as was my grandmother Elsie in Felixstowe, Suffolk. There were reasons to be concerned because I remember one night when the family had to evacuate our house very quickly as mobs of Muslims versus Hindu-Sikhs were on the rampage. It meant that my family having to sleep in a ditch several yards away from the comfort of our house. It was a long night and looking back, my mother had to be very maternal especially as all the children were very young and frightened. Luckily, everything was back to normal the next day but decisions had to be made by my parents on the question on when to return to England?

It was also at this time that I can vividly remember all the banners, flags and posters in the streets in Quetta awaiting the arrival in India of the last Viceroy of India, Lord Mountbatten who was officially the Head of the British Administration in India. He was charged with overseeing the transition of British India to Independence.

As Independence neared, the Country began to descend towards sectarian civil war. When the decision in favour of partition was made, the parties next faced this nearly impossible task of fixing borders between the new states. In August 1947, India gained its independence from the British Raj. The Northern, predominately Muslim sector of India became the nation of Pakistan, while the southern and majority Hindu sectors became the Republic of India.

It was also at this time, that many American troops were pulling out of Quetta via the railway and we as young boys would wave to them in a friendly manner. They too returned the compliments and in addition, threw out dozens of food tins and chewing gum, the latter tasted sweet and were long lasting! We had never seen or chewed such delight. When the last trains stopped going by, we were very sad as we did not want them to go and more importantly, lost our daily chewing gum ration!

Myself with the balloon, my sister Maureen,
my brother Geoff and my Mum in Quetta

My days of playing in the Indian and now Pakistan sun were coming to an end as the family decided to relocate to England and specially to Felixstowe in Suffolk where my grandmother from my mother's side lived with her older children. It was hard for me to say goodbye to all my Indian friends and some of their families as I had built a wonderful relationship with them all. As a gesture of our friendship one of the father's took us on Tonga rides which was a light carriage drawn by a horse and was a popular mode of travel. They were fun to ride in and cheaper to run compared with an automobile. Having such pleasure, resulted in us visiting the nearby villages and watch the ladies and men cook wonderful bread, chapattis and curries.

Many farewell parties were organized by my parents and their many friends. It was an exciting time with our two loyal servants helping to organize and look after myself, my brother Geoffrey and sister Maureen. Gommersal our male servant, was a wonderful man who not only cared for me but got himself involved in my many activities such as bird watching and riding bicycles. He was visibly moved by our intended departure for a new life in England. I often thought about him when I was growing up. Where did he go, who's servant had he become, did he live a long life? It was not my decision to leave but of my parents who were worried about the internal politics and safety of their children.

6

When it was time to leave, my father would stay in Quetta for 3 months, so my poor mother took responsibility for looking after four of her children, me being 7 years old and Peter the youngest, a mere 5 months old. This involved a few weeks on board ship from Karachi to London, so it was a hard task for her considering my adventurous spirit as a young and energetic boy.

P and O Chitral (Reproduced by kind permission of P & O Heritage Collection).

The Ship that transported us was called the Chitral which was launched in 1925 and served in World War 2 as a troopship and was eventually scrapped in 1953. On leaving Karachi on this ship, I could vividly see my father's yellow shirt getting smaller and smaller as we were waving goodbye to one another. Soon it was pastures new for my family minus my Dad.

What a wonderful journey on board this ship! It was to go through the Suez Canal, stop at Port Said in Egypt, travel through the Mediterranean, stop in Gibraltar, travel through the tumultuous Bay of Biscay and finally to London.

I soon made a couple of friends on board and decided to explore the ship, not at the top but right below the deck along the luggage compartment. It was great fun hiding from each other not knowing that at any time, this section of the boat would be locked for some time on the journey. Boys will be boys!

My parents' wedding in 1941.   My father in his Baluchistan`s Police Uniform.

Another excitement was that the ship was going to travel through the Red Sea and I had never experienced a red coloured sea before. Can you imagine as a young boy the disappointment that I had when there was no red sea apart from its name. The Red Sea is the extension (or inlet) of the Indian Ocean, located between Africa and Asia. The entrance to the sea in the south is through the Gulf of Aden and the somewhat narrow Babel Mandeb (Strait). I never thought that I would be back in Aden serving as an infantry soldier with the 1st East Anglian regiment in January 1964, some 25 years later on. It was also here that I saw so many dolphins bopping up and down swimming along our boat for a few miles. I am not sure whether the boys on the boat or the dolphins themselves, enjoyed this spectacle the most!

From the Red Sea, the Chitral travelled through the Suez Canal, a marvellous engineering feat. It is an artificial sea-level waterway connecting the Mediterranean Sea to the Red Sea through the isthmus of Suez and is single-lane.

The passengers were now awaiting our arrival in Port Said in the anticipation of buying or better still, bartering for goods. As we docked the merchandise sellers in `bum boats`, quickly came along the boat. There were probably 20-30 of these little boats all of them fully loaded with various goods, including as far as I can remember hats and leather bags. Soon everyone was in the selling and buying mode and it was fascinating to see the merchandise being hauled up onto the ship in a basket where it was viewed by the prospective buyer and then bartering undertaken. I too got into the action but wanted my favourite chewing gum, so I ordered a few packets but the sellers were not happy that I sent only my treasured three -penny bit coin for this order! I could not wait for the ship to leave as the 2 men in the boat wanted to come aboard as they were furious. My excuse was my inexperience in dealing with such adult matters!

We then sailed through the wonderful Mediterranean Sea before stopping at Gibraltar. Gibraltar is the British overseas territory located on the southern end of the Iberian Peninsula. We spent some time on the `Rock` to visit and of course seeing the mischievous monkeys called `Barbary Macaques`, considered even today by many to be the top attraction in Gibraltar. As far as I can remember, we were told that they were used to human interaction but I was not sure personally as they looked menacing!

After leaving Gibraltar, the boat headed to the Bay of Biscay (lying along the Western coast of France) and we were told by the shipping crew to expect some rough seas. They were right in their forecast as the boat tossed from side to side and many passengers were sea-sick. Some of the fiercest weather conditions of the Atlantic can be witnessed in the Bay of Biscay and the area is home to large storms during the winter months and we were on board in the latter part of February 1950! Soon we were heading for London and thinking of a new life ahead in cold England.

LIFE IN FELIXSTOWE, SUFFOLK IN THE 1950`S

The Chitral docked on the 2 March 1950 and we were greeted by my Uncle Arthur and Auntie Oriel, who had also lived in India in their youth whilst their father (My grandfather) had served in the Indian Army Service Corps. On leaving the ship, we travelled to Liverpool Street station and had another 2/3 hours journey to stay at our grandmother`s house in Chepstow road, Felixstowe.

It was strange to see the houses all packed together with limited space to play. Houses were smaller and were certainly overcrowded in inner-city areas.

This was our abode for several months until my father arrived from India, so my grandmother must have been `shell shocked` to have so many children around her in the semi-detached house at Chepstow road

My first bed was shared with my Uncle Will who was on leave from the Royal Navy. He was fun and as I soon awoke from what I thought was a long sleep, he showed me his vast collection of coins which he had saved from his naval trips abroad. He then introduced me to his match box collection which was a delight to see and soon I got the `bug` in collecting my own personal match boxes. The other early fascination was his collection of naval cap badges such as HMS Collingwood, Dryad, Raleigh, Ganges and The Royal Yacht Britannia. Seeing all these naval memorabilia was a great advert to join the Royal Navy but the Army had the greater influence on me to join later on when I was 18 years old. Things were not the same for me when his leave ended and he had to return to naval duties. His party trick was to jump over his Mother`s front fence with ease and this athletic feat was most impressive to us. It was only years later as we got bigger and more athletic, we thought how easy it was to do it ourselves!

Myself and my uncle Will outside our house in Cobbold Road, Felixstowe

Felixstowe is an Edwardian seaside town and civil parish between the river Orwell and river Deben on the North Sea coast of Suffolk. It had and still has beautiful gardens and the Spa Pavilion which was used mainly by those financially well off holiday makers who in the 1950's could afford to go. We and many locals did not have the money then to enjoy the luxury of tea and cakes. The Port of Felixstowe, which in my time was small and catered for ships carrying Carlsberg beer, timber, wheat and maize. Today the Dock is the largest container port in the UK.

It did not take me long to make acquaintances as everyone wanted to be friends with the arrival of the little `Indian` boy. These early friends included Jimmy Green who lived in the same road, Graham Vine, Michael Ware, John Cousins, Chris Davison and Keith Adams, all of them enjoying sport. All but one, remain my friends to this day.

When my father arrived in England we moved to 8 Cobbold Road in Felixstowe close to the wonderful seaside. It was opposite to perhaps the most striking building on the front called Harvest House. Originally built as the Felix Hotel, it became Fisons headquarters (a pharmaceutical and horticultural chemicals company) and today, it has been converted to apartments for residents of retirement age, many with fabulous views over Felixstowe's north sea.

School trip 25 June 1953 to Regent Park Zoo in London.
Back row with tie undone is yours truly!

11

Coming to England was certainly a culture shock to my father. Food in India had been plentiful, despite the wartime conditions. In austere, ration-strapped post-war England, it was a vastly different story. Our weekly meat ration permitted one shilling and two-penny's worth of meat per adult, so it was a major treat to have real meat. Butter was unobtainable and margarine scarce with dripping being the common substitute. Fresh fruit was only available during the summer and those families lucky to have a garden nurtured their own apples, plums and pears. Any uneaten fruit to include blackberries were bottled and bananas were unheard of. I remember seeing the first one being eaten by a boy with the skin still on and not peeled!

Coal was in short supply and my father and I would frequently `tour` the beach in search of coal being washed up. There is still coal today that is washed up on the beach after a stormy night. Since clothing was rationed, `hand-me-downs` were the order of the day. My favourite Uncle Will would promise me some of his worn out shirts and coat when he had no use for them. I must have looked a sight wearing clothes that were for a man and not a boy. When our shoes wore down, we either used metal studs (Blakeys) on the heels of the shoe or in many instances, placed cardboard in the shoe itself!

My father had difficulty finding a job at first and he was always at home `directing` odd job duties especially, for me being the eldest, so I had to grow up fast. For example, I was the lead in tidying and dusting of our rooms which was inspected by him on each Saturday morning. If not to the required standard, it was done again to please him. I remember one `inspection` when I was 10 years of age when the fault he found was the dust on top of the door! I was not tall enough to reach it in the first place but he was determined to stop me playing out with my friends. Beds was also made daily and completed before 8am each day. This type of regimented order would prove to be of huge benefit to me when I joined up in the Army!

Obviously, he seemed unsettled and unhappy with his new surround. Number 8 Cobbold road was cold especially when the cold east wind would appear and I and my two brothers would share one bedroom but with only two beds. We took it in turns to sleep two in a bed. Our bedroom floor was covered in linoleum. In winter time, it would be absolutely freezing, so you devised a system of somehow getting under the blankets straight into your clothes, without touching the lino, otherwise your bare feet would be left there freezing. We did however had the luxury of corona bottles filled with hot water as a substitute for hot water bottles!

My mother had no drying facilities, apart from a clothes-horse which would be draped in front of the coal fire. The steam and mist from the damp clothes, allied with the smoke from our fire which never drew properly, would make us all choke the second we entered the room. This was our house in the 1950's which I thought was normal for everyone in Felixstowe at the time. However, thinking about this now it makes it sound more like the 1850's. Looking back if anyone asked me what it was like living in these conditions I would have said it was a jolly good childhood and living by the sea was a plus.

Luckily for us we did have the beach to visit every day and my father with Peter would play against myself and my brother Geoffrey, under floodlights (the lamps) on the promenade nearly every night in the winter months for at least an hour. This was great fun. We use to run across the breakwaters in the sand and of course this built up our fitness and conditioning. In the summer months, it was swimming or athletics training under the watchful eye of our instructing father.

The one thing that we loved to do as well, was to see who could throw the stone pebbles from the beach the furthest? At first, my Dad would win but soon I was beating him, a result of practicing at every available opportunity. I would throw into a wind, with the wind and aiming at targets, which were generally washed up tin cans. I loved the thrill of hitting these tins with accuracy.

When we were hungry, after our energetic exploits, my mother and sister Maureen would bring the cooked curry to the beach nearly twice a week in the summer months. The smell soon attracted favourable comments from the visiting tourists, so it was a family comment that we, the Tancred's were the first to use the phrase `takeaways curries`!

At times my father was very strict and I used to frequently visit some `motherly helpers` at the Barnardo's House at the bottom of Bath road not far from where I lived. The friendship was developed from my delivery of newspapers to them. Kindly, cups of tea with few biscuits were served in an atmosphere of caring and calmness, completely different from my house on certain days. I did ask them on several occasions could I become a Dr Barnardo's boy. This was refused as I already had a mother and father!

I used to roam and play in the gardens near the present Spa Pavilion with the many friends especially Graham Vine. On occasions we were given a `dressing` down by the local policeman, a certain PC 'Gunboat` Meadows. He put the fear into us and we would never do anything wrong if he was about. What a field day he would have today.

Outside our house in Cobbold road, I would chalk three stumps on the walls of Harvest house opposite. With daily practice, I soon became accurate in my bowling and the great shame in hindsight, is that it was not 22 yards away but much shorter. This accuracy sadly did not transfer to the correct sized- pitch, otherwise I believe I would have become a first class bowler in cricket.

EAST SUFFOLK COUNTY EDUCATION COMMITTEE

SWIMMING CERTIFICATE
440 YARDS

THIS IS TO CERTIFY THAT

WILLIAM TANCRED

OF Felixstowe County Modern SCHOOL

HAS SATISFIED THE EXAMINER BY SWIMMING 440 YARDS USING RECOGNISED STROKES.

Date 20.7.1955.

Organiser of Physical Education.

A certificate for swimming in the North Sea, Felixstowe. No swimming pools in 1955!

Slowly throughout the 1950's, families around us installed electric immersion heaters in their water tanks, which provided reliable hot water. They put extra plugs in the rooms, so electric fires could be plugged in. The more affluent acquired a fridge, a phone and a TV. We never had any of these things, until the 1960's. In 1953, for the Coronation, there was one local family with a TV, so all the Tancred's paid a visit to see it in black and white the event of the day. However, we did have a radio which was our main source of entertainment for most families of the 1950's. I used to stay up with my father listening to all the boxing world title fights that took place in the USA, such as Sugar Ray Robinson versus Randolph Turpin, Don Cockell versus the great Rocky Marciano and a host of other boxing matches. My father also took me on my first trip to London, not only to see the sights but to shake hands with a boxer called Len Harvey who at the time was running a pub. Len was of course a former British boxing champion at 3 different weights.

1953 was also a time of the terrible floods that hit Felixstowe badly. On the 31 January 1953, freak winds drove a storm surge down the North Sea. By evening

14

this had reached the east coast of England where sea defences were over-topped and damaged by the waves. Memories of the deaths (41) and severe destruction caused by the 1953 floods remain as strong as ever. As a 10 year old boy, I remember excitedly getting up early to see the immense damage on the promenade and the flooding around Langer Road Park. Bloated dead cows were floating on the flooded park and the beach was strewn with debris and a badly damaged £1 note, luckily with the numbers still intact which my father lost no time in confiscating!

The most enjoyable activity for Felixstowe children in the 1950's was the ABC Minors, the cinema show for children held every Saturday morning at the now Palace Miniplex Cinema in Crescent Road costing an entry fee of 6 pence. I can still partly sing the song that we all used to shout out at the top of our voices if memory serves me right.

We are the boys and girls of the ABC

And every Saturday we line up to see

The films we joke and shout about with glee

We like to laugh and have our sing song

Such a happy crowd are we...eeee....

We're all pals together

We are the boys and girls of the ABC.....

We watched cartoons, short films and then the real picture which was usually an absorbing serial, mostly cowboys and Indians or cops and robbers with lots of chases and escapes, the 'baddies' always losing. At the commencement of the show, there were announcements and invitations to the youngsters whose birthday it was to come on stage. On the stage they were greeted with huge cheers and given a small present. Often we spotted the same youngsters coming up every week to get their birthday present. My brother Geoffrey had a birthday every month! Many times the audience shouted, "Get off the stage, you had

15

your birthday last Saturday!"

It was an absolute delight in seeing films such as Laurel and Hardy, the Bowery boys,` Flash` Gordon, the Three Stooges, Just William and Abbot and Costello. What laughter, the whole of the Felixstowe cinema joyously laughing in harmony. I cannot think of anything these days that would give children the same sense of camaraderie as those Saturday morning pictures. Missing one was unthinkable!

Every Easter Charles Manning on the sea front would open up his seaside attractions to all the local children for free. I suppose looking back it was one way to check that all the rides and equipment were in good working order and safe to use. This reasoning did not occur at the time because the whole place was `jam packed` with kids screaming and shouting with sheer enjoyment. So Easter was always a lovely time for the local school children in Felixstowe.

Playing marbles was equally enjoyable for me as fortunately, I never had to buy one because I always won and so my pockets were always full on returning home. Frequently, holes in my pockets occurred due to the number of marbles won and carried. Looking back now, all I started with was a couple of ball-bearings which Jimmy Green and I managed to swap. No pocket money for me in those days so from a young age I learnt to survive on my wits and athletic prowess.

The other game I excelled at was conkers. We used to challenge each other with ferocious conker competitions during play time at school or outside the school gates, where many boys would be in action. Some boys also baked their conkers to make them firm and hard, so these conker competitions were very competitive. Having an oven was the key to many successes however.

My first school was Causton Junior School and I soon made many life-long friends as a result of playing sport. In fact, both the headmaster Mr Pryke and my form master Mr Stocker loved cricket, the latter also inspired us with his stories of the Bomber Command in World War 2. Little was done in terms of academic development so the forthcoming 11 + was going to end in failure for many of the boys. In India, I had excelled in my primary school and on my arrival in England aged 8, I knew all my tables both backwards and forwards.

My school in India was a private one and my general knowledge was more advanced than my peers in England at the time. I do wonder if this is the reason that so many English Ex-pats of my age who returned to the UK in the late 40`s have achieved so much in life. Now in my new environment, academic work was at a standstill and this continued into my secondary education. Many of my school friends today feel that the education system badly let them down. Angela my wife, six years my junior had a totally different educational experience attending one of the first Comprehensive schools built in 1956 (Colfox in Bridport, Dorset).

Causton Primary School class.   In the middle of the third back row wearing a tie and white jumper is me!

In my secondary school many of the male teachers had recently come out of the Forces, having done short term teacher training courses which were made simpler and quicker after the War to encourage men into the teaching profession. Most of them seemed to have passed few exams themselves, judging by the lack of any letters after their names on the speech day programmes.

However, there were some good, enthusiastic teachers whose lessons I grew to love in such subjects as history, geography and physical education. The one teacher everyone feared was a Mr Orford or `Bunny` to us and he taught maths. If he disliked you, you would be made to sit at the front, so he could watch you, a position I frequently took up!

I spent about four long, deadly boring years in metalwork and woodwork, subjects which I was useless at and to me, a waste of time. However, I did enjoy the working the bellow so that the fire was not extinguished! It was great

17

exercise for a young boy who wanted to develop muscles.

On one occasion, we all had to do a project set by Mr Cooke the Metalwork teacher and I decided to make my own discus, as throwing implements were expensive to buy. All the boys in the class wanted to help as this was a most unusual project to say the least. I made the metal ring, a few others planed the inside of the wood shaped like a discus whilst someone was experimenting with the lead weight it go in the middle. It was in great anticipation that I went to throw it for the first time on the school playing fields watched by all the helpers and a few of the admiring girls. After two attempts, the discus broke up in pieces, so it was back to the metalwork room and start again. I never did use the completed one for any competitions as it was a talking point for my father to show this hand- made discus amusingly to his friends. Soon after this, my father managed to find a rubber discus with which to practice and which did not break up on landing.

It was in Physical Education and Sport that my life -long friends were made. Jimmy Green, Chris Davison, Derek Dockery, John Cousins and Felix Newsom were regular members of the football and cricket teams. We had fun and as a team, won most of our inter-school competitions. One fixture stands out for me in those early days. Our PE master Mr Westhorpe, organised in his words a `plum` fixture at a private school called St. Felix. We set about this prized fixture with an attack against the startled defenders of this school and within 15 minutes the score was 5 - 0 to us. At half time, the score increased to 9-0. We were very pleased to go in with this lead and expected to be congratulated by Mr Westhorpe on our performance. He was very upset to say the least and said, `If you carry on playing this way, you will lose the fixture and the post- match cakes and tea next season`. We carried on playing like we did in the first half and finished the game 14- 0. We thought we had done really well but Mr Westhorpe was right, we lost the fixture the following year. On reflection, we should not have made such a score because cakes were such a rarity in the mid-fifties and indeed a great loss to our deprived team. A great win but a sad day.

In cricket we were a force in the county schools and many of the players went on to play regularly for Felixstowe and the surrounding towns in the County. I played a good standard county schoolboy cricket and had I concentrated on this sport, perhaps would have reached a high level. All the boys were never coached here in Felixstowe and I am sure many of the school friends mentioned above would have done really well had they been exposed to effective coaching.

In addition to representing the school in cricket and football teams, I started to shine in the shot, discus and javelin athletics events. I took part in the Suffolk County championships at the newly opened Coronation ground on the 1 May 1956 in front of the HRH the Duke of Edinburgh in the discus event. I progressed from here to compete in the Southampton All-England School Championships in 1957 but this time in the shot put event. The championships spread over two days, officiated by a huge number of timekeepers, judges, and marshals. Most of them were volunteer teachers and locals who were fanatical supporters of athletics.

Fine specimen of young boys. School`s gymnastics team.
Tallest boy in the back row is the young Tancred!

THE TWENTY-THIRD ANNUAL COUNTY CHAMPIONSHIPS

In the presence of
H.R.H. THE DUKE OF EDINBURGH, K.G., K.T.

Felixstowe, 1st May, 1956

Presented to .... *William Tancred*

who gained ...*Fourth*... place

in the ...."*Throwing the Discus*"............... event

C. S. Westhorp
Honorary Secretary

My first ever Discus throwing certificate gained at the opening of the Coronation Park in Felixstowe, 1956

19

The busy programme demanded military type planning and at any one moment a number of different track events could be in progress. Elsewhere in the arena, the field event athletes would be battling it out in earnest.

This excitable activity took place before thousands of noisy and enthusiastic spectators, matched by the brilliant organisation and the exceptionally high standard of the entrants, many of whom would become future international representatives. It appears today however, that these prodigies find the transition from school-age to senior success very difficult due to either injury, apathy and other interests which they find more attractive and less demanding.

I was also apprehensive of staying two nights with my unknown hosting family but I need not have been concerned for they turned out to be like a second family but with more food on the table.

They provided a comfortable bed and a wonderful breakfast so I was well looked after in competing in my first Schools Championships. I arrived to be greeted by rain and my team manager, who was also responsible for giving out the athlete's shorts and county vests. To my alarm, my issued shorts were so small they scarcely covered my `crown jewels`, so I warmed up in my father's old track suit bottoms! On seeing my rivals my heart sunk. They were big boys and were obviously shaving with one boy having a beard. I felt completely intimidated and failed to qualify for the final.

It is well known today that all those born in July/August of the school year are at a disadvantage in physical development/maturity when compared to those born in September/ October, but of course there are exceptions. The latter also have an advantage in that they have received coaching and skills training before the summer born. Anyhow, I learnt many lessons from this ordeal, one being that I was in the wrong event!

I vividly remember going on the train from Ipswich station to London Liverpool Street station dressed in short trousers so as not to pay the full fare as an adult. My father only gave me this small amount to go to an athletics course at Motspur Park Surrey. I felt very uncomfortable sitting with other adults and even more so when the rail ticket inspector slid the door open and said, "Tickets please". At my turn, I handed my ticket for inspection and he asked, "What's your age son?" I replied in a practiced softly high pitched voice, "Twelve Sir". He paused, looked at me sheepishly and then announced to all, "These boys are getting bigger each day!" As the train was approaching London I swiftly went to the toilet to change from short trousers to long ones so as not to be further embarrassed. The only problem, I had to do this `acting` on the return journey back to Ipswich.

Another activity that comes to mind at school was the weekly trek from school in the summer months to go swimming in the sea opposite the current disused yacht pond now being converted into a large car park. (In fact this yacht pond was used by me and a few friends to gain confidence in swimming in water on our own). I do not think we minded swimming in the cold sea as it gave us an opportunity to leave school and to learn to swim under instruction and with the added bonus of gaining swimming distances certificates. I still admire my 440 yards certificate that was gained in the North Sea in 1955! I do not think many of the youth of today would have readily accepted this approach to swimming.

When not playing sport or engaging in my favourite lessons of history and geography, my friend Felix Newsom and I would disappear to Felixstowe Ferry and search for washed up bullets, gun cartridge magazines and if lucky, hand grenades! Bullets and its finding were not rare in those days but one lunch time in June 1956, we came across a grenade. To our delight we decided to take it to school to show all our friends and I put it into my pocket. On entering the school`s premises, the head master Mr Girling asked us where we had been and to empty our swollen looking pockets. When I showed him the grenade, he panicked and asked his deputy Miss Bailey to call the police and fire brigade and evacuated the school whilst awaiting the arrival of these emergency services! After an hour, things got back to normal, although I do remember a few smacks of the cane for my misdemeanours.

Another event around this time was with my friend Graham Vine who happened to `secure` the services of a very large tractor tyre tube, so that we could go boating in the sea near where the recently re-opened Spa Pavilion stands. We paddled along nicely, singing at the top of our voices "Well I never felt more like singing the blues...." the number I hit *'Singing the blues'* in 1956 by Guy Mitchell. So we were about 500 yards away from the shore and panic was arising as we could not paddle back to shore. We noticed a group of spectators who were waving frantically and so we did the same! However, it had become apparent to the shore spectators that we were in serious trouble. Before long, a coastguard launch arrived to pick us up and returned us to the spot which we had left a couple of hours earlier. We were greeted by a couple of lovely old ladies who smothered us with blankets, served with a cup of tea and biscuits and treated far better than at home! We never did report this incident to our parents because their reaction would have been opposite to these kind old ladies.

Boys at the school were also introduced to gardening which again was not a subject that I took well. It gave me the opportunity to see how plants, vegetables, and fruit grew and soon I followed other boys in tasting and chewing the home grown produce. So good it tasted that I threw some of the vegetables and fruit over the fence to collect them after school in our paper bags with Graham Vine.

I was used to having a paper bag because I delivered papers in the morning, evening and Sunday mornings just to gain some pocket money in which my father was slow to oblige. A Saturday delivery job was also on the work list and all this done with school and sport activities.

With my pocket money I would buy my mother her favourite pear drops and our special sweet shop was Mr Hope (`Luggers`) shop opposite Causton school. Lovely eucalyptus sweets, well it was for me, sherbert, which fizzed in your mouth or liquorice laces and of course bubble gum which lasted for ages especially dipped in sugar granules.

`Lugger`Hope was a kind old man but we youngsters were too fast for him to cope with the little finances that we had and I am sure he made no profit when we left his shop.

Looking back to my formative years, I have never come across so many nicknames given to people that has lasted a lifetime in their lives in Felixstowe. For example, there was Tarty Smith, Tug Wilson, Taiter Hammond, Gobbi Smith, Gasher Gage, Boommer Abbott, Narky Turner, Nogger Knight, Chalky White and Ninky McKinnon.

It was fun using these nicknames when we went scrumping because if caught, the real names would not be recognised. Such childhood pursuits probably made us run and become more agile and it was a shame that those not possessing these traits got caught. No one as far as I am aware `snitched` on the others if caught! Many of the boys and I needed some association to help us to develop and keep out of trouble so some joined youth clubs, sea scouts, young farmer associations and other organisations.

My choice along with John Cousins and Jimmy Whitman was the 1st Felixstowe Sea Scouts with the Scouts Hut based in Bath road not far from where I lived. It was a wonderful organisation and Skipper Rupert Bullock was the Scout master.

We played numerous games, the toughest being murder ball, where the ball was placed in the middle of the gym and when the whistle went, you raced to get the medicine ball back to your line before the other team could stop you. It soon became apparent who were the front runners in each team. Often after this game, you would be black and blue from all the wrestling for the ball.

The highlight for me at the Sea Scouts was the opportunity to gain badges ranging from activities, challenges and recognising achievements. My poor mother must have felt this to be a chore because nearly every month, I came home with a badge to be sewn on my Sea Scout uniform. Looking back, the scouts enabled me to know all the roads and streets of the town, the art of camping, rowing and sculling in lovely Beccles and learning first aid and many more activities that were useful in life. I proudly gained the award of the Queen`s Cord and now regret not staying on longer to achieve becoming a Queen`s Scout. I was getting taller and wearing shorts, so it was time to wear trousers and be more of an adult.

Suffolk AAA Youth champion in shot, discus and javelin events with proud mother

John Cousins, Jimmy Whitman, `Nogger` Knights and myself ,
prior to our 24 hour walk and camp with the
1ˢᵗ Felixstowe Sea Scouts.

At this time in my early teens, I was beginning to make a name for myself in local athletics but Felixstowe had no throwing or weight-training facilities. As the family lived close to Allenby Park, we tended to use this small Park for our throwing which included the javelin, discus and shot put. Needless to say this did not last long and we were politely asked to move on and practice elsewhere! It was time to join Ipswich Harriers who at the time had facilities on the present Ipswich Town FC practice pitch.

No sooner had my father and I had settled into what were thought ideal practice facilities we came across a certain Alf (later Sir) Ramsey, the Town manager who asked my father and I what were we doing throwing a javelin on his beloved training pitch? My father objected and told the then Mr Ramsey that his boy would become a champion and he should applaud him and not make him feel not wanted. Father carried on and asked me to do certain mobility exercises and conditioning drills and after a while, Mr Ramsey asked my father to take the Town players for half an hour in the same vane and soon everything was forgotten! I told my father Mr Ramsey was the Manager of this great club and his reply was," Does he know who I am"? Alf Ramsey was knighted for his wonderful services to football which was applauded by Dad when he heard of Sir Alf`s knighthood.

On another occasion at the Town practice pitch, I was asked by my father to throw a cricket ball for distance throwing. So with an illustrious group of Ipswich town players watching me, I unleashed the cricket ball from one side of the goal post right over the top of the other, some 100 yards. They were amazed by the distance thrown and better still, it did not damage their precious pitch! A great team with a top-class manager, all of whom wished me the best in my chosen sport. To think of those early `encounters` between two very determined individuals and then to remain friends is something to treasure today.

Ian Swindale (England discus thrower), myself, my brother Geoff, Mark Pharoah (Former British discus record holder) and Peter Cook (Suffolk AAA hammer champion) at Northgate School Ipswich, on a coaching course.

My father and Joe Sharp founded the Felixstowe athletics club around 1956 and quickly attracted many enthusiastic members, mainly runners and keep fit enthusiasts. Training sessions would be held at Langer road playing field or the Coronation Sports ground depending on its availability for this newly formed athletics club. The club ran for a few years before is termination due to a lack of volunteer officials and coaches including having some financial problems.

The club did organise certain trips to create an interest and develop motivation amongst its members and one excursion that comes to mind is the Great Britain versus the USSR at the White City stadium in Shepherd`s Bush, London in 1956. Arising very early in the morning, the coach full with many of the local athletics team on board headed off from Felixstowe excited and in high spirits with the prospect of seeing top international athletes in action. As we disembarked from the coach eager to find our seats in the stadium we were informed that the fixture was scrapped due to `Nina and the five hats`. Apparently, Nina Ponomareva the USSR discus champion who spoke no English when apprehended at C & A in Oxford Street, London was accused of not paying for the five hats by the store detectives. Due to these charges of shoplifting and the tensions between Whitehall and Moscow, the two day international was called off. Everyone was dejected and we then travelled back in sombre mood instead of one of jubilation. This incident would always be known as `Nina and the five hats`.

Looking back my father was ahead of his time with regards to scientific training and sports conditioning. He was an avid reader on up-to-date training methods and was influenced by books by the great German technician Toni Nett. It was also at this time that I was beginning to use regularly, The Discus Throw, a flick book by the USA coach Dean Cromwell. By flicking the pages, one could observe the discus throw from start to finish, much in the way as cine-cameras do today.

I also attended two more All-England Schools` Championships in the 15-17 Intermediate Group. In 1958 at Houghton-le-Spring County Durham, I finished 4th in the javelin and 2nd in the same event at the 1959 Championships in Nantwich, Cheshire. All of these events coincided with me attending Ipswich Civic College, now Suffolk New College and studying for my General Certificate of Education `O` Levels in 1957/9. I studied five subjects - English Language, Economic history, General Science, Geography and British Constitution. I passed all the subjects and intended to take British Constitution and Economic History at A Level after the summer recess.

The teachers at the Ipswich Civic College were good and inspiring and I particularly liked the English Language teacher Mr. Harwood including Mr Worsnop the Geography teacher who also loved sport. Mr Cranford the British Constitution lecturer although not friendly, knew his subject and wanted the best from his students. Many students found his lectures initially confusing and gibberish but once I understood the basic concepts of constitution including the process of legislation, the subject became easier to learn. It became my most successful subject and if I went to University, it would have been my degree discipline. Even though I had these good lecturers, I learnt so much from the Teach Myself books (black and yellow cover) covering the syllabus of the GCE by Crick or someone with a similar surname. I did not pay a penny for these books, as a young lady cashier in the Ipswich Ancient House bookshop took pity on me and allowed me to study the books sitting in the corner of the shop.

It was the late fifties and the dawn of pop music which was an exciting draw away from studying. Finance was required if you wanted to purchase the latest records or attend concerts. My friends and I were unfortunately too poor, so during our lunch breaks, we used to go the `Listening booths` in Footman`s, the Ipswich department store that later became Debenhams, to listen to the latest records. We promised to buy them when our listening was over but luckily, the girls working there put no pressure on us to buy but were happy to speak to us and have a possible night out.

I liked to listen to *Move It* by Cliff Richard which reached No 2 in the UK Singles chart and is credited with being one of the first authentic *rock and roll* songs produced outside the United States. The other song that kept me singing was by Emile Ford and the Checkmates, who was the first *black* British artist to sell I million copies of the single `What do you want to make those eyes at me for?`

Before going back to college to study for `A` levels, I started work at Felixstowe Docks to earn much needed money and enjoyed working with the Dockers, some of whom having married local girls whilst they served in the Royal Air Force and had now settled in Felixstowe. During lunch breaks or if no boats were docked to unload, I impressed these older men by throwing pebbles across the dock basin to hit some Petroleum Tanks in the distance with the sound of a `ping`. Most could not believe that anyone could throw so far let alone a 16 year old. A group of the older and worldly- wise Dockers made instant friends with me and said, "When the next boats come in we will have a bet with them that you could hit these tanks and then claim cigarettes, bottles of spirits and tobacco from each boat" So in the first month, so much `booty` was won that I was told to rest my arm until the next boat came in! I just loved it but in the meantime aspirations for further studies were dwindling.

My father was still very active at 42 and I remember fondly that he saw an advert to walk from John `O` Groats to Lands End. This offered £1000 for the winner of each man and women to finish, which in those days was enough to buy a house in 1960. He told the whole family that he was capable of winning and set about training. The training involved going to the beach from our rented property and then walking back up a flight of concrete steps, performing this several times. I accompanied him regularly but with not too much enthusiasm. If raining, it was up and down the stairs where we lived at 8 Cobbold Road, which had 3 levels. If that was boring, he used to perform his walking mileage by going behind the sofa in the small lounge and walk to each side of the wall counting loudly one, two, three...., up to 500, all this while the family were trying to watch the television!

The big day arrived and he announced that he was leaving to win the prize. A big cheer from all us greeted his announcement and at long last, all of us thought there would be some peace in the house for a few weeks. He travelled to Scotland with another colleague from Felixstowe, Leslie `Tiddy` Bowdedge, a local Scouts master. On Friday 26 February 1960, a ramshackle army of more than 700 walkers set off from John O`Groats for Land`s End 900 miles away. All types, sizes, all nationalities were there with many totally unprepared, including my father, for the weather in the north of Scotland and the 10ft drifts that greeted them.

There were Cockneys, North Country farmers, university graduates, mechanics, clerks, waitresses, at least three peers of the realm and the unemployed. One man had a wooden leg, another totally blind. None had any of the waterproof, high-tech gear that is available today and importantly, all were expected to provide their own food and accommodation and complete the race in 28 days.

The organiser Billy Butlin made huge efforts to police the race with checkpoints but cheating was rife with competitors cadging lifts in lorries and cars. Nonetheless, the race was an enormous national event as it proceeded south with extensive media coverage.

All competitors wore a number so were clearly identifiable and town bands and lord mayors turned out to greet them. Sadly my father only completed some 200 miles and retired hurt due to blisters he burst with pins which caused infections. His companion carried on his own for another day before he retired exhausted and hungry. The men`s winner Jimmy Musgrave, of Doncaster completed the course in just 14 days 32 minutes which worked out as more than 60 miles a day! The women`s race was won by a 19 year old apprentice hairdresser from Liverpool, Wendy Lewis in 16 days, 19 hours and 30 minutes. More than 170 competitors finished within the 28 day cut-off.

My father at the start of the Billy Butlin walk – John O'Groats to Lands End

On returning home on crutches, the mood in the family home was bleak with no laughter coming from anyone least alone from the returning walker! When things did settle down my father installed in all of us that in any endeavour that we take on, make sure that every stone is turned over and that preparation and planning is of paramount importance.

Around this time, I also joined the Felixstowe and Trades Labour Club with Jimmy Green, Tarty Smith, John Horton, Roy `Ken` Dodds and a few more. I learnt to play billiards and snooker not of a high standard but I did win the club`s darts individual title in 1961 and was presented with my first cup, so minute that you could easily lose it, if put in your pocket. Also, we played football for Walton FC and sometimes for Felixstowe Juniors and travelled the county with our fixtures. They were some good footballers namely Jimmy green, John Cousins, Chris Davison, Mel Chandler, Tater Hammond and Brian Bullock. So much fun and good mates, who were not distracted by the fast growing up girls in the town and surrounds.

Myself with my friend Jimmy Green aged 17

My father at this time was feeling the pressure of the daily commute from Felixstowe to Ipswich where he worked at Reavells, an engineering firm close to Ipswich railway station. I used to visit him on certain days, so that we could walk to Portman road and train. However, I remember one day seeing a sports car drive up with an attractive lady beside the driver. On asking the officer in charge of security who these two people were, he replied it was Richard Attenborough and his co-star the lovely looking Pier Angeli. They were making the film called *The Angry Silence*, a portrait of Industrial Relations in early 1960`s Britain time and raised important issues around relationships between employees, managers and owners. I changed my mine straight away that I would like to become an actor if you were to play opposite so lovely and sincere lady as Pier Angeli!

The other film I remember being made in the mid-fifties was The Yangtze Incident starring the great actor Richard Todd. It told the true story of HMS Amethyst, a frigate caught up in the Chinese Civil war. It was partly filmed on the rivers Orwell and Stour which run between Ipswich and Manningtree. I approached the film set on the banks of the river Orwell as I had heard the ship guns firing thinking Britain was being attacked. I was told to leave as quickly as possible as the film crew did not want to film an English boy with his bicycle in tow. Still, I was excited and relished the opportunity to tell my friends and family. It was interesting to learn afterwards that Simon the cat was awarded the Dickin Medal after surviving injuries from a cannon shell, raising morale and killing of a rat infestation during his service on board this ship. The Dickin medal is awarded for conspicuous gallantry or devotion to duty serving in military conflict.

I remember selling a few evening papers to film star Anthony Steel, a fine looking man who spoke very well and to actors Bonar Colleano, Victor Maddern and Michael Balfour. The latter three did not in my view, had the presence or manners as the debonair Mr Steel. If I could not look like him, I thought acting after all, might not be for me. The film they were making was called `The Sea Shall Not Have Them`, a 1954 British war film which also included the fine actors Sir Michael Redgrave and Sir Dirk Bogarde. Again it was filmed in Felixstowe and was about a British aircraft which is forced to ditch in the North Sea and an RAF Air Sea Rescue launch is deployed to search, struggling against bad weather, mechanical problems and a fire in the galley.

Relating to films, I remember my father asking me what was on at the local cinema after delivering newspapers and informing him one afternoon, a film called *The Flaming Torch* starring Bob Mathias and Ward Bond was showing. He told me instantly, "We off to see it, Bob Mathias is the greatest all-round athlete ever"!

Bob Mathias had won the 1948 London Olympic Games decathlon at the age of 17 years and 263 days, a phenomenal achievement for such a young man. The decathlon is the ultimate test of all round athletic prowess. It was a gripping film and I along with my father, were in awe of young Mathias, with the actor Ward Bond playing his high school coach. He went on to defend his title successfully in the 1952 Helsinki Olympics, a feat accomplished by Britain's Daley Thompson several Olympics later. As an update Ashton Eaton of the USA did the same in 2012 and 2016 and is the current world record holder.

Surprisingly, Bob Mathias retired aged only 21 and subsequently became a politician and before his retirement ran the USA National Fitness Foundation. Sadly he died of cancer aged 76.

He was an inspiration to me in developing all-round athletic ability and in attempting all the 10 events in the decathlon. As a note, I did attempt to compete in one decathlon and in 1965 attained 6015points which ranked me 10th in the UK decathlon rankings. I failed to continue further decathlons as my hurdling and pole vaulting techniques were not particularly good but who knows with good coaching and better facilities, what I might have achieved in this gruelling event?

Breaking the Suffolk AAA Junior Javelin record with a throw of 213ft 11in/65.20m,
Bury St. Edmunds 1960 (Archant)

After all the excitement in living in Felixstowe the family then moved to Ipswich at 433 Nacton Road although I continued to visit my friends from school and the social activities of the Felixstowe Labour Club.

It was a semi-detached house situated in a busy road far away from the freedom of living in a sea- side town. My father was happy as he could cycle most days to work but I wished to move on to a make a life for myself. Perhaps working in the dock gave me the independence and impetus to try something different and I was hoping that perhaps National Service would still be an option.

2. THE ARMY

1ST EAST ANGLIAN REGIMENT

You are in the Army now! 18 years of age and just missing National Service but volunteering for 9 years service with the Infantry. In the middle of the second row, with a nervous smile, is Private Tancred! (Studio Five)

I was 18 years of age, although National Service had finished call-up by a few months, I decided to enlist with my father's blessing (as he thought it would 'toughen' me up) with the 1st East Anglian regiment at Bury St. Edmunds in 1961. I was given a number which I can still remember today as 23873001 (as I can with my mother's Co-op 'Divi' number 51255) and marched off to get a haircut with a group of other enlisted boys. It became apparent they were all from different parts of the land and with different personalities. There were silent ones, talkative ones, slow ones and morose ones. After the haircuts, we were taken to the cook house and experienced our first army meal. I was happy to demolish the lot that was offered on my plate as I was hungry and thought this free food was very palatable. Others thought that the food dished out by the catering staff was not fit enough even for a dog.

Shortly after the meal, we were then introduced to our platoon sergeant, a veteran of the Korean War who stood no nonsense and reminded us that we might be the darlings of our mothers but we were certainly not his. We were marched to our barracks which had enough beds for 25 recruits and showed how to make our beds and how to leave the blankets and sheets when we arise at 6.30am the next morning. Having a father like mine who 'trained' me in bed making at a very early age posed me no difficulties whatsoever!

The night for most of us was long as many could not sleep and one or two were crying and missing their homes. Next morning at 6.30am we were awoke by the corporal in charge of our barrack room by clanging two dustbin lids and told, `Get hands off cocks...on socks!` I was not surprised or alarmed by this introduction to the new day and had a chuckle to myself as I was getting dressed.

After breakfast, we had our daily inspection and marched to the parade ground for drill. The sergeant major took a delight in getting us to march properly and in time. Many of the recruits found this difficult, some swinging the left arm and left leg together or others not marching as a unit. Gradually over time our drill improved but a few recruits were discharged as being not army material.

With my three mates on passing out and proud of the marksman`s rifle badge

I loved the physical training in the gym which always smelt of horse liniment. However, for those with no sporting or physical activity interest it was a place of torture and pain. All around the gym there were wall-bars and climbing ropes at either end. Most of the time was devoted to physical training exercises coupled with medicine ball activities. Circuit training was also the order of the day and was disliked by most of the recruits. Circuit training is a form of body conditioning or resistance training using high intensity aerobics. It targets strength building and muscular endurance. An exercise `circuit` is one completion of all the prescribed exercises in the programme. When one circuit is complete, one begins the first exercise again for the next circuit. Traditionally, the time between exercises in circuit training is short, often with rapid movement to the next exercise. As an interest, circuit training was developed by Morgan and Anderson in 1957, at Leeds University.

Another much hated physical training and conditioning activity was the Assault Course. Although intimidating at first, there was always satisfaction at the end of this challenge. You were faced with awesome adrenaline fuelled obstacles such as rope swings, high walls, tunnels, crawls, monkey bars and to top it off, a zip wire. We were placed in teams of 8 men for the competition to find the best team and were often `encouraged` to win by the shouting of the drill sergeant who happened to be a manic depressive. Eventually after 8 weeks training we were finally permitted to send a letter home to our parents or girlfriends or some other acquaintances.

I informed my father in my very first letter that I had settled in well, thanked him for his disciplinary behaviour to me which made my army training so much easier compared to most boys and alerted him that we had central heating due to the stoves being placed at the end of each barrack room. It was far warmer than the days and nights spent in my home either in Felixstowe or Ipswich.

My father wrote back to say he was glad that things were working out well for me and enjoying the disciplined life but thought the British army were getting soft due to the central heating situation!

At the end of basic training at 18 years of age, I became fitter, learned to mix socially, understood Scots, Welsh, Irish, Brummie, Norfolk and other weird accents, how to con the cookhouse staff to get extra rations, how to wash, iron and mend clothes and never to volunteer!

The winning East Anglian Brigade`s Minor Units Team at the Army Athletics Championships, Aldershot 1961. I am the tallest in the middle of the back row with QSMI George Talkington (later Lt. Colonel) in front, second left. (Studio Five)

The most interesting `skive` that I learnt in the Army from an old `sweat`, was in order to look busy, just carry a bill board under your arm and walk anywhere, as everyone would think you were busy doing a job and no one would question you, not even a drill sergeant! It worked successfully for me as well as I was not stopped or questioned on my walkabouts which proved his theory correct.

I also finished as the best recruit for my intake and after a well-earned leave was due to go to Aldershot to complete a Physical Training Course which lasted 13 weeks. It was demanding course but I found it enjoyable and worthwhile with a bonus of learning different sports both in terms of theory and practice. I also came into contact with many like- minded people from all walks of life and more importantly, was very impressed with the talent of the Army Physical Training Corps staff and their facilities. The desire for me now was to gain more experience and transfer from the Infantry to this Corps as a Physical Training Corps Instructor. To do this I had to attend and pass what was called an Advanced Course and again it was of a 13 week`s duration.

My first advance course at Aldershot. The white singlet individual is my instructor Jonny Irons and on his left Capt Stanley Blacknell. On the back right, far right is Sgt. Eddie 'Fibber' McGee. I am on the back row in the middle! (APTC)

I passed the course but the Army Physical Training Corps felt that I was too young at 20 years of age to progress and transfer to the Corps and needed more maturity and experience. So I was informed about the situation and told to rejoin my Battalion. The Battalion was now based in my home town of Felixstowe, so much for enlisting to see the world! Still it was fun to be based in my home town for a few months before the next posting rumoured to be abroad.

1st East Anglian Regiment Football team at the Felixstowe Sports ground, Dellwood Avenue. Front row, second from the right Merv Tomkins who played in the reserves for Ipswich Town FC and back row, first left Malcolm Beaton our APTC Instructor, known in the game as `the bull-dozer`! I am in the back row, fourth from the right and played centre half for the team

During this period I along with two other boxing enthusiasts, went to the Empire Pool Sports Arena in November 1961 to see the fantastic Great Britain versus the United States of America amateur contest when unbelievably our boxers beat the mighty United States 10-0. The stars seen included Alan Rudkin who went on to become a Commonwealth and European bantamweight champion and the `rat catcher`, Dick McTaggart the 1956 Melbourne Olympic Lightweight gold medallist who reputedly came from a very large family of 18 children with many of his brothers being accomplished boxers.

For me the contest of this historical night was the bout between our `Blond Bomber`, Billy Walker against the giant Cornelius Perry in the heavyweight contest. It did not last long as Walker knocked him out in the first round and the whole place erupted in delight and amazement. Billy Walker would go on to be a very successful British heavyweight boxer and businessman like his elder brother George. From here onwards, I was a `hooked` on boxing! What a cherished memory to have seen this boxing match live!

I still managed to attend an athletics course in October at Motspur Park, Surrey under the watchful eyes of the national coaches and was told that I had needed to get stronger and bigger if I was to be successful as a thrower. This was good advice because other talented throwers had these attributes.

After attending this course, I caught the evening train from Liverpool Street heading to Ipswich and in the buffet carriage some of the Ipswich Town FC players including the manager Alf Ramsey and John Cobbold the Chairman were enjoying the banter. I suppose in those days, some of team travelled to the London fixtures by train and not the bus or in some cases today by flying. Anyhow, Mr Cobbold (politely called Mr John) recognised me and offered a drink to which I replied, "A coffee sir". He immediately offered me his tankard and said, "Try this". After a cautious swallow, my throat felt it was damaged due to the mixture of vodka, brandy and other mixtures of spirits in his tankard!

On returning home, I mentioned this incident to my father and said he was a kind man to which my father replied, "He is always happy due to his love of alcohol"! I did meet him again at Portman road by having a kind invitation to watch a match in the Director's box only to remember half of the game, due to the free flowing champagne given to me before the match!

By the time, John Cobbold celebrated his 21st birthday in 1948 he had become a Director of the club and was the youngest Director in the Football League. In addition, he was also the grandson of the 9th Duke of Devonshire and Chaired Ipswich Town from 1957 until 1976 and apparently did not know too much about football. Two lovely stories about him have been reported. The first one being at Leicester one afternoon, he patted Bobby Robson on the shoulder when Ipswich Town were 2-0 down and said to him, "The team are playing really well so Bobby what special training have you implemented?" The Ipswich manager was momentarily mystified and after a couple of seconds, replied to John Cobbold, "We are not winning 2-0 but losing 2-0 and we are the away side. We have changed to yellow as Leicester are the home team and as a result, they are playing in blue"!

The second story relates to a sponsorship deal. At the unveiling of this major sponsorship deal John Cobbold spoke to the invited media, "It has been mentioned that the club will squander the sponsor's money on wine, women and song. It is an absolute lie. We do not do a lot of singing here at Portman Road". He was eccentric but was an incredible generous man and is sadly missed.

Whilst on weekend leaves during this time, I used to go St. Matthew's Bath Hall and the Ipswich Gaumont to see the pop stars do their stuff and marvel at the music they provided. On one occasion, I was approached by Long John Baldry at the interval and we started to talk to one another. He probably noticed me as I was 6ft 4in tall and he stood 6ft 7in, so we had something in common. However, things got a little tense as I was not of his inclination and wished him well. He did make a public acknowledgement of being gay in the 70's. Nevertheless, he played a key role in the growth of the British rhythm and blues movement. Also at this venue was an up and coming Rod 'the mod' Stewart who needed feeding looking at the size of his legs but boy hasn't he done well and now a Knight! He did not kick footballs to the audience in those days! Money was tight and I believe from all the rumours, he still is!

As a solo artist in 1967, Long John Baldry recorded a pop song 'Let the Heartaches Begin' that went to be No 1 in Britain, followed in 1968 top 20 hit titled 'Mexico' which was the theme of the UK Olympic team that year.

Within a few weeks, the 1st East Anglian regiment were to go to Aden in the latter part of 1963. Aden at the time was one the few remaining British Colonies, set sweltering at the southern edge of the Arabian Peninsula. I was eager at the prospect of overseas service and had never been abroad since my arrival in England. It also provided an opportunity to get into some sunshine and leave the cold winter behind. I did think at the time that the regiment would primarily be deployed in Aden for internal security and thus not 'technically' on active service. Things turned out to be very different with this posting.

When the Regiment was ready to leave for Aden, I could not go to my utter disappointment as a result of passport difficulties. It appeared that as I was born in India of British parents, that naturalisation papers were necessary before a passport could be issued. My father was informed and his reaction and letter to the Passport Officer at Whitehall, London was posted (see his copy letter dated 20 January 1964). It's very amusing as illustrated in his second paragraph he states that, 'I am not a Pakistani or Indian, but a British subject by birth. Of course if you agree that if a cat had kittens in a fish shop, the off-springs were kippers, then you may be right in assuming that I am anything but British'.

It worked and within two weeks the official passport was delivered and I proceeded to travel to Aden with a few other late departing soldiers. My father although an extremely disciplined man, was also a character and 'loved' writing to anyone with his wit and sarcasm. He also wrote personally to Liberace (1919-1987) the American pianist, singer, actor who was worth over $110 million at the time of his death and to one of the Rothschild family, who were the richest family in the world, for money to help him in his new hobby of looking after birds. When no money was forthcoming, he called them, "Tight sods"!

Ready for Aden in my `civvies`, January 1964 (Sarony)

41

433, Nacton Road,
Ipswich.
20th January, 1964.

The Passport Officer,
Whitehall,
London.

Dear Sir,

It is with regret that I have to write to you on a matter of extreme urgency, and that is in connection with my son's passport, Corporal William Raymond Tancred, of the First East Anglian Regiment, who has been refused one on the grounds that because he was born in Quetta, Pakistan and myself in pre-India, that Naturalisation papers are first necessary before a passport is issued to him.

I am not a Pakistani or Indian, but a British Subject by Birth. Of course if you believe that if a cat had kittens in a fish shop, the offspring were kippers - then you may be right in assuming that I am anything but British.

Both my father and his relations and my father-in-law and his relations have loyally served in the British Army both in times of peace and in Wars, and, I am positive, if we were in a similar crisis, all this damn nonsense would never have arisen.
I, myself, did security work in East Persia.

My family and I have been residing in this Country since early 1950 and my son has been in Her Majesty's Forces for close on three years. Now to be told that he has to do a further 14 days in the Country before a passport is issued and then after Naturalisation papers are signed, is utter tripe.
Besides, it has taken your Department a whole month to make this finding - for it was over a month since his passport application was forwarded to you. This unwarranted delay has resulted in my son missing his flight to Aden, where his regiment has been posted.

You are quite at liberty to ascertain any facts required by reference to Somerset House. The Commonwealth Relations Office may likewise be approached.

However, I intend taking up the matter with the Prime Minister and if need be requesting for my son's immediate discharge from the Services.

Yours faithfully,

(A. N. Tancred.)

My father's humorous and amusing letter to the Passport Office in January 1964

42

On arriving in Aden, I became the Regiment's physical training instructor in charge of keeping the troops fit and occupied when they were off duties with team games and swimming pool activities. I arose at 5am daily to beat the heat and lime coated all the football pitches. I was under the command of Captain Mickey Rouse of the Army Physical Training Corp who would later become my Staff Officer as Lt. Colonel at the Royal Military Academy, Sandhurst from 1965-1968. He was a first rate officer, much respected and commanded his men exceedingly well. He also encouraged me to do other sports such as Basketball which was often played against the RAF at Khormakser.

Walking in the streets in Aden while off duty

Drinking `coca cola` with my mates in relaxation mode. Bob Durrant far left, myself far right.

43

Mixing with other colleagues was fun and there were many days of laughter and drinking tiger beer. Some soldiers would play pranks with the dhobi wallas or the laundry workers. They were unbelievable in that with so many clothes to be washed, pressed and returned without losing any item to each soldier was done on an identity marking of dots, lines, squares and no names. However when they wanted payment they would ask who is Corporal Mickey Mouse, Private Desperate Dan or Tarzan and similar names. Everyone used to have a laugh until the sergeant asked for the real names and payment to be made instantly to these hard pressed laundry workers.

Visiting the Aden State Police Marine Section. On occasions, we were sent to the dock area to check transport and Army deliveries with the Police.

There were also tense times whilst on the occasional patrols for me which included the Radfan hills and the district of Ma`alla, which during the period of rising insurgency, the flats became targets for the Arabs firing rockets from the hills. There were further incidents for example when an Arab with a camel pulling a cart along a road which over-looked Waterloo barracks, stopped and fired bullets from a machine gun hidden under the tarpaulin of his cart. The bullets hit the compound where troops were resting and off duty. After I left Aden there were a few men beheaded when captured, sadly one being a young officer that I trained at Sandhurst. Unfortunately, there were further losses during this conflict and the posting turned out to be one of action.

All those Armed services personnel who served in Aden during this period were awarded the General Service Medal and Radfan Clasp for the campaign and operations that fell short of a full-scale war.

It was also in Aden, that I used to do some throwing and weight training in the evening, as it was cooler. I was also making good strides in my throwing performances and motivated as the Middle East Land Forces athletics championships were to be held at the camp in the next month.

The day arrived (7 March 1964) for me to compete in the Championships and I won all four of the throwing events and set a new Middle East Land Forces records in each (shot 48ft 2in/14.68m; discus 167ft 0in/50.90m; javelin 192ft 7in/58.70m; hammer 139ft 6in/42.56m). The discus throw ranked me 3rd in the UK rankings for the event. A few weeks later, I went on to win all four throwing events in the Inter services Athletics Championships with the Army coming out top.

Waterloo Barracks -1st East Anglian Regiment 1964.
Shamsan Mountains in the background.

45

Breaking the Middle East Land Forces javelin record with a throw of 192ft 7in/58.70m.
Note no tartan run-ups but throwing on loose sand. (Aden Chronicle)

I was now making a name for myself as a discus thrower and my days as an infantry man were coming to an end, as I was to go on my second 13 weeks Advanced Physical Training course in Aldershot to be followed by a another 13 weeks Probationers course with a view this time, to transfer to the Army Physical

Training Corps (APTC). Aden had made me experienced and mature!

Before attending these courses in Aldershot, I won both the Army and the Inter Services Championships shot and discus titles and was also placed 3rd in the AAA`s in the discus event. As a result of the AAA`s performance, I was selected to represent Great Britain against the Benelux Countries for my first Great Britain international in Ghent. I performed well with a throw of 165ft./50.30m and finished 3rd in the competition.

My roommate was Jeff Teale, a blunt, no nonsense former miner and shot putt thrower who introduced me to the readings of Karl Marx, the revolutionary socialist. In the short period in each other`s company, we discussed Marx`s theories about society, economics and politics. There were other characters in the team from different walks of life who shared my dream of doing their best in whatever pursuit took them. For example, there was Jeffrey Archer or now Lord Archer the celebrated author and former Conservative Party chairman who was our representative in the 200 metres and was I believe, President of the Oxford University Athletic club. He spoke quickly but very eloquently and was very charming to all and walked about with his devoted umbrella. You could not have met two different personalities but they loved athletics as much as I did.

Ghent is a lovely city, full of Flemish architecture and a splendid night life which all the throwers at the time could substantiate. We were under the `command` of Chief Petty Officer John Dutton of the Royal Navy the hammer thrower, who was much older than us and showed us the `ropes` to move about at night. We all arrived back early in the morning to catch the flight back to London. The trip ended in an administrative `cock-up`. When we arrived back at Heathrow with our luggage still standing at Brussels airport, the British team vented their frustrations on the poor organisation with mumblings of discontent to put it mildly.

I managed to get another international vest this time against Poland who had in the discus event the former world record holder Edmund Piatkowski who also at one time was their heavyweight weight-lifting champion and the 6ft 8in tall Bergier, who won the discus contest narrowly from his compatriot. Although Piatkowski came 2nd, I was struck by his quickness and strength as he was not tall by a discus throwers build. I came away with the belief that you did not have to be really big but fast, technically proficient and strong to throw the discus long distances.

My discus teammate was Roy Hollingsworth then current British discus record holder who went on to represent Great Britain at the 1964 Tokyo Olympic Games. It was interesting to note that when I was at Sheffield University in the late 80's, I taught his son Eric Hollingsworth who eventually became Australia's national athletics coach. Other personalities in the team were Ming Campbell who later on in life became Sir Ming and Leader of the Liberal Party, Robbie Brightwell the team captain at the Tokyo Olympics Games and Ann Packer who went on to win the 800m women's title and the eventual long jump winners for both the men's and women's Lynn Davies and Mary Rand.

The last major performance before attending the military physical training courses was for representing the Rest against the Olympic team at Portsmouth. Although throwing well, I failed to qualify for the required Olympic distance and now concentrated on my military career which was to transfer to the Army Physical Training Corps.

I managed to pass all the necessary tests and examinations required for the Advance Course this time and after a short break, went onto the demanding Acting Sergeant Instructors Probationer's Course. You were expected to pass everything and it had to include first class tests for gymnastics, a sport I was not built for as I stood 6ft 4in tall in my socks. Luckily for me Gary Fuller another probationer on an earlier course had passed, he too being 6ft 4in. and was an eventual Army Light-heavy boxing champion in 1965 and a Great Britain Basketball player of some distinction, so we had a lot in common as also, we were the first really tall men trying to get into the Corps. He was such an accomplished boxer who could 'knock out' an opponent quite easily, so many people commented that his opponents should have marketing/advertising adverts on their soles of their feet to capture a large audience! Gary was known as the Living Legend to all his colleagues and was a real character.

Being weak in the gymnastics field, it was my bad luck to have as my Staff Instructor Jack Pancott, a British Gymnast who competed in both the 1960 and 1964 Olympic Games. He was a tough man, took no prisoners and did not care whether you were a British International athlete or any other top competitor, you had to do anything that he asked you to do whether it was handstands on top of the parallel bars or front somersaults! I had the greatest respect for him and tried everything that was asked by him, even when I fell off the high bars and damaged my useful right arm that was needed to throw and lift weights.

TRANSFER TO THE ARMY PHYSICAL TRAINING CORPS

AND INTERNATIONAL ATHLETICS

My father and I after competing against one another. Great fun while it lasted

After this gruelling 13 weeks I successfully completed all the requirements to transfer to the APTC and was welcomed with open arms by the Army's athletics fraternity. I was extremely proud to have achieved this and to get accepted into the Corps and to receive my cross swords badge was a 'dream' come true. (I and another 1st East Anglian Infantryman Denis Arnold are the only soldiers from this regiment to have transferred to the Army Physical Training Corps).

My transfer to the Army Physical Training Corps in 1965 as a Sergeant Instructor and looking very happy. (APTC)

I went on a short leave before being posted to the Royal Military Academy, Sandhurst as Sergeant Instructor (SI) in Physical Training. This military establishment is based in Surrey and is the place where all officers of the British Army are trained to take the responsibilities of leading the soldiers under their command. I thought this to be a wonderful posting and was eager to arrive and start working and not training.

I remember the very first day reporting to the Sergeants' Mess and informing them that I was new, single and ready to move in before heading to the Gymnasium and report for duty On entering the Mess I saw my friend John Jennings sitting at the dining table with no-one sitting opposite him. Assuming it was free, I sat down and was having a normal conversation when I heard a cough behind me and everyone stopped in their tracks to await the next move from the gentleman behind me. He was a much older man, coming to his end of long service but this chair apparently had been his for these past two years. He abruptly mumbled something to the effect of, "Get off your arse and find another chair to sit on!" Although his rank was slightly higher than mine I was not used to this bullying attitude and asked his name which he gave as Staff Sergeant Jackson. I told him that I did not see his name printed on the back of the chair! I then moved this chair to the end of the mess table and got myself another chair in order to continue my conversations with John. Needless to say, I was reported to the Academy Sergeant Major RSM Phillips who kindly had some words with me and Jackson the reporter of this incident. He diplomatically asked both of us to shake hands and not let this incident happen again. Staff sergeant Jackson never claimed the chair again and also wished me the very best every time we met up carrying out our duties on the Campus. This was my first `baptism of fire` in living quarters at the Royal Military Academy, Sandhurst!

After lunch I reported to the Gymnasium to see Lt. Colonel M. Rouse who had been my officer in-charge in Aden who welcomed me at Sandhurst as did the RSM Gordon Staveley who would look after us. The Regimental sergeant Major (RSM) is primarily responsible for maintaining standards and discipline and acts as a parental figure to his or her subordinates. Gordon Staveley was in fact a fine man who took no nonsense from anyone and was a Korean War veteran.

I was then introduced to the other Physical Training staff, most of them known through my previous Army training and athletics competitions. They were very talented young men who had represented the Army in their chosen sports, some were internationals and others aspiring to make the 1968 Olympic Games. John Jennings from Dewsbury and I, soon became firm friends and this friendship still exists strongly today. The former Army Medic was a tenacious, hard-working Instructor, who eventually became an Army Captain and was an outstanding Army football and rugby player. At the time we were the only two instructors who were single so the bond was strong to say the least. John was small in stature compared to me and we were fondly known as `Batman and Robin` to the Officer Cadets!

The Physical Training Staff at The Royal Military Academy, Sandhurst in 1965. In the blazer, front row the very likeable Lt. Colonel Micky Rouse who had been my staff officer in Aden. On his right was the RSM Gordon Staveley who was much respected and feared at the same time! On the back row, far right one of my best friends John Jennings who finished up as a captain and I in the middle of the back row.
(Kind Permission RMA Sandhurst).

This posting was not always smooth as many times we were lucky to escape minor punishment after playing `games` with some of the Officer Cadets and other ranks. There are two incidents that I can remember fondly today which involved the Senior RSM Phillips and an Officer Cadet, Mr A. Beevor.

After acting as judges at the Officer Cadet boxing match both John and I with the help of the other PT Instructors, had to dismantle the boxing ring, load it onto a three-ton lorry then take it to the storage shed. At the back of the lorry there was a tarpaulin sheet that could be drawn like a curtain in order that no one could see inside. Well to our amazement and delight, we saw RSM Phillips and the Adjutant who was on a white horse, inspecting the buildings in the grounds. John shouted out, "Get into step with the horse RSM, you letting the side down"! All this I might add, said behind the curtain. Well, we all broke into laughter and even louder when we saw him trying to get in step with the Adjutant`s white horse! No sooner when entered the Gymnasium our RSM Gordon Staveley looked at us angrily and said, "Which b......shouted out those words to the senior RSM in the British Army? We paused and both John and I said in harmony, "I did it sir"! He then broke into laughter, shook our hands and said, "He thinks far too much of himself". Perhaps any other RSM would have

52

given us a reprimand and be confined to barracks for several days.

The other incident involved Officer Cadet Beevor who happened to be in both John and my squad for Battle Physical Training which was usually performed in the Confidence Area away from the Gymnasium. The aim of this training was to develop every officer to be physically fit to perform his/her duties efficiently. However, one night when both John and I were on guard duty at the Old College at Sandhurst, Beevor with his two fellow officer cadets accompanied by three ladies entered the building and went up the stairs. On reaching this position, one young girl smiled at me and I swiftly returned the compliment. She turned to Beevor to enquire who we were. His response was that we were just ordinary Physical Training Instructors. This comment was like a `rag to a bull` for John, who said to me, "I will get him for undermining the Corps. (Old College is one of three buildings on the Sandhurst Estate and opposite the parade ground used for drill practice and passing out parades)

In the morning after performing our guard duties, we assembled at the battle physical training area to take the training lesson, when John noticed Officer Cadet Beevor wearing a hair net under his helmet! When asked to remove his helmet a hair net was shockingly exposed. Asked why he wore a hair net, he explained that it prevented his hair falling over his eyes. John immediately produced a pair of scissors from his pocket and started to cut his hair from just above eye height and immediately asked him if he could now see properly? Beevor replied, "Perfectly clear staff" He then   put back his helmet. I was horrified by John's actions but he replied that any officer wearing a hair net would have been ridiculed by his men and respect would have disappeared overnight. In the circumstances John was right but perhaps he could have done this another way? Thinking we were to be charged for this action was swiftly disregarded by Officer Cadet Beevor who said to me afterwards that," Staff Sergeant was right and I will never wear a hair net again especially in public"!

Later he publically admitted that he did not like Sandhurst and you can in some ways see why, but he has acknowledged a debt of gratitude for his time in the Army.

Antony Beevor passed out of Sandhurst and became a regular officer in the 11th Hussars, served in Germany and in bases in England before embarking on a new career as a military historian of note. He has published several novels, while his works of non-fiction include The Spanish Civil War; Crete and the Battle and the Resistance, which won the 1993 Runciman Award. Berlin: The Downfall 1945, became a number one best seller and has been translated into twenty

–four languages. He is also a contributor/lecturer to the King`s College, London series of seminars on Armed Forces into the 21st Century, commissioned by the Economic and Social Research Council.

As a matter of interest, his father was in the SOE (Special Operations Executive) during World War II, sometimes referred to as `the Baker Street Irregulars` after the location of its headquarters. It was also known as `Churchill`s Secret Army`. Also, I had the pleasure of reading a fascinating book on Patrick Leigh Fermor by Artemis Cooper, Antony Beevor`s wife. Patrick Fermor, amongst other things, played a prominent role behind the lines in the Cretan resistance during World War II. In the film `I`ll Met by Moonlight` film star Dirk Bogarde plays the part of Patrick Fermor who captured the German General Heinrich Kreipe under the `noses` of the Germans.

Other Officer Cadets whom I had the honour of Instructing in physical training in 1965 was the late King George Tupou V of Tonga, known then as Prince George. A huge man, probably over 20 stone who spoke eloquently and sounded very `posh` but I could see he felt very uncomfortable in his PT clothing. He would rather have been in the Officers mess and enjoying his status amongst his friends. Right from the onset he informed me Sandhurst was a shock to him and he was not used to be yelled at by the Guards personnel. So we had to treat him differently and gently persuade him that Physical training was good for him plus everyone at Sandhurst had to pass some basic training tests otherwise, he would have to go on a PDC trip (Physical Development Course). He hated the idea of any perspiration and doing any form of exercise, so it was a great challenge to the PT staff. On one occasion he was asked to jump and hang on a bar so that he could lift his chest to the bar. So big was the man that all he could do was to raise his toes before landing back on his feet. This was after two instructors raised him so he could hang onto the bar. He was destined to do a PDC course but the timely death of his father prevented this and he had to return to Tonga to be crowned King in 2006. He was still in my opinion, a fine man who had a wonderful sense of humour especially away from the `sweat` of the Gymnasium and any yelling instructors!

Tonga lies 1320 miles northeast of New Zealand and is dependent on tourism, fishing and crop growing. It also boasts a formidable rugby union team who have beaten some of the top nations.

I was also very privileged to have been the physical training instructor along with my best friend John Jennings to the Sultan of Brunei who was in Ypres 40 platoon at Sandhurst. They were fantastic young men who were destined to do well in Army life. Most finished their careers as Lt. Colonels. After nearly 49 years we met up again, this time as old men but with the same enthusiasm as in our youth.

The Sultan or Mr Bolkiah to us in 1965 was not particularly fond of any form of exertion but was a trier! He was extremely friendly but when seen away from Sandhurst looked very ordinary despite being one of the richest men in the world. One night at the local cinema at the interval, the lady with the ice creams asked if either John or I were Sandhurst Physical Training Instructors. We both put up our hands and in a flash, all the ice creams from the tray were passed down to us. We immediately told her to stop as we had not ordered anything but her immediate reply was that the man sitting in the Circle behind us had paid. We looked up and saw the smiling Mr Bolkiah with his thumbs up. In the morning, during the start of the PT lesson we informed him that no bribes were allowed and furthermore, we were in strict training and ice creams were off the desert list!

The Sultan has been ranked among the wealthiest individuals in the world worth billions. Today he owns the Dorchester and many other similar hotels around the world and is reputed to have in his personal collection over 7000 high performance cars. All the Brunei wealth comes from the reserves of oil and natural gas. He succeeded to the throne as the Sultan of Brunei following the abdication of his father in October 1967.

It was only years later that I had the chance of an audience with His Majesty to meet him again when I was the Director of Physical Education and Sport at Sheffield University in 1987. My task was to help the University recruit suitably qualified overseas students to study for a Diploma in Sports Studies and I approached Brunei's Minister of Education with my intended assignment. On my return to Sheffield to my utter disappointment, a letter from his Private and Confidential Secretary had crossed, informing me that His Majesty had no objection to receive me in audience when I arrived in Negara Brunei Darussalam! It's a shame that we did not meet and discuss my visit intentions and how my life after leaving the British Army had changed to other challenges. Also, I did hear of rumours that having an audience with his Majesty resulted in a `gift` of a Rolex watch!

Even as an international athlete while serving in the Army I had to do duties like any other instructor and the posting was demanding as you were expected to train the Officer cadets on a daily basis, sometimes going on long runs twice a day. It was hard to train some days as energy levels by the evening, were low.

However to keep me company was a radio with `pop` music blearing out while I was weight training. Such noise blasting from the Gymnasium attracted Lt. Colonel Rouse to the training area and he watched me train. He took such a delight in seeing me train with such vigour that after I had finished asked me if it was possible, could I bring the radio into the large gymnasium in the morning to use for Officer Cadet Circuit training. To the delight of the cadets and the instructors, lessons and efforts improved dramatically if music was on display. This radio support continued throughout my time at Sandhurst and perhaps, I instigated the idea of using music with training throughout gymnasiums in the country in 1965? To this day music is part and parcel of exercise. Looking back if I could have marketed my idea of music and exercise, I might have been the second richest man in the world.

Family relaxation at the Spa Gardens Felixstowe. Self, Peter, Mum, Maureen and Anita with nephew Stephen in the pram. To think he is now 50 years of age!

Office of His Majesty
The Sultan and Yang Di-Pertuan
of
Negara Brunei Darussalam.

فابت کباوه دولج شهرا ملیا
دارن سری بکن اسلطان دان بغند رروان
نکارا بروني دارالسلام

Ref: HHPO 101/1967/X

Bandar Seri Begawan, 26 Mac 19 87

Dr. W.R. Tancred,
Director of Physical Education
and Recreation,
The University of Sheffield,
Department of Physical Education
and Recreation,
Goodwin Athletics Centre,
Northumberland Road,
Sheffield S10 2TZ,
UNITED KINGDOM.

Dear Sir,

      I am commanded by His Majesty Sultan Hassanal
Bolkiah Mu'izzaddin Waddaulah, Sultan and Yang Di-
Pertuan of Negara Brunei Darussalam to refer to your
letter ref: WRT/LM dated 10th February 1987 concerning
your request for an audience with His Majesty, which
has been received by His Majesty.

      I am pleased to inform you that His Majesty has
no objection to receive you in audience when you have
arrived in Negara Brunei Darussalam.

Yours faithfully,

(PSJ PENG HJ ABD MOMIN)
Private and Confidential Secretary to
His Majesty The Sultan and Yang Di-Pertuan of
Negara Brunei Darussalam.

Letter from the Private and Confidential Secretary to His Majesty, the Sultan of Brunei
to receive me for an audience with His Majesty

57

Ypres Company 1965. Extremely talented young Officer Cadets who went on to reach senior positions in the British Army. In the front row, fourth from the right is His Majesty, The Sultan of Brunei. Along with John Jennings, I had the great pleasure of training this company in physical training at Sandhurst. Incidentally, we all met up again after some 50 years in London for dinner and many drinks! (Mike Capper)

Anyhow, other talented sportsmen used music while performing with weights such as Colonel Mike Campbell-Lamerton of The Duke of Wellington's Regiment. A big man at 6ft. 4in, he was the captain of the British Lions in the difficult tour of New Zealand in 1966. He enjoyed weight training but if no music played, he found working-out that much harder. Mike Campbell-Lamerton was a most wonderful character who I admired from afar. He appeared to have many lives, once treading close on a mine while on active service in Korea and then in Cyprus, he fell 60ft/18.28m from a helicopter in full combat gear, sustaining severe back, hip and leg injuries. The fact that he recovered to play international sport is a tribute to his perseverance as well as his ability.

Captain Pringle Fisher of the Royal Army Dental Corps was another advocate of having music with weight training. He was an elegant rugby union flanker who captained Scotland in the 1960's and won 25 caps. He also played basketball for Scotland and Great Britain at the 1960 Olympic Games. A very modest man, who was much respected as an officer and gentleman to all of us at Sandhurst.

Although I did not see Colonel John Blashford-Snell in the weights room, he was a great supporter to the Army Physical Training Corps in that as a Staff Officer he saw first- hand of the importance of cadets having the desired physical fitness to lead men. He was a very experienced and knowledgeable Officer who had seen active service in many areas around the world and renowned as one of the world's highly respected explorers.

There were some odd sports fixtures that the Staff Sergeants Mess had organised which included cricket and rugby at venues that we used to play on but a fixture against the Broadmoor Hospital was by any standards most unusual. A high – security psychiatric hospital at Crowthorne in Berkshire, it housed many patients with severe mental illnesses, many of whom had personality disorders. It was strange to go through the gates and security checks to play but I do know that at this fixture we let the Broadmoor inmates win! The fixture as far as I am aware did not continue as a permanent annual one.

Another character but this time that I had the pleasure to serve with was Staff Sergeant Eddie McGee or to all of us in the Gymnasium` Fibber` McGee. He told many us so many stories, some being true and others just blatant lies. The strange thing to me was that he did not tell lies to gain any advantage but always told so many lies regardless. However, he was senior to many of us and had seen service in the Suez Canal conflict in 1956. Maybe, some of his interesting stories could have originated from this Egyptian experience?

He was undoubtedly a fantastic survival expert and learned his tracking and self–defence techniques and the art of survival during his years as an Army paratrooper with the British Special Forces. He was also an expert in karate, ju-jitsu and aikido. I was also impressed with his climbing techniques whether it was in the trees or on scaffolding. Eddie was most skilful, agile and moved silently like a cat.

On leaving the Army Physical Training Corps, he ran the National School of Survival Centre from his home village Nidderdale and to supplement his Army pension, worked as a successful bodyguard.

He is famed as the SAS tracker who helped the Police to corner the triple killer Barry Prudom in 1982 Using footprints in the early morning dew on the 5th day of the search, he tracked down Prudom, from Malton Cottage to a fresh liar he had made in the undergrowth. Cornered by Police marksmen, Prudom, armed with a gun and machete, refused to surrender to the police and shot himself.

At an Army sports reunion later on in the year in Aldershot, I met up with a very friendly gentleman   Bill Nankeville who also at one time served with the Army Physical Training Corps. He was a former AAA one mile champion and had competed at both the 1948 and 1952 Olympic Games in the 1500m. We got on famously sharing our athletics memories and personalities met. He had two sons David and Robert and is the father of Bobby Davro (Dav after David and Ro after Robert) the TV impressionist.

Some years later on a long walk with my wife Angela near Blakeney, north Norfolk, we came across an elderly gentleman riding a bicycle who wanted some directions. We told him where he was and thanked us. I also told him that he seemed fit for his age. He replied, "I have always kept fit since being a PT instructor in the Army". I told him that I too served in the Army and was an Army Physical Training Corps Instructor. He then bellowed out that he did not like any Instructors and, "If I ever saw that bloody Sergeant Nankeville again, I would punch him"! With a surname like that, he too must have known Bill but in different circumstances.

1965 was also the year that I was beginning to make progress as a discus thrower and was being selected regularly for Great Britain internationals. In the match against Poland I was again competing against Piatkowski and Bergier who finished 1st and 2nd but I was getting closer to them with my distances.

The other full international was against West Germany who had the gigantic Jen Reimers all 6ft. 10ins and weighing around 21 stone. He won the event but was slow compared to the two Poles in the previous competition. However, I was intrigued by the other West German Neu who only just beat me for 2nd place with his unusual double turn discus technique starting with a 'heel-ball-toe'. I tried to copy this technique when I was on home soil but had difficulty in staying in the circle and furthermore, losing my speed in throwing which was my asset.

Further international representations this time for England were against Czechoslovakia who had in their team the mighty Ludvik Danek who won the contest with a throw of 200ft 2ins/61m, the first time I had seen someone throw over this magical distance. He subsequently went on to break the world record and became the 1972 Olympic Champion. A giant of a man who was fast, rangy and at one time a national ski jumper of some repute illustrating his enormous leg strength and power.

I might add that he could handle his drinking better than most people I knew. After this match he and his team mate took me to his favourite restaurant and showed me how to drink out of a wine glass pipette with a yard of ale. Again, he won this contest!

The other England match that year was against East Germany in East Berlin. In order to compete, I had to get `clearance` from the Army and travelled with my passport not as a soldier but as a Government Official. I can still remember seeing guards with rifles at each corner of the stadium and the buildings looked bleak, the food was practically inedible and the accommodation dismal.

During this fixture, we had the opportunity of moving through Checkpoint Charlie which was the name given by the western Allies to the best known Berlin Wall crossing point between East Berlin and West Berlin during the cold war. At the most visible Berlin Wall checkpoint, checkpoint Charlie is frequently featured in spy movies and books. A popular cafe for Allied Officials, Armed Forces and visitors alike, Cafe Adler (`Eagle Cafe`) is situated right on the checkpoint and provides an excellent view to look into East Berlin while having something to drink and eat. Today, Checkpoint Charlie is now an Allied Museum since the Reunification of Germany.

It is interesting to note that the England team were strong enough to compete against East Germany in 1965 but that soon changed due to their doping programme. East Germany conducted a decade`s long programme to feed performance enhancing drugs to their athletes known officially as STATE PLAN 14.25. The drug regimes, given either with or without knowledge of the athletes, resulted in victories in international competitions, including the Olympic Games. East Germany had been a pioneering state in doping, so much that it was considered to be the inventor of doping.

Systematic doping of athletes ended with the fall of communism in East Germany in 1989 before German reunification a year later. Many former athletes including the throwers I competed against in this fixture suffered from health problems related to steroid consumption. Sport was indeed used as propaganda to achieve international prominence.

Looking back to those days, I often think that perhaps if I had better training facilities I would have done better in my discus throwing. I was improving but when on leave from the Army, I travelled home to Ipswich to see my coach who happened to be my father. As I mentioned earlier, Dad was most enthusiastic and would spend hours of his leisure time to help me to have success. He constructed a weight training area for me and my brothers Geoff and Peter to train in the back garden all–year round, summer and winter! For throwing, he would go to a path leading to Ransomes factory off Nacton Road in Ipswich and mark the discus and shot put circles with chalk. We would all throw our various implements under his watchful eyes. Most times I would lose the discus in a field which had about 18 inches of grass on it. Many times I showed frustrations but he would often say "Stay calm"! Calmness is an important factor in competition especially under pressure.

Throwing practice from a road with chalk marked circle

Dad and myself at Ipswich Airport`s `long grass` field

The factory shift workers often passed by offering their support and watching us train in amusement as many of them had not seen so many different throwing implements. A couple of these workers said, "Good luck Bill, you will beat those bloody Russians." They had no idea what I was up against!

Well I did not have the luxury of decent facilities nor was I State sponsored but had in abundance the `bulldog spirit`. Later on I did use the cellars of Ipswich Airport to do my weight training, which had poor ventilation, was cold and damp with no heating in the winter and worse of all, black soot was found in my nostrils when my nose was blown! Training facilities needed to be improved if I was to excel in the world of athletics. How I envy the training facilities available today for our athletes.

A rare family photograph with my brothers Peter, Geoff, Dad and me, at Bury St. Edmunds Suffolk competing in the Suffolk AAA championships. (Archant)

It was at this time while attending an athletics course in London that I met Ron Pickering the National Coach to Wales from 1961 to 1966. During the course, he left an indelible mark on me with his sheer enthusiasm for the sport. His talent as a brilliant coach and teacher with a larger than life personality and ability to inspire and motivate people soon became evident to all. Also as a coach he expected dedication, commitment, high moral standards of discipline and behaviour. After leaving his post of coaching in Wales he became the `voice of athletics` working for the BBC.

He started my weight training thinking in that he maintained that force or strength is as important to the explosive event athlete as breath is to the runner. What is more, whilst runners and coaches may argue over the relative merits of various running based training programmes to improve performance, no one can seriously doubt the absolute specific need of weight training for the great majority of athletics events. I was indeed very fortunate in meeting him as he had the specialist skills and knowledge of coaching throwers at international level.

On another occasion, I met a newly appointed national coach who did a lot of talking but on setting him questions, his replies were devoid of any basic technical knowledge. I had the impression `that a blind man was speaking about colour`. From there on, I avoided any contact so as not to embarrass him but many others `caught` him out, so in the end he resigned his position.

Another change for me around this time was the influence of Jim Fox who went on to win the team Modern Pentathlon gold medal at the 1976 Montreal Olympic Games. He was a full time athlete at Sandhurst and worked tirelessly at his five events namely cross country running, swimming, pistol shooting, riding and fencing. It was at the latter event where he caught out one of the biggest cheats in sport. In an epee bout against his friend Major Boris Onishchenko of the Red Army, a world champion and a silver medallist from the 1960 Rome Olympics, Jim accused him of cheating. The British team protested that Onishchenko`s weapon had gone off without actually hitting anyone. The competition director seized Onishchenko`s weapon and brought it to the bout committee.

It was found that the Russian`s weapon had been illegally modified to include a switch that allowed it to register a touch without making any contact whatsoever on his opponent. He was subsequently disqualified from the competition which inevitably forced the Soviet Union to scratch from the team event. As a result of this cheating, he was escorted from the athlete's village by Soviet Officials the night of his disqualification and reported to be `back in his home city of Kiev` the next day. Some two months later it was reported he had been called before the Soviet leader Leonid Brezhnev for a personal scolding and was dismissed from the Red Army on a dishonourable discharge. Furthermore, he was stripped of all his sporting honours and finished up as a taxi driver having fallen from grace.

I envied Jim`s position as a full time athlete and knew from his dedication that if one is to reach the top, then full time attention must be given. Maybe, I was in the wrong regiment or sport as athletics was not favoured by the powers at the top to be to be considered important enough for full time training? However, this change did happen when I purchased my discharge from the Army to pursue a teacher training course at Loughborough College in 1968. The grateful recipient of this change of attitude was Kriss Akabusi the 400 metre bronze medallist from the 1992 Barcelona Olympics. It was during this period of full time athletics training his true potential was realised. Good luck to him because with that kind of support, you are bound to succeed. In my case training Officer Cadets all day and performing the necessary guard duties at night did hamper my throwing progress.

Preparing to put the shot at Bury St Edmunds (Archant)

Myself with RSM Phillips, the senior RSM in the British Army and Jim Fox who went on to win a team gold medal at the 1976 Montreal Olympic Games at The Royal Military Academy, Sandhurst (Kind Permission RMA Sandhurst)

Rounding off this interesting chapter of my life in 1965 was my association with a wonderful character called Fortescue Finnis, known as Mickey to us but Fortescue to the senior officers! The pranks he used to play would have got us a court martial but he was treated as a bubbly fellow.

He used to teach the Commandant`s wife how to ride a horse as he was a fine horseman , having competed in the Modern Pentathlon at the 1964 Tokyo Olympic Games. He ordered the wife to, "Lift up your arse higher" whilst trotting in full view of us. As we laughed, he thought it most funny, so this time he shouted, "Get your arse to move up and down", to which she replied, "Anything you say Fortescue". Had it been anyone else, we would have been reported and `docked `a week`s wages!

Training during the winter months of 1965, was enjoyable and there was something to aim for as in 1966 there would be the British Empire and Commonwealth Games in Kingston, Jamaica and the European Championships in Budapest, Hungary. So with that in mind, I was anxious to compete early and qualify for both Games.

It stated off well at the Suffolk AAA championships when I broke the AAA National record with a throw of 182ft 10ins/55.72m some 5ft/1.52m off the UK National record. Many congratulatory letters and telegrams were received but the one received from Captain Phillip Oulton was rather special. He was a big man from the Cheshire regiment stationed at Sandhurst and was passionate about athletics. His speciality was the shot and discus, although he did not achieve huge distances, his enthusiasm was infectious.

Prior to this competition, the RMA Sandhurst Cadets had a match against other Officer Cadets from NATO countries at Breda, Holland. I went as one of the coaches to the team under Phillip Oulton. It was for five days and just before the competition, we travelled to Ruhr Valley to see the Mohne and Eder dams famed by the Dambusters raid in 1943. Operation Chastise was an attack on the German dams on the 16 and 17 May 1943 by the Royal Air Force No 617 Squadron lead by Wing Commander Guy Gibson who was eventually awarded the VC for this attack.

The Mohne and Eder dams were breached causing catastrophic flooding of the Ruhr valley and of the village in the Eder valley. The operation was very costly as 8 of the 19 aircraft were lost. Barnes Wallis the brilliant scientist who invented the `bouncing bomb` was distraught at the operational loss. However, the name `The Dambusters` and their story, will always be in the forefront.

We left this memorable visit in high spirits and the Officer Cadets could not wait to compete against their opponents in Breda. The cadets did well and I enjoyed the coaching experience with the occasional uplifting talks by Phillip Oulton. To cap it all, the winners of each event were given medals that were presented by Princess Beatrix later Queen of the Netherlands and her husband, Prince Bernhard of Lippe-Biesterfield.

On my return from Breda, I was selected by the AAA in a match against Cambridge University and was close to my recent AAA national record with a throw of 179ft 5ins/54.70m. Shortly after this fixture, I was asked to attend a training weekend under the watchful eye of National Coach John Le Masurier. He was a mild natured man, laid back yet hugely effective in his approach to coaching. I respected him straight away and we both learned from one another and from this meeting, he used to travel to Sandhurst to coach me for the remainder of this season. I might add he was the coach of Mary Rand who went on to win the 1964 Tokyo Olympics long jump event and Chris Carter a former British champion in the 800m.

National coach John Le Masurier who coached me for a period in the sixties here taking advice from him. (Mark Shearman)

On this course was Joe Bugner then a first year junior who I believe won the All-England discus title for the under 15 year age group. I thought he was a confident young man especially when he told me all afternoon that when he got stronger and bigger he would beat me easily! Well he did get bigger and stronger but he was more adept to boxing at the highest level than in discus throwing.

Josef `Joe` Bugner took up boxing and had a relative short amateur career. The last bout in Ipswich against George Baker, the Suffolk heavyweight champion and scrap metal dealer, I saw him win. My father and I wished him luck in his professional career at the event as he announced he was going to turn professional at an unusually young age of 17!

In March 1971, he is remembered to have beaten national hero Henry Cooper for the British, Commonwealth and European title in a 15-round controversial decision which as a result, was Cooper`s last professional fight. Bugner twice held the British and Commonwealth heavyweight titles and was three times European heavyweight champion. He also went the distance with both Muhammad Ali and Joe Frazier which is outstanding considering their greatness in boxing.

After retirement from boxing, he went into the film industry as a small time actor and also did some sports advertising. Today he suffers from being diabetic and has a serious back injury sustained from all the training and fighting in his youthful years, something that I have in common with him today.

The last time we spoke to each other was in a hotel prior to his fight against Winston Allen of the USA at Bloomsbury in 1982. We wished each other well and it was not long after that he relocated to Australia where he lives. (Below from Athletics Weekly)

Bill Tancred advises first-year-junior Joseph Bugner.

On Saturday 18 June 1966 I had the honour to throw against Russia at the White City and performed well in this much loved stadium which held large crowds and was the first Olympic stadium in the UK. The stadium was demolished in 1985 to make way for the BBC White City Building.

After the match, we had the Dinner for athletes and officials at The Dorchester in Park Lane which was sponsored by the News of the World. It was a wonderful evening and I got on very well with my Russian opponents especially after a drink or two, with no politics discussed, just exchanging jokes.

On the 9 July, I won the first of my seven AAA`s titles at the White City and to become British champion was most pleasing. During the contest, it started to rain which made spinning the discus rather difficult. To have a better grip in these conditions I used sticky resin (from pine trees) on my fingers so by the end of the competition, the hands were black and tacky. I did not know at the time that Her Majesty the Queen was presenting prizes to the winners of each event and as my event was running late, I was told by the senior official that I had no time to wash and clean my hands. So as I went to shake her hands, she immediately asked what this sticky substance was. I informed her that it was resin to help to throw the discus in inclement weather. No doubt today she shakes hands with everyone but wears white gloves to this day, because of the shaking experience with me that day or that`s what I believe!

Incidently, it was John Pennel the four time pole vault world record holder and USA 1964 Olympian, who introduced the `resin` to me at the 1963 AAA Championships at the White City. Resin was used as an aid to help him with gripping the new flexible *fibreglass pole* which made a huge impact in the event against the old *metal pole*. He went on to become the first man to vault over 17ft./5.18m

The next selection was for England at the British Empire and Commonwealth Games to be held in Kingston, Jamaica from the 4 to 13 August 1966. This was the first time that the Games would be held outside the so-called White Dominions but the last time as the British Empire and Commonwealth Games. In future they would be known as just the Commonwealth Games.

The model pose wearing the 1966 British Empire and Commonwealth Games blazer
(Archant)

The athletics events were held at Independence Park and this was the final athletics competition at the quadrennial competition to feature events measured in Imperial units rather than metric units.

This was my first Games and was the most enjoyable to say the least. I enjoyed meeting all the other Empire and Commonwealth athletes in the village which was excellent. Apparently, there was more variety in food compared to the Tokyo Olympics of 1964. Each team manager had a car for running about with some rumoured to go site seeing around the island! The University of West Indies` site of the village was set well out from the noise and hustle of the town.

However, the training facilities were not adequate so in an unprecedented move, the athletes used the National Stadium to train. By some terrible oversight no place had been made available for training. Furthermore, there was a bumpy grass field useless for hurdlers and jumping specialists because no pits existed and it was particularly dangerous for runners with square ends and ups and downs. If it had not been for the disordered training facilities, the result of a conflict between the local organisers and the Jamaican Empire Games

Federation, everything would have been fine.

The favourite relaxation was to listen to all those wonderful steel drums. I was captivated by this kind of music which to me was extraordinary and the use of *calypsos* for carnival performance was stimulating. This and *Reggae* showed that there was good deal more to Jamaica than rum!

I was witness to some outstanding performances in seeing for example Harry Jerome (Canada) winning the 100 yards in 9.41 sec; Wendell Mottley (Trinidad) first in 440 yards with a time of 45.08 sec and the majestic Kip Keino (Kenya) winning the mile in 3 min 55.34 sec.

In the discus event I was outclassed as the humidity affected my spinning of the implement and I finished a disappointing 9th place. I was not used to throwing in such temperatures and was completely overawed by the sizes of my discus rivals. The winner of this event Les Mills, a hugely muscular man from New Zealand threw the implement 184ft 4in/56.18m, followed again by another large man from Canada George Puce who threw 183ft 9in/55.94m and 3rd was the gigantic Robin Tait from New Zealand with a throw of 180ft 5in/55.02m. All of these throwers, I would meet later at the 1970 Commonwealth Games in Edinburgh, Scotland.

Les Mills went on to become a very successful Gym owner and gives his name to *Les Mills International* (Gym programmes used throughout the world) and eventually became the *Mayor of Auckland* New Zealand`s largest city from 1990 until 1998. The other New Zealander Robin Tait, had the distinction of representing his country at six Commonwealth Games.

It was pleasing however, that my roommate John FitzSimons won the gold medal in the javelin with a throw of 261ft 9in/79.78m and I returned home happy knowing the experience of competing in the `friendly Games` was worth all the training and sacrifice in making a successful athlete.

It was also a good time to be involved in sport as the nation basked in the glory of the magnificent England football World Cup win. The 1966 FIFA world Cup final was one of the most controversial finals ever. The match was played between England and West Germany on the 30 July at Wembley Stadium. The British television audience peaked at 32.3 million viewers making the final the most watched television event ever in the UK. England won after extra time to win the Jules Rimet trophy.

My first AAA discus title win with cup in 1966 (Archant)

No sooner we were back it was the European Athletics Championships in Budapest, Hungary from 30th August until the 5 September. This was going to be harder than the British Empire and Commonwealth Games as the stiff competition would be coming from the Eastern Bloc countries that included the mighty East Germans. I was proved to be right as the East Germans finished 1st (Thorith), 2nd (Losch) and 3rd (Milde) and I failed to qualify for the finals in this enormous stadium.

The Nep stadium had a capacity of 100,000 and was built between 1948 and 1953 using a large number of `forced` volunteers, including soldiers. Less than one year later, on the 23 May 1954, the English football team suffered its worst nightmare by being beaten at this stadium 7-1. Now named after the brilliant Ferenc Puskas, who was widely regarded as the best striker in the world in his

73

time and Hungary's greatest ever footballer. Today, it is an all-seated having a capacity of 38,652. It's a shame that only last year (2015), I along with my wife Angela, walked very closely to this stadium, not knowing it had changed its name otherwise for memory sake, I would have jumped to the chance to see it again.

A new IAAF ruling was applied for the first time making gender verification for female events mandatory. As a consequence, all women competitors were forced to have sex checks. Several of the greatest women athletes missed this year's championships, among them world record holders Iolanda Balas (high jump) from Romania, as well as Tamara Press (shot put) and Tatyana Shchelkanova (long jump) both from the Soviet Union.

Great Britain won gold medals in men's long jump with Lynn 'the leap' Davies jumping 7.98m and the great character and horse racing tipster Jim Hogan the marathon in a time of 2 hrs 20.04 sec. Some other gold medal winners from Europe included the suave Frenchman Michel Jazy winning the 5000m, Eddy Ottoz (Italy) in the 110m hurdles, and the large Hungarian Vilmos Varju in the men's shot put. I watched Vilmos with interest because in between rounds he was drinking coffee which was so thick, it hardly poured out from his beloved flask. The outstanding competitor from these Games was Irena Kirszenstein from Poland who won both the women's 200m with a time of 23.1sec and the long jump with a distance of 6.55m. East Germany won eight gold medals.

After the Championships closed there were the usual banquet celebrations with 'free flowing' alcohol and in my case 'snaps' by the glass full. The word 'snaps' is similar in meaning as the German word 'schnaps', in the sense of 'any strong alcoholic' drink. Well, I was lead well by Miklos Nemeth from Hungary and John FitzSimons both very friendly javelin throwers. Nemeth would go onto to become the 1976 Montreal Olympics men's javelin champion and whose father was the 1948 London Olympic Games hammer winner, so he came from a great family tradition of throwers.

We said our farewells around 1am and left to find the station to return back to the athletes' village in a 'fog' of not knowing where I was? Luckily for me, I spotted another drunken athlete, Laurie Tait the 110m hurdler. Thinking we were on the right train, we both fell asleep for a quick 'cat nap'. After an hour or so, I noticed nothing familiar and tried to ask people in the carriage in slowly speaking English and arm gestures, where were we going and if wrong , how to get back to the Budapest station. Panic set in when being told, we were going further east and away from Budapest.

I awoke Laurie and changed trains so we could catch another one this time heading west to Budapest. Luckily and being in a sober state, we managed to get a taxi just in time to pack up our bags and head back with the team to the airport for home.

It was some years later that my father and I were walking near Hyde Park London and spotted Laurie performing his art on the pavement. He immediately recognised me and informed my father that his son saved his life due to the horrible experience on the train in Budapest. He felt at the time we would never have got home safely again to good `old Blighty`.

Long term family friend Ken Bloomfield, Dad and self with young sister Anita in the front at Felixstowe

It was already a long season but two more internationals were arranged before the end of the season. In September, Great Britain was against Sweden in Stockholm at the 1912 Olympic stadium. It is the smallest athletics stadium used in a summer Olympics and has seen more world records broken than any other stadium around the world.

Making up the team included Jeffrey Archer for his only one full GB representation and although not ranked in the top 10 of British 200m runners, made the team as so many athletes dropped out because they were either tired from a long season or beyond their best so late in the year.

On the other hand, I was pitted against the fast improving giant of a man called Ricky Bruch. He stood 6ft 6ins tall (1.98m) and weighed 310lbs (140kg).

Larger than life, he turned up with a bowler hat, brolly and spoke English most eloquently, so would have been a promoter's dream in getting 'bums on seats'!

Although he did not win the event, the winner being the very tall Lars Hagland, Bruch beat me but the distance was not outstanding. During his career however he did win a bronze medal at the 1972 Munich Olympic Games and equalled the world record in June 1972 with a throw of 224ft 5in/68.40m.

He trained with tenacity and maniacal intensity for the 1984 Olympic Games in Los Angeles but this was all in vain as he was snubbed by the Swedish Olympic committee from competing. He wanted revenge so Bruch continued fanatical training and entered small competitions without any stiff competition. He also managed to use the wind to his advantage in having a number of discus circles around the stadium and depending on the wind direction he could use the appropriate discus circle.

By employing this perfectly legal ploy, he eventually in November 1984, set a new world record with a throw of 233ft 10in/71.26m at the age of 38. Bruch was not only a workaholic he enjoyed himself along the way. He has also written a biography *Gladiatoms Kamp* (The Gladiator's Battle released in 1990) and was the star of the documentary 'The Soul is Greater than the World'.

Sadly, he passed away on the 30 May 2011 after his toughest battle, pancreatic cancer at 64 years of age.

The last international fixture was between Great Britain, Finland and France in wonderful Paris on the 1 and 2 October 1966. I came 3rd in the match and had the satisfaction of beating the two Frenchmen Alard and Drufin, including Mike Lindsey, who at his prime was GB's leading shot and discus specialist.

The banquet was held on a riverboat travelling slowly on the river Seine with all three nationalities on board. Soon as the wine flowed, the noise became louder and louder and the French started singing and asked us to reply. This went on for 30 minutes or so, when all of a sudden the bread rolls covered in cheese were thrown in our direction, one hitting Mike so hard that he went 'red in the face' so we all thought this was it! Food was thrown at each other and all control was lost and the boat had to return back to the starting point. Many of the throwers were so inebriated they had difficulty in walking and had to be put into taxi's to go to the hotel. Next morning, the coach taking the athletes back to the airport was quiet and many athletes looked pale and frail. It was the end of the athletics season. So much for European harmony and friendship!

Back at Sandhurst, military training of the Officer Cadets continued along with my aspirations of improving as an athlete. I enjoyed training these Cadets as they were fine young men who were a credit to our nation. Within one term, you can recognise who the real leaders of men will be. It was an honour and privilege to be their Physical Training Staff Instructor, as was serving in the Army Physical Training Corps.

The Army Physical Training Corps Instructors were also well respected by most regimental personnel at Sandhurst and one former RSM comes to mind which is interesting. On my infrequent visits to the Sergeants mess bar, I came across an elderly gentleman who everyone called Sir, including myself. He always wished me well in all my Army and International competitions and I thought no more of it until some senior soldiers told me who he was.

It turned out to be Regimental Sergeant Major (RSM) John Lord. RSM Lord was a parachutist and was captured in Arnhem and taken prisoner, along with a great number of other Arnhem prisoners to Stalag X1B at Fallingbostel. This camp was in a dreadful state when all the prisoners arrived and RSM Lord immediately took over the administration and worked tirelessly to improve it until liberation in 1945. When liberated, the officers and men who arrived at the camp could not believe the high state of morale amongst the prisoners and the excellent bearing and turn out, all due to the RSM.

He spent 15 years at Sandhurst as the RSM and never disclosed his excellent war record to anyone.

It`s well worth noting that The Academy`s stated aim is to be `The National Centre of Excellence for Leadership`. All British officers, including late-entry officers who were previously warrant officers, as well as other men and women from overseas, are trained at the Royal Military Academy, Sandhurst. The Academy is the British Army equivalent of the Britannia Royal Naval College, Dartmouth; Royal Air Force College Cranwell and the Commando Training Centre Royal Marines.

Another Officer Cadet at Sandhurst at this time (1967) was O/C Mark Phillips who later on in his military career finished as a Captain serving in the Royal Dragoons. As a cadet I found him hard working and polite with a fondness for the horses. He was then a reserve member of the British Equestrian team for the 1968 Mexico Olympics.

I met him again at the 1972 Munich Olympic Games where in the 3 day team event, he won a gold medal. Soon after this he met and married Anne, Princess Royal with whom he had two children.

After he retired from the Army, he continued to style himself Captain Mark Phillips-which was allowed as junior cavalry officers whose civilian work involves equestrianism, may continue to use their rank. He remains a leading figure in British equestrian circles, a noted equestrian course designer and a columnist in the Horse and Hound magazine. It was an honour to have been his physical training instructor during his period of military training at Sandhurst.

Prior to the athletics season getting underway, I was invited to attend a reception for Ipswich sporting personalities by the Mayor Mrs Marjorie Keeble. In her light hearted speech at the Ipswich Town Hall, she said "With all due respects to Mr Ray Crawford (Ipswich Town's centre forward) there are other games besides football which deserve recognition." This was true and it was a pleasant evening mixing with them and exchanging stories.

Along with Ray Crawford who played for England, were motor cyclist Dave Bickers, hockey player Dinah Onyett, Suffolk netball player Rita Flude, cyclist Gerald Coles, Derek Clarke of the RAF and decathlon team captain at the British Empire and Commonwealth Games plus a few drunken officials clutching their sherry glasses and slurring in speech when talking to us. No one could understand the vote of thanks from one them but we all left happy and content at this rare event at the time in the Town Hall.

The athletics season got off to a good start by throwing the discus 180ft 5in/55.00m in the AAA's match against Cambridge University including a personal best of 54ft 8in/16.66m in the shot put. The discus result convinced me that I could break the British discus record this summer because this distance was unexpectedly long so early in the season. It was also pleasing to hear that brother Geoff had been selected in the hammer event in a AAA's match against London University. Although smaller in stature, Geoff was technically efficient and fast. So it was hoped that the youngest brother Peter would follow in our footsteps and throw for the AAA's which would make it a noteworthy family of brothers in the throwing events. This happened for Peter in a match against Birmingham University, making a brotherly field event trio achieving such distinction unique.

I went on to win the Inter Counties Championships for Suffolk AAA's at the White City with a throw of 166ft 7in/50.78m beating John Hillier from Kent and Barry Lynn representing Middlesex in the process. Hillier went on to coach Lawrence Okoye the current UK discus record holder with a throw of 223ft 10ins/68.24m set in Halle, Germany on the 19 May 2012. I also finished 3rd in the shot put which enabled me to gain the valuable points for the County. In doing so, the Suffolk County team eventually took the Minor Counties award in 1967 for the first time ever which was a great achievement for Suffolk in athletics.

As soon as this fixture was finished, I was called up to compete for the British Army against the German Army in the discus and shot events in the BAOR Stadium at Sennelager. I was in good form and broke both Army shot (55ft 9in/17.00m) and discus (179ft 7in/54.76m) records to win both events. Past holder of more than a dozen Army Field event titles was Eric Cleaver at 41 years of age was by far the oldest competitor and still good enough to gain a creditable 2nd place. During his youth he represented Great Britain several times and finished his Army career as a Lt. Colonel.

Spectators were treated to a splendid attempt at 7ft in the high jump by the German international, Lieutenant Wolfgang Schillkowski, at a height he holds the German record. He was close to this but had to settle for a winning jump of 6ft 10in/2.08m.

Among the large crowd was Colonel Soellner, Commandant of the German Armed Services Physical Training school, who won the gold medal for rowing at the Berlin Olympic Games in 1936.

My teammate Dave Bayes won a close encounter in the hammer with a throw of 183ft 10in/56.04m. A strong man who trained hard but played harder when not on duty was an inspiration to us who were younger than him. I felt sorry that he never won a full Great Britain vest as he was so close. He was splendid company to have a drink or four with and his sense of humour and jokes were legendary. He could tell jokes from 6pm until the shouts of "last orders" would be given by the Bar staff. The famous Ken Dodd and Dave would have been a great pair on stage.

One joke of his I can recall went something like this - A train left Waterloo station and in one carriage there were only two people sitting opposite one another. After 5 minutes, the male passenger noticed the title of the book being read by a woman called *Sexual Statistics*. He then asked her, "Is it a good book?" In which she replied," Very, very interesting. Do you know that the Red Indian has the longest male organ and the Polish has the widest?" He replied, "Is that so. By the way, my name is Tonto Polanski and what's yours?" Dave would then go on like this all night. A lovely bubbly character you would like to take with you to liven up a party.

The other notable team mate was Tony O`Neill, a formidable all-rounder who was in the Army Physical Training Corps and was the athletics specialist. Tony could also consume beer as though there was no tomorrow and could look as bright as a button next morning when everyone else was suffering from hangovers. His knowledge of athletics particularly in the statistics of performance records was truly amazing. He could tell you who threw such and such, the day, the time and whether that thrower came 2nd or 5th, he could be spot on. He became a voluntary athletics statistician with the National Union of Track Statisticians (NUTS).

RESULTS

Event	First	Second	Third	Fourth
100 yards	UFFZ H Swoboda (G), 9.9sec	KAN Brenner (G)	Cpl Bukasoqo (B)	Sgt Fitch (B)
220 yards	PZGREN H Moser (G), 22.3sec	KAN Brenner (G)	Lieut Skippage (B)	Sgt Fitch (B)
880 yards	SCHTZ H Ochsenbruch (G), 1min 53.8sec	PZSCHTZ Barthelt (G)	Lieut Ling (B)	S/Sgt Kitchener (B)
One mile	GEFR H Franke (G), 4min 10.1 sec	Cpl Gibson (B)	GEFR Buhr (G)	L/Cpl Gue (B)
Three miles	SSI P J Freeman (B), 13min 59.6sec	Pte Wood (B)	SU Liess (G)	GEFR Falke (G)
120 yards hurdles	Lieut R Legge (B), 14.4sec (British Army record)	Lieut Houston (B)	GEFR Stahl (G)	GEFR Stegmann (G)
3000 metres steeplechase	GEFR G Molders (G), 9min 9.6sec	Cpl Venus (B)	L/Sgt Piotrowski (B)	STUFFZ Spreng (G)
4 x 440 yards relay	German Army, 3min 19.2sec			
High jump	Lieut W Schillkowski (G), 6ft 10in	FHJ Delfs (G)	Spr Bridges (B)	Pte Berryman (B)
Long jump	GEFR G Brunner (G), 23ft 1½in	FHJ Delfs (G)	Lieut Legge (B)	Cpl Phillips (B)
Triple jump	L/Sgt M Varney (B), 44ft 4in	Sigm Wells (B)	GEFR Seibel (G)	GEFR Brunner (G) retired hurt
Pole vault	Cpl J Fenge (B), 14ft 0in (British Army Record)	SCHTZ Strobel (G)	SI Lyons (B)	UFFZ Swoboda (G)
Shot	SI W Tancred (B), 55ft 8¼in (British Army record)	FHJ Schoon (G)	Cpl Byam (B)	OLT Motzkus (G)
Discus	SI W Tancred (B), 179ft 7in (British Army record)	Capt Cleaver (B)	LT Knobel (G)	FHJ Schoon (G)
Hammer	Sgt D A Bayes (B), 183ft 10in	OLT Breindl (G)	Sgt Hughes (G)	OLT Motzkus (G)
Javelin	GEFR H Neumann (G), 218ft 11in	S/Sgt Hart-Ives (B)	UFFZ Zumpe (G)	Capt Tinniswood (B)

German Army 91 points, British Army 85.

Setting a new British Army shot record 55ft 8in/16.97m in Sennelager, Germany 1967
(Both above from The Soldier Magazine)

I was fortunate to know Tony really well and he has provided me with help from Peter Matthews, with a record of all my discus competition throws over 58m with dates and the year, including all my full GB appearances and records which appear in this book.

In the triple jump, Mike Varney who was also another PT Corps man went on to become a qualified Remedial Gymnast and subsequently, the physiotherapist for Tottenham Hotspur Football Club for almost 30 years. So in the Army team were some very talented individuals but we lost the athletics match against the German Army by 6 points but beat them soundly in beer drinking afterwards!

Winning the discus event in the London versus Milan fixture. On my left, is Mike Lindsey who was a formidable British shot and discus thrower. I represented London because at the time, I was a member of the Polytechnic Harriers athletics club.

(Photograph by Alberto Cavallini)

I went on to win my 2nd AAA title national title later that year with a throw of 169ft 9in/51.76m at the White City beating John Watts and Mike Lindsay. John was a very muscular Royal Marine who would later be my team mate at the 1972 Munich Olympic Games. Strong as an ox, well-conditioned, he could easily have represented GB in Judo had he concentrated on this Sport. A fine man, who stood for no nonsense and had strong principles.

The International season started off with the Europa Cup Semi–Final in Duisburg, Germany on the 22 July. Germany was the eventual winners, Hungary 2nd with Britain 3rd who failed to qualify for the final. I managed to secure 3 points after a throw of 177ft/53.95m

The next big test was a tour for Great Britain with a match against Hungary in Budapest on the 29/30 July and then in Sczecin, Poland 2/3 August against the

Poles. The Nep stadium was again the venue for this encounter and I was against the world ranked Hungarian Geza Fejer who threw 180ft 2in/54.92m to win, 2nd his compatriot Janos Farago who narrowly beat me with a throw of 178ft 1in/54.29m. Great Britain beat the Hungarians 113 points to 99 in the men's contest and the women finishing 1st as well 73 points to 51.

After this match the team flew out to Sczecin which is located near the Baltic Sea on the Oder River. Again, I finished 3rd behind the two Poles but I was getting closer to these giant throwers. At the banquet, I presented Edmund Piatkowski with a pair of stockings which I had promised him. The banquet erupted into fits of laughter. It was not directly for him to wear but a present to his wife!

The next GB international was against the mighty USA at the White City on the 12 August 1967.The team were trounced 139 points to 84 points on the Saturday. Again, I finished 3rd with a throw of 174ft 6in/53.2m and John Watts 4th with a throw of 160ft 2in/48.82m The winner was the friendly Gary Carlsen, a 22-year old Southern Californian University student and 2nd Bill Neville, both of whom were regular 200ft/61m discus throwers. On this occasion, Carlsen threw the implement 198ft 7in/60.54m to win with Neville placed 2nd with a throw of 184ft 4in/56.18m.

After the banquet, which was held at the Grosvenor House in Park Lane, London and sponsored by the News of the World, Gary Carlsen and the other `heavy` throwers asked where was Soho and if close could we visit? They had heard about it in the States and it was on Gary's `bucket list` already at his young age.

For those not familiar to the location, Soho is an area of the City of Westminster and part of London's West End. Long established as an entertainment district, for much of the 20th Century, Soho had a reputation as a base for the sex industry in addition to its night life and its location for the Headquarters of leading film companies.

Since the 1980's, the area has undergone considerable gentrification. It is now predominately a fashionable district of upmarket restaurants and media offices, with only a small remnant of sex industry venues.

However, in 1967 there was much to be seen and our American visitors were not let down and one of them went off with a scantily dressed buxom lady for the remainder of the night. For Gary, it was his best evening ever and Soho the best district in the world.

I soon had to get back into shape as I was selected by the British Amateur Athletic Board in conjunction with the British Olympic Association and a certain number of UK's senior athletes to go to Font Romeu for 2 weeks altitude training (30

August to 10 September) in preparation for the 1968 Mexico Olympics.

The National Centre for altitude training at Font-Romeu (1,850m above sea level) was just opened primarily for French athletes to hold their training camps in their preparation for the Mexico Olympic Games that were to be held at altitude. Font-Romeu is set in the wonderful and scenic Pyrenees on the French side of the French and Spanish border which is approximately 10km away.

The centre had all the necessary facilities in order to train hard, often under the watchful eyes of a national coach and also a leading physiologist named Dr Griffiths Pugh. Dr Pugh is best known for his contribution to the success of the 1953 British Everest expedition led by John Hunt during which Edmund Hillary and Tensing Norgay made the first ascent of the highest mountain in the world.

Dr Pugh highlighted the importance of having adequate oxygen and fluid for the climbers high on the mountain. His insistence was given not from an armchair but from experience on mountains and supported by meticulous scientific observations in the field. It therefore carried weight with the climbers, who could be sceptical of scientists whose work was confined to the laboratory.

He was chosen to come to this training camp due to his research on the effects of altitude on athletes` performance. He predicted correctly that the altitude in Mexico would decrease times for long distance events but the reduced density of the air would give small advantage to sprint events.

We got on really well together as he was also interested on the impact of throwing in high altitude and in training with weights. When not training and over a coffee, we discussed life in India, where his father was a barrister in Calcutta and the British Army life and my service with the PT Corps. He had served as a Medical Officer during World War II. Dr Pugh was a most interesting conversationalist when you got him interested.

However, Griffiths Pugh was a complete British eccentric. There are plenty of anecdotes of his absentmindedness and one springs to my mind on the numerous occasions he could not remember where he parked his car and would often go back home by train and report it missing to his local police station. The police would eventually recover it!

However, the funniest story of his eccentric behaviour relates to his experimental work in 1951. A visitor to the Hampstead offices of *The Medical Research Council* was confronted with the most extraordinary sight of a semi- naked man lying in a large Victorian enamel bath full of brim with water and ice cubes. The man's body was chalk-white with cold and covered in wires attached to various instruments. His ginger hair contrasted sharply with the pale pallor of his face. The man in question was Dr Griffiths Pugh and the visitor had stumbled across him conducting a typical eccentric experiment into the effects of hypothermia. He had to be rescued by his laboratory assistant who was luckily close by otherwise he might have frozen to death because he hardly moved in the enamel bath!

Dr Griffith Pugh talking to me on the track at Font Romeu (Athletics Coach, BAAB)

Taking a break from altitude training in Font-Romeu

The other athletes who attended this training camp Included Mary Rand, Lillian Board and Tony Wadhams the triple jumper. On one of our very few rest days we managed to go to Andorra which was located in the eastern Pyrenees Mountains and bordered by Spain and France. It is the sixth-smallest nation in Europe.

I can still remember it vividly as being very warm with many tourists, including us, visiting the shops for any bargains and the general sight-seeing. It was a wonderful day and we got to know about each other in a different environment, sharing different stories and life experiences, with plenty of army jokes thrown in.

Mary Rand was indeed the `Golden Girl` of British athletics having won the long jump at the 1964 Tokyo Olympic Games by breaking the world record, the first British female to win an Olympic gold medal in track and field athletics. She had also won a silver in the pentathlon and a bronze medal in the 4 x 100m women`s relay. She was a fantastic all-round athlete with a lovely engaging personality.

Indeed after this, she used to travel to Sandhurst`s athletics track at the Oak

85

Grove in her red sports car to see her coach John Le Masurier who happened to be coaching me at this time. So when she appeared everything and everyone were at a standstill! She had that magnetic appeal at that time. There is a plaque commemorating the world long jump record (22ft 2in/6.76m) by Mary at the 1964 Olympic Games in the market place in Wells, Somerset where she had come from.

Mary Rand with some of the British athletics team in Budapest, 1966

Lillian Board was a most charming, polite and bubbly girl who was destined to win a silver medal in the 400m women`s event at the 1968 Mexico Olympics being beaten just before the line by Colette Besson of France, by a mere 0.09 sec. She was so close in being an Olympic athletics champion.

Lillian Board, Olympic silver medallist 1968, running at the White City Stadium
(Mark Shearman)

I used to go to her parents house in Ealing and met her kindly father George and her sister Irene together with Lillian`s boyfriend, David Emery who I believe was a budding journalist at the time. We would talk about the love of athletics and about life in general but things were to change for poor Lillian.

In September 1970, she was sadly diagnosed with terminal colorectal cancer (or bowel cancer) and told she had two months to live. She then travelled in November 1970 in the hope of seeking a cure to the village of *Rottach-Egern* in the Bavarian Alps near Munich, West Germany to be treated by the controversial physician, Dr Josef Issels at his Ringberg Cancer Clinic.

Straight away she was placed on a strict diet of healthy food and with spring water and herbal tea as her only drinks adhering to his belief in non-mainstream treatments. Following this, she then had her tonsils and two front teeth removed as Issels believed they helped spread infection. Very soon her conditioned worsened and she sadly died in Munich on the 24 December 1970. It was an extremely sad day and a great loss to all her family, friends and to the sport of athletics.

The other athlete who was with us at Andorra and specifically Font-Romeu, was Tony Wadham who was at Loughborough College of Education, made a few GB representations but unfortunately failed to make the Olympic Team for Mexico City, the places going to Fred Alsop and Derek Boosey.

The last full international match was against West Germany on the 22/23 September at the White City. Hein-Direck Neu with his unusual `heel-ball-toe` start of the discus turn won the event, closely followed by Klaus-Peter Henning and then myself 3rd with a throw of 171ft 1in/52.19m.

Neu who spoke very good English and had a career as a Sports master in West Germany, was tested positive for anabolic steroids in 1978 when he last won his national title and served a ban of 1 year. At the age of 69, he gave an interview to a German newspaper and declared that he had taken anabolic steroids for years and all his colleagues did so as well, stating that even sports officials and physicians in West Germany were involved and everybody informed.

After the hectic training and competitive season it was back to military training at Sandhurst with a view of a complete break from athletics training and enjoying life once more. This involved lots of parties and general relaxation before the winter`s hard and dedicated training which would be necessary, if I was going to make the 1968 Olympic Games.

However, during the season I met a few agents who were looking out for models to exhibit shirts and fitness clothing. These agents liked the look of me and requested that I should go to London to show my potential! They were members of The Association of London Model Agencies. After 3 or 4 shoots, I was wanted and they offered me a contract and promised regular work such as modelling for Clothing catalogues. With this new direction I went back to Sandhurst full of joy and awaited Army clearance to do this part-time modelling role. Two weeks later, the news came back that I was a soldier first and a model second, but I was not allowed to sign the contract.

On the left is the Great Britain v USA plaque for the shot put 1969. On the right is the Great Britain versus USSR plaque for the discus 1966.

Athletics Competitors photograph 1969 European Championships

Modelling tracksuit for keep fit enthusiasts

Who knows had the contract been signed I might have been a model and not a regular soldier from that time. It was rare I suppose and flattering to be recognised as a potential model for a sports person going back to 1967 when the sport was amateur with no agents to advise and help. Today, modelling goes hand in hand with top sport. Although disappointing, it gave me the momentum to start training in earnest to break the British discus record and make the Olympic team next year.

So with this in mind and my firm commitment I believed that with proper and dedicated training I would break the discus record. As a result, my training schedule would consist of the following training protocols:-

☐ GENERAL: Agility exercises, mobility training, general fitness maintenance, circuit training, `athlete` preparation and long distance continuous running (30 minutes).

☐ SPEED: Speed running, tempo runs 200m x 5-10 and resistance running.

☐ STRENGTH: Rope climbing, Power lifting, Olympic lifts (aim - maximum strength, explosiveness and speed), multi-bounds (30-60m), depth jumps (70-90cm) and reactive strength activities.

☐ TECHNIQUE: Drills and perfection work.

☐ MENTAL TRAINING: Mental `toughness`, achievement of goals and self-confidence skills.

My typical Weekly PREPARATION PERIOD at that time was as follows:-

Before each session started and finished, I used the appropriate warm up and cool down protocols.

☐ MONDAY - Conditioning work (medicine balls, rope climbing, jumps and running).

☐ TUESDAY - Strength training.

☐ WEDNESDAY - Agility exercises, technical drills, mobility training.

☐ THURSDAY - Strength training.

☐ FRIDAY - Conditioning work (tempo runs, hill work and plyometrics).

☐ SATURDAY - Technical work, mental preparation.

☐ SUNDAY - Rest or active relaxation.

Ready for throwing 60ft 4in/18.39m shot put in a match against Wales at Glamorgan.
Far right is John Walters who at the time was the leading shot put thrower for Wales
(G. Roberts)

The COMPETITION PERIOD was as follows:-

Appropriate warm up and cool down protocols used:-

    ☐   MONDAY - Strength training.

- TUESDAY - Speed training/Jumping activities.

- WEDNESDAY - Throwing/technical training.

- THURSDAY - Strength training.

- FRIDAY - Mobility exercises/throwing (easier session), mental preparation.

- SATURDAY – Competition.

- SUNDAY - Technical easy throwing and stretching.

My brother Geoffrey going through the `paces` with dumbbell presses.

Now its my turn!
Note we used the cellars of the former Ipswich Airport for our weight training.

After six weeks of dedicated training, I was getting stronger, more powerful and fitter. My winter`s throwing was also improving at this stage of the year and was anxious to compete in indoor shot putt competitions to judge the improvement in a competitive environment.

I was also heavier due to having extra rations of steak cooked for me by the wonderful and sympathetic chefs in the Sergeants Mess, served at 10.30am prior to the main lunch. I was also drinking 4/5 pints of milk a day delivered to the Gymnasium by a very friendly and grateful milkman.

After all the hard training things were going well as I was getting stronger and heavier with additional protein and drinking gallons of milk.

My first indoor shot competition was at RAF Cosford in which I finished 2nd with a throw of 54ft 9in/16.7m, the winner being Jeff Teale with a putt of 58ft

2in/17.73m. Teale would later on be GB`s only representative in the event at the 1968 Olympic Games where he finished an admirable 10th place.

As a result of coming 2nd in this national indoor event, I was selected to represent Great Britain in the shot putt for the first time in this event against West Germany on Saturday 24 February. This was new territory for me in competing internationally in this strongman event. Whilst warming up I noticed the very large mountain of a man Heinfried Birlenbach who subsequently won the event easily with a putt of 63ft 7in/19.38m, 2nd place going Gloeckler at 59ft 2in/18.34m and myself 3rd with 53ft 9in/16.38m. Birlenbach stood 6ft 8ins tall and weighed 120kg and was good enough to win the European indoor Championships that year and finished in 8th place at the 1968 Olympic Games.

My throwing outdoors was improving and after a minor competition in Ipswich, I knew with favourable wind conditions that the British record could and would be broken. This happened on May 18th at the Milton Road track in Cambridge with a throw of 187ft 10in (57.26m), some 10in over the Olympic qualifying distance. I also improved my shot putt distance to 55ft 6in/16.91m. So at long last, my throwing was making an impact as I was singled out by the East German authorities and asked by them to compete against the mighty East Germans in East Berlin at what was called the International Olympic Day on the 19 June.

Just prior to this invitational, I was chosen to compete for England against Scotland, Wales and Ireland in Grangemouth, Scotland. The stadium was built in 1966 for the citizens of Grangemouth partly funded by BP. As far as I remember, there were many refinery works and was polluted. I won the competition with ease and with a modest throw of 168ft 7in/51.40m but the wind was coming from the wrong direction and not conducive to any great distances.

The next match was very different as I received an invitation to compete in East Berlin on June 19th against the formidable trio of Thorith, Milde, and Losch who placed 1st, 2nd and 3rd in the 1966 European championships plus 3 others, who I had not heard of before but were warming up with such distances that were overwhelming to me. There were 19 of us in this pool, all of them from either, East Germany, Russia, Bulgaria and Czechoslovakia which included the giant Ludvik Danek, my old banquet drinker from a previous meet. Needless to say, I had a disastrous afternoon, just finishing with a mere 163ft 0in/49.68m. Thorith won the competition close to his East German record and looked a potential winner for the impending Mexico Olympic Games. For me, it was back to the drawing board.

At this time I started questioning my suitability of staying in the Army as I felt with regular `guard duties` plus training hard for the impending Olympic Games, this did not mix well. Also, I always wanted to teach or lecture when my athletics career had finished and to progress in the PT Corps in those days was either to take up a short service commission in another regiment or go through a remedial gymnastics course (physiotherapist) and wait for promotion. As it stood it was a bit like waiting for `dead man shoes`! So I decided to apply for entrance to the world renowned teachers training establishment, Loughborough College of Education.

Before the interview, I did some research on what was required to pass. I was not lacking in any confidence issues about any practical activities but apprehensive on any questions that might arise such as reading books and newspapers columns including dates of Teacher Acts etc. Most of my `informers` told me `tell them you read the Times and Guardian which will show your class`!

The day started by being interviewed by someone from the Education Department, a certain Mr `Paddy` Brown who seemed more happy to talk about my athletics career and Mr Ian Paisley who was the loyalist politician and Protestant religious leader, as he too was Irish. Luckily, I had read about him and informed Mr Brown that he was famous for his `thunder` and was known to his supporters as `the big man` whose reported words were `no`, `never` and `not an inch`. He was happy to have met me and showed me where to go for the next part of the interview, the PE and Sports Skills test.

At the North Gym I was met by Mr Eric Blackadder who apparently had responsibility for gymnastics at the College and 5 other potential students. All of them looked like little schoolboys compared to my size and age. We were asked to do a handstand against the wall together, when two of them crumbled to the floor. They obviously were not strong enough to hold their bodyweight on the hands. One even complained of getting a headache! From this activity, we proceeded to throw a rugby ball to each other followed by trapping a football thrown by the young man purported to have a headache from the demanding hand stand against the wall!

The last test was to perform a forward roll and even then, some failed to perform this accurately. As a member of the Army Physical Training Corps, I was asked could I develop this demonstration further. With the whole group watching I did a completed handspring, headspring followed by a forward roll with a resounding applause from the group. To think the gymnastic activity was my weakest in the PT Corps, coming here to perform like this was most pleasing to say the least.

On leaving Loughborough, I was told that I should receive an official letter shortly and my performance all day was most acceptable, so I left and decided then that if successful, I would `purchase my discharge` from the Army and commence a new career in teaching.

Before making a firm application to leave the Army I wanted to see my superiors to ask if I could be excused Guard duties with a promise that if I made the Olympic team I would on my return from Mexico, catch up all the guard duties I had missed. After a few days I was told to report the see RSM Phillips, the senior RSM in the British Army who marched me in as though I had committed a crime to see the Commandant Major-General Peter Hunt. I asked him to be excused guard duties until after the Games but he swiftly told me that I was a soldier first and an athlete second. That was the end of the meeting and I was swiftly marched out with the RSM shouting Left, Right, Left, Right, Left in what was about 2 seconds. Even to this day, I was not sure whether it was he who said I was a soldier first and a model second in an earlier request to sign a contract for a modelling agency!

On retirement, Major-General Peter Hunt became Constable of the Tower of London and I met him again to have a brief conversation about athletics and my progress in civilian life, all done in a pleasant and relaxing manner far different to our Army relationship. He was also at one time, the President of the *National smallbore Rifle Association.*

Sergeant Instructor Bill Tancred APTC British Discus champion; Major-General Peter Hunt CB, DSO; AcRSM C. Phillips and Sergeant Jim Fox REME British Modern Pentathlon Champion 1968 (Kind Permission RMA Sandhurst)

After this encounter, I applied to purchase my discharge and had to await the Ministry of Defence decision. Everyone was surprised and sorry that had made this decision especially my Senior Master of Arms Lt. Colonel Mickey Rouse OBE who I had known from my service in Aden with the 1ˢᵗ East Anglian regiment.

I was also influenced to leave because a few APTC men were being commissioned not on merit but on long service which to my mind was not right. For example one newly promoted officer nicknamed `Tricky Dickie` once said to me, "How many O levels do you have Staff"? I replied, "Seven Sir". He then went on to say he had two and they were in, "Maffs and Geogo." Enough said.

Although selected for the next match against Switzerland on the 29/30 June in Berne, I withdrew as I wanted to defend my Army title at Aldershot on the same weekend. As a result my brother Peter made his debut for the Great Britain team in taking my place. At the Army championships I managed to break both the shot and discus records with throws of 55ft 9in/16.99m in the shot and 181ft 10in/55.44m in the discus.

As the trials were approaching it was important to win the national AAA`s title and with this in mind, I managed to win with a throw of 174ft 1in/53.36m, beating off the challenge of Arthur Mckenzie and my old Royal Marine foe, John Watts. It was a comfortable win and more pleasing in beating two touring Americans, one of which Mike Louisiana, had thrown well over 200ft/61.00m in the States.

Both John and Arthur were also trying to throw well as this was the last major event to qualify for the Games. They were good friends as well and John to this day has remained friends. On the other hand, Arthur`s contact gradually disappeared over time. Even to this day, I will always remember our greetings to one another. When we used to meet up, I always said, "How are you Arthur"? To which his reply would be, "Canny Bill!"

Arthur served in the Police force and had many stories to tell on our frequent international trips together, so it was no surprise to me that when he left the Police service after 31 years as a Detective Inspector he turned to writing. He commenced writing in 1979 when on Police duty in Hong Kong. His plays include *Pickets and Pigs* set during the miner`s strike and *Gym Boy,* set in a Gym, frequented by men of a certain age. He wrote for long-running TV series *The Bill*, and his film, *Haringan*, starring Stephen Tompkinson as a hard-bitten detective sergeant on the North East Sink Estate, was shown in 2013. He was a very talented man who was fun to be associated with and was obviously a good story teller inspired by his successful Police career.

Arthur McKenzie and myself prior to competing for Great Britain against Sweden in Stockholm 1966

The first 70 athletes named for the 1968 Mexico Olympic Games were announced on August 6 which was a lovely birthday present as I turned 26 years old that day. In the team were many great and respected athletes including Lynn Davies the defending champion. Lynn had won the gold medal in the long jump in 1964, earning himself the nickname `Lynn the Leap` with a leap of 8.07m. He also eventually became the President of the UK Athletics Members Council.

Confirmation of the selection came via a letter from Buckingham Palace signed by the President of the British Amateur Athletics Board, His Royal Highness Prince Philip the Duke of Edinburgh. As it was also my birthday, the local postman had a hefty bag of letters which included congratulatory ones to deliver.

Of course my mother and father were absolutely delighted including my immediate family, relations and friends. My father had spent much of his leisure time in supporting, coaching and advising me on the journey. A great day all round.

BUCKINGHAM PALACE.

August 4th, 1968.

Dear Mr. Tancred,

I am delighted to inform you that you have been selected by the British Amateur Athletic Board to represent Great Britain and Northern Ireland at the XIXth Olympic Games in Mexico City in October, 1968.

Many congratulations and I send you my best wishes for a happy and successful visit to Mexico.

Your event is:

Discus

The official letter inviting me to the 1968 Olympic Games

Myself throwing the discus at Loughborough College (Barry Bell)

100

Letter informing me that I had been selected for the 1968 Mexico Olympic Games team
(Archant)

There was another full GB international to take place against Poland at the White City on the 31 August/1 September and I finished 4th with a throw of 178ft 9in/54.48m. Before the team were due to leave, the British Amateur Athletics Board arranged a GB versus the Rest fixture for all us to have a competitive match because the next real test was going to be in October and at high altitude.

As soon as this match terminated I travelled back to Sandhurst, knowing that my discharge papers had arrived and as long as I paid £100, I could leave the service on the 17 September. Loughborough College had also accepted me and I was ready for the new challenge.

However, there were a few anxious moments when the Commandant at the PT School in Aldershot Lt. Colonel `Pip` Dawson and a few senior officers of the PT Corps asked to see me urgently in Aldershot to persuade me to stay. I was offered a staff car and travelled the few miles from Camberley to the PT School in Aldershot. The meeting was very cordial and they `mapped` my military career over the next 15 years and said that I would be an outstanding officer in the Corps if I stayed in.

The British Army 1968 Olympians at Whitehall, London to meet General Sir Geoffrey Baker at The Ministry of Defence. I am on the far right of the picture and far left is Major R. Mortimer, the Modern Pentathlon Manager. (Crown)

I was told to think about it and return in two days with my answer. So after two days I returned and said my decision was still the same. Without any further ado, Lt Colonel Dawson with a red face ordered me back to Sandhurst as he did not want to see me again!

So on the 17 September 1968 I was discharged from the Army after 8 years service but would be in the Regular Reserves for another 4 years. My military conduct from my red book *Regular Army Certificate of Service* states `Exemplary and I was a distinct loss to the Army`.

So I said my farewells, went through the gates at the RMA Sandhurst for the last time and caught the train to my parent`s home in Ipswich. Very soon later after packing I made my way to Loughborough to begin a new chapter of my life as a civilian and student albeit a mature one.

3. LOUGHBORO ROUGH COLLEGE, 1968 OLYMPIC GAMES AND ATHLETICS

I arrived at Loughborough railway station with just a suitcase which was used for my various Army postings and was somewhat battered as I had it for 8 years. As soon as I came out of the station I asked a local how far was the College Campus in which he replied that it was just over a mile, so being a former infantry soldier, I proceeded to walk which took me approximately 30 minutes. I believe today that they have shuttle buses to transport students to the Campus or to the railway station.

On arrival I reported to Mr Basil Stamatakis who was the head of athletics and Greek born. He was delighted that I had made it and welcomed me with both arms as the College needed a shot and discus thrower of a decent standard and I fitted the bill very well. After all the administration was over, he showed me the way to the History department on the other side of the campus to see the head who I believe was a Dr. Widdop?

Within a few minutes, I got the feeling that he was not sympathetic to sportsmen and was shocked when I stated I would be leaving shortly to Mexico for 6 weeks! He searched and presented me with 10 history books for some `light reading` whilst training and competing, so that I would not be behind when I eventually returned to Campus.

I then proceeded to make my way to Gimson Hall with my `battered` suitcase and the prized 10 history books. My room was on the top floor and to be shared with another tall student named Maurice Trapp. Maurice was a very gentle person with a polite persona and was amused when I asked him if there was a spare locker which I could use. He confirmed that there was a spare locker and I quietly grinned. I told him it would be ideal for the 10 prized history books which I had no intention of taking to Mexico! His chin dropped and then he burst out laughing. Smiling, he added that he had a key so that he could ensure the books would be safe until my return. Later on in life Maurice would become the Vice President of New Zealand Rugby and was a successful New Zealand rugby coach.

After this brief enrolment, I headed off to London to meet the team members of the Olympic squad who were all smartly dressed, for the long flight to Mexico City. It was exciting to be among the best sportsmen and sportswomen from different sports and disciplines. I was extremely honoured to have secured selection and was looking forward in competing against the best in the world.

On arrival in the Olympic Games Village we were allocated our rooms which would be shared by four of us. So, if anyone snored it was bad luck and in our case we had the gold medallist in this `event`, a certain hammer thrower by the name of Howard Payne. I was familiar to this all-night disturbance having been in Army barrack rooms with 25 soldiers, most of them being nightly disturbers.

The training facilities were good and the catering excellent. In fact, I thought the food to be so good that Jeff Teale, our shot putter and I, stayed for long periods eating all the different types of nationality foods that were offered. In no time, we added weight to our expanding girth but on reflection, this was not sensible as it made us `sluggish`.

We were visited by many celebrities whilst eating and this included HRH the Duke of Edinburgh, who asked me personally, "Is the food good?" I replied, "It beats Army rations Your Highness!" He walked away smiling and probably thought of his `food rations` when he served in the Royal Navy.

On one occasion, having a large breakfast we were joined by Percy Cerutty who was one of the world`s leading athletics coaches in the 1950`s and 1960`s. Eccentric as they come, this Australian pioneered a home-spun system of `stotan` training, embracing a holistic regime of natural diets, hard training in natural surroundings and mental stimulation. He is famed to have coached Herb Elliott to a series of world record performances culminating in an Olympic Gold medal at the 1960 Rome Olympics for the 1500m. Incredibly he was never beaten at this distance or the mile.

We would often discuss our training methods, why we ate so much, his training philosophies, and of his love of the British flag and his parting words would always be, "Beat those bloody Russians!" A most interesting man but obviously strange in his demeanour.

Myself outside the Mexico Olympic Stadium

Taking a `breather` after training (M. Shearman)

On the left is me with the British Team taken outside the stadium ready to march in. On the right - Don`t worry ladies, I`ll carry your luggage! On the back row on the left is Barbara Inkpen (High Jump) and on the right Maureen Barton-Chitty (Long jump). On the front left is Sue Scott-Reeve –Herrington (Pentathlon), myself and Anita Neill (Sprints). (The Times)

My discus training was going well but I found my speed weight training and lifting tiring as the altitude was effecting my recovery. Still I thought it must be the same for every other discus thrower. I was impressed by the great American discus thrower Jay Silvester who was the world record holder and favourite. I met up with Gary Carlsen again who was in a more serious mood than when I last saw him in Soho. Al Oerter, the triple gold medallist had not arrived as he wanted to just fly in a couple of days before attempting to win his fourth gold medal.

Other greats seen and watched with interest were Randy Matson who was to become the gold medallist in the shot put, my old discus foe Ludvik Danek from Czechoslovakia, Janis Lusis the Russian eventual gold medallist in the javelin, Bill Toomey the decathlete, the Hungarian hammer thrower Gyula Zsivotzky and Les Mills the shot and discus thrower from New Zealand.

Les Mills practising at the training area in Mexico

The Mexico Olympics opened to a new kind of furore, not politics, not race or war, but altitude. Coaches and doctors warned that strenuous efforts at 7,000ft above sea level could be dangerous. Several nations had set up special training camps in high mountains, the Russians at Alma Ata and the USA at Lake Tahoe. The Mexicans, who were used to it, claimed the altitude would make no difference, but the fears of sea-level dwellers were well founded.

Just before the Olympic Games opened on the Saturday 12 October there had been a mass student demonstration in the City, several people being killed which made the organisers feel tense that trouble could take place. To everyone's relief, the Games opened without any problems. The stadium was full and the track was the first Olympics to use an all-weather surface which today is usual at every major international competition.

The events requiring great stamina suffered at Mexico but in others unbelievable records were set. The 100m, 400m, 4 x 400m relay and long jump records set in the rarefied atmosphere, remained for numerous years. Even allowing for altitude, the Kenyans from the Kisii Hills were wonderful athletes. Two years earlier, they had dominated the same events at the Kingston British Empire and Commonwealth Games in the steamy, lowland heat of Jamaica. Pride of place for me was the great Kip Keino. In the 1500m there was no doubting his mastery, even though the world record holder, Jim Ryan (USA) turned in a first rate run. Try as he might, Ryan could not hold the Kenyan on the final lap and Keino won in a time of 3 min 34.9 sec, an Olympic Games record.

The Americans dominated the sprints as usual. Here for the first time, the 10sec barrier was broken in the 100m and then the 20 sec barrier in the 200m. Soon after this event, won by Tommie Smith with John Carlos coming 3rd (both from the USA), they both raised a clenched fist to the crowd at the victory ceremony, thereby giving what was eventually known as a Black Power salute.

Peter Norman, Tommie Smith and John Carlos performing the Black Power Salute (M Shearman)

Undoubtedly, this Black Power salute was a political demonstration conducted by these two *African-American* athletes, which I witnessed in surprise and not knowing at the time the significance of it. As the American national anthem (`The Star-Spangled Banner`) started to play, they raised a black gloved fist and looked down until the anthem had finished. Also Tommie Smith, John Carlos and the Australian Peter Norman the silver medallist, all wore *human rights* badges on their jackets.

This action performed by these two athletes is regarded as one of the most overtly political statements in the history of the Modern Olympic Games. When they left the podium they were booed by many of the spectators. Smith later said, "If I win, I am an American, not a black American, but if I did something bad, they would say I am a Negro. We are black and we are proud of being black. Black Americans will understand what we did tonight".

Poor Peter Norman, who was sympathetic to his competitors` protest, was reprimanded by his country`s Olympic authorities and ostracized by the Australian media. Furthermore, he was not picked for the 1972 Munich Olympics despite having qualified 13 times over. An absolute disgrace.

Sadly Norman died in 2006 and incredibly, both Smith and Carlos were pallbearers at his funeral.

Perhaps the greatest performance for me at these Games was to witness first-hand the men`s long jump final. In the afternoon of Friday 18 October, Ralph Beamon went into orbit, stunning two world record holders and the reigning champion (Lynn Davies of Britain), with a giant leap of 29ft 2.5in (8m 90cm). It was Beamon`s one and only jump in the final! The defending champion Davies told Beamon, "You have destroyed the event so should we all now retire from long jumping!"

The record stood for 23 years until Mike Powell of the USA beat it at the 1991 World Athletics Championships in Tokyo. Beamon`s world record jump was named by *Sports Illustrated* magazine as one of the greatest sports moments of the 20th century and I was there to witness it.

Another sensation was to see the first man to jump over the bar backwards to win the gold medal with a height of 2.24m. His name was Dick Fosbury of the USA. He revolutionized the high jump, inventing a unique `back-first` technique, known as the 'Fosbury Flop', adopted by almost all high jumpers today.

His method was to sprint diagonally towards the bar then curve and leap backwards over the bar, which gave him a much lower centre of mass in flight (it was already below his body) than traditional techniques.

It is interesting to note that many School teachers and club coaches in the

UK tried to use this newly found technique with their high jump specialists and unless the school had the necessary landing facilities, many injuries were forthcoming as the athletes just had the hard sand to land on!

In the triple jump, the world record was broken three times, the title eventually going to Viktor Saneyev of the USSR with a jump of 17.39m. He would later win gold medals at the 1972 and 1976 Olympics and a silver medal in 1980, a phenomenal Olympic athlete.

Another phenomenal Olympic athlete going for his fourth successive gold medal was Al Oerter, known as `the man with the golden arm` and my rival. He entered the competition not as the favourite, this `tag` being given to his bitter rival, the wonderful technical discus thrower Jay Silvester, the world record holder (224ft 5in/68.40m), also from the USA.

On entering the stadium, Silvester had a terrible start as he nearly knocked himself out by hitting his head in the tunnel and was concussed for a while. Anyhow, Oerter was in tremendous form and broke the Olympic record for his fourth Olympic gold medal with a throw of 212ft 6in/64.78m, Milde of East Germany 2nd with 206ft 11in/63.08m and the 3rd place to my friend Ludvik Danek with 206ft 5in/62.92m.

Poor Jay Silvester had to settle with 5th place with a throw of 202ft 8in/61.78m. I had failed to qualify for the final and went back to the village feeling very low but determined that this setback would make me stronger in future major competitions.

I did speak to Al Oerter the next day near the village and congratulated this supreme athlete on his extraordinary achievement here in Mexico. We sat down and had a coffee and discussed his training regime in particular his mental preparation. He was very open about his `secret` of success. He seemed to `peak` at the right time even though never the favourite.

To start off, he asked me," What did you think of when trying to go to sleep before the Olympic competition?" I replied, "I have thrown far enough in the qualifying round to qualify for the final or I have set a British record in round one. Do you think the same?" "No", replied Oerter, "I think in round one, that one of my rivals has set an Olympic record, so how do I react to that? Or, the wind direction has changed, so how do I adjust my technique? Or, someone outside the circle is trying to put me off, again what do I do?" So from my point of view, in 1968, his mental preparation was way ahead of his rivals because he thought of every possible competitive situation.

He also provided some 10 strategies for success in life and sport namely:

    ☐   VISUALIZE - Picture the euphoria of winning in your mind and try to experience what it will actually feel like to accomplish your goal.

- [ ] SET SPECIFIC GOALS - You need to otherwise there is nothing concrete to work on.

- [ ] BE MOTIVATED - In order to be successful, you must be dedicated and have a positive attitude.

- [ ] HAVE TOTAL SELF BELIEF - No negatives. Do not ever think that you cannot achieve your goals.

- [ ] HAVE A FOCUS- Stay in the zone of what you really want. Focus on the successful outcome.

- [ ] BE DETERMINED - Anything is possible, do not waver and work at it.

- [ ] REMAIN OPTIMISTIC - Never have negative thoughts. It`s having a `can do` attitude.

- [ ] PLAN A STRATEGY FOR SUCCESS - Think about every step along the path to achieve your goal. Try and order the stepping stone stages until you reach it.

- [ ] WORK HARD - Go that extra mile. It will be worth it in the long run.

- [ ] ENJOY - Enjoy what you are doing and praise yourself when things are going well.

Most certainly, this was great opportunity for me to discuss discus throwing, physical training, mental preparation and competition with the greatest discus thrower of all-time. He gave an insight into winning with the mind and muscle for sustainable fitness.

Oerter retired after these Games but made a comeback in the mid-seventies and even threw at the 1979 AAA`s Championships coming 2nd with a modest throw of 195ft 7in/59.64m but beating all the other British throwers. This was the last time we met up and I remember fondly asking what he thought of our throwers in which he replied, "I am on vacation seeing Europe and they think they are as well judging by their performances!"

He did get serious again by attempting to qualify for the American team in 1980 for the Moscow Olympics but finished 4th in the US trials. He nonetheless set a personal best that year at the age of 43 with a throw of 227ft/69.19m which is most remarkable.

After retiring for good, Oerter became a celebrated abstract painter and in 2006, he founded the *Art of the Olympics*. Regrettably, he died of heart failure at the age of 71.

After failing to qualify in the discus, I had the opportunity to watch the other athletics events taking place which included the qualifying, finals and if the opportunity arose, the other sports and its participants.

The Blazer badge for the 1968 Olympic Games.

Great Britain won 5 gold medals and the Olympic champions included David Hemery (400m hurdles), Chris Finnegan (middle weight boxing), Bob Braithwaite (shooting), Rodney Patisson and Ian MacDonald-Smith (sailing) and Derek Allhusen, Jane Bullen, Ben Jones and Richard Meade (equestrian).

I managed to congratulate Hemery's great performance in winning the gold medal in the world record time of 48.1sec in the 400m hurdles. He remained sober after his victory but the middleweight boxer Chris Finnegan was worse for wear, almost out on his feet after his heavy drinking session with his `mates`. What a difference comparing the two sports when each one reaches the pinnacle of performance! However if it was me winning a gold medal, I would have accompanied Chris on his drinking celebrations.

Other great sporting celebrities seen were Vera Caslavska from Czechoslovakia who won 4 gold medals in gymnastics and was `lucky` to be at the Games after the recent Soviet invasion of her country. However, she did cause an incident, while standing on the medal podium after the balance beam event final where Natalia Kuchinskaya of the Soviet Union had taken the gold medal in debatable circumstances. Vera Caslavska quietly turned her head down and away during the playing of the Soviet national anthem. This action was a silent protest by her against the recent Soviet invasion of her homeland. She also repeated this display at another Gymnastics medal ceremony.

Subsequently she was banned from future sporting events and international travel for many years by the new regime and also made her an outcast from society. Caslavska`s position improved greatly in the 1980`s after the intervention of the members of the International Olympic Committee and after the fall of communism, her status improved dramatically.

It was very exciting to see Harold (Hal) Connolly, the 1956 Melbourne Olympic hammer champion and his wife Olga Fikotova, also an Olympic gold medallist from the Melbourne Games (Women`s discus) come over to talk to us throwers. It is interesting to report that Connolly`s left arm was 4in shorter than his right and to become an Olympic champion with this disadvantage was even more noteworthy. Also during these Games of 1956, he began a relationship with the Czech discus thrower Fikotova and married her in Prague the following year with the great middle distance runner Emil Zatopek as their best man. Their romance hit the headlines during this period as it was during the Cold War, a name given to the state of political and military tension after World War 2 between powers in the Western Bloc (USA, NATO and others) and powers in the Eastern Bloc (The Soviet Union and its allies in the Warsaw Pact).

Harold and Olga Connolly walking in the Olympic village in Mexico

The heavyweight boxer George Foreman was in a jubilant mood in the village after winning the gold medal, knocking out the Soviet Union heavyweight Jonas Cepulis. Later on, he would become a two-time world heavyweight champion and outside the sport, he became an ordained minister, author and entrepreneur. He is also known today for his promotion of the George Foreman Grill, which has sold over 100 million units world-wide and thus made him many dollars.

The introduction of doping tests resulted in the first disqualification from doping. Swedish pentathlete Hans-Gunnar Liljenwall was disqualified for alcohol use. He drank several beers just prior to competing in the pistol shooting discipline to calm his nerves. This was just the start as doping became a real issue that survives today.

The Olympic Games closed on the 27 October and could be described as eventful, colourful, record breaking and a wonderful experience that will never be forgotten.

After this spectacular closing ceremony, some of the athletics team headed to Acapulco by bus for a different Mexican experience and relaxation by the sea. It involved drinking, seeing the night life, having some boat trips, swimming and watching the brave young men performing cliff dives.

One character we met here in a bar was the very amusing ex-boxer called Terry Downes who was a former world middleweight champion. He had many stories to tell and could be the `life and soul` at any party. Downes was famous for a number of quips. After a brutal fight early in his career against Dick Tiger, the talented Nigerian, Downes was asked who he wanted to fight next. He replied, "The bastard who made who made this match" in reference to his manager at the time, Mickey Duff.

Arriving in Mexico City.

Relaxing in Acapulco –being an athlete can be fun after all the training!

Soon we were flying back to Britain to await further invitations and the commencement of my teacher training course at Loughborough College. As soon as we touched down in Heathrow Airport, there were masses of people awaiting our arrival including many of the media who were trying to interview the `Olympic Stars`. All very exciting but everyone was glad to be back after so long away.

I travelled back home, stayed the night and then headed to Loughborough College. At the time I felt very honoured to have been accepted by this great institution and could not wait to start. After all, Loughborough had (and still has) a strong tradition of teacher education and a history of successfully producing teachers who are in great demand by schools and colleges in the UK and abroad. Furthermore, it had a galaxy of international sports stars such as Dave Travis (Commonwealth javelin champion), Clive Longe (British international decathlete) from athletics, Keith Fielding , Louis Dick, Brian West international rugby players and many top class cricket and tennis players.

I went and saw the appropriate personnel, filled in the necessary forms, allocated to a PE group but decided to drop my second subject history, so went to see Maurice Trapp, who did indeed keep the history books safe, collected them from the privately closed locker and gave them back to the head of the History department who was startled but relieved that I was not going to be his student.

Within two weeks I had settled in but was rather dismayed that no real weight training facilities existed apart from a squat rack at the end of the North Gym, where the gymnastic apparatus was stored. I was assured that this lack of weight training facilities would improve by next year as a new PE Centre would be built and accommodate a weight lifting room. At the time I wondered where all those talented and international athletes trained when no weights facilities existed?

I also managed to get a single room in Gimson Hall, close enough to the Refectory and the Athletics track and the pub called `The Blackie`, which was frequented by myself and most of Gimson and Ling halls residents on Friday and Saturday nights prior to the glorious discos. All in all, after leaving the Army, I thought this was a holiday camp.

Members of Gimson Hall, Loughborough looking smart on a Sunday afternoon outside the famous athletics pavilion. I am on the back row far left. Many of these students went on to have successful teaching careers. In the centre sitting down is Duncan Case the Warden who came to our wedding in Bridport.

I was in a group of `Mature students`, all of us being older and more experienced than the `normal` entrant. The senior being Terry Keogh an ex-Squadron Leader from the RAF, Mike Hill also ex-RAF, Mike Elia a London Cypriot and an engaging individual, Ken Hill an Irishman who had `done everything` that no one else had done or seen and myself, ex-Army.

There were other mature students who were a year above us which included a very knowledgeable and experienced John Pinches who had worked in the first Leisure Centre in the UK at Harlow in Essex. We would often mix and share our life experiences and support each other.

There were some wonderful tutors notably Mr Lewis who taught Methodology of Teaching Physical Education. He was a firm disciplinarian who promoted excellent time keeping and smartness. As a former soldier I fitted in very well with his philosophy and thought him to be the best as he taught us `how to teach with meticulous planning and preparation`. Although not liked by many students at the time, those who continued in teaching, years after would state strongly he was the best teacher mentor.

Another man I respected was the Greek born academic, Basil Stamatakis who with Robbie Brightwell taught athletics. Mr Stamatakis was technically one of the best throws coaches I had ever encountered. He had an analytical eye and could spot a mistake as soon as one threw an implement. The only problem at first was his heavily accented speech but in time, you could understand what he was saying. I clearly remember to this day his instructions to, "Get into two halves, one half here, the other half there and the other half over there!" On receiving these instruction the group of us , probably 15 in number, were completely confused and stood still but laughing until tears ran down our cheeks!. He then commented, "Don`t you understand English gentlemen"?

Robbie Brightwell who was my team captain in the British team taught us the track events. He was an enthusiastic lecturer and was respected by all. After all, he was the Captain of the British athletics team at the 1964 Tokyo Olympic Games and the gold medallist at the 1962 Belgrade European Athletics championships in the 400metres event. Incidentally, he was also born in British India (Rawalpindi) and came to England in 1946.

Representing Loughborough College in a match against the AAA

The one subject that felt uncomfortable to me was educational gymnastics taken by a lecturer called Colin Raine. This was completely different to formal gymnastics in that it involved activities that allowed the child to self-test or create movements that defy gravity to enhance components such as flexibility, balance, coordination and strength. This was taught in a non-competitive manner, with emphasis placed upon the success and skills achievable by each individual student.

I think if you were 6ft plus and weighed nearly 17 stone and pretending to be `a falling leaf` did not abode well for your macho image! I tried my best but my heart was not in this subject along with other heavy rugby players.

New components for me at the time, was the study of Motor Skills and Its Acquisition. I was captivated by this subject, learning about the stages of learning (cognitive phase, associative phase and the autonomous phase), feedback and learning, types of tasks and transfer of training for example. The subject was taught by Clive Bond, a softly spoken man who inspired the `thought process` in me.

Comparative Physical Education was another new subject and was taught wonderfully by a tall and suave gentleman called Clint Sayer, who was the Head of the Physical Education Department. His lectures were fascinating and interesting and at the time, I had never studied other nation's sport organisations. Of particular interest was the Master of Sport pyramid used by the USSR to encourage soviet sportsmen and sportswomen to attain increased mastery in world sports. The USA had its well funded Collegiate system with full sports scholarships. I was beginning to understand how British athletes were inferior in support (facilities and finance) when compared to these two super powers in global sport.

Although I had been exposed to anatomy and physiology studies in the Army, we studied this subject again and was taken by a certain Dr Henry Robson, who was medically trained and knew his `stuff`. Quite eccentric, he would just walk in and talk about anything relating to his subject but you had to be alert otherwise you would be lost as he just `rattled` along. Before each lecture, he would visit the gentleman's loo and always managed to stain his trouser legs with urine after finishing urinating. He would always say, "You are a happy bunch to teach and it is most pleasing to see".

What a privilege to come to Loughborough College. It was so good that I never wanted the course to finish and it was completely different to my regimented 8 years lifestyle in the Army.

However, The Army Physical Training Corps taught me so much in terms of man management, teaching methodology, opportunities in gaining so many technical/coaching qualifications in numerous sports and gaining confidence in everything, but you have to plan and prepare for success. So with that `up your sleeve`, I had a fantastic start when I entered this other great institution.

Before the end of the year, two invitations were received to attend functions relating to the British Olympic team which gave me the opportunity to meet up again with fellow athletes but in a different environment.

The first one was a reception at Lancaster House, St James on Saturday 9 November 1968 from the Prime Minister Harold Wilson. A short man, probably 5ft 8ins tall and appeared interested in sport as he moved around and talked to his invited guests. This Prime Minister is generally recognised as a man of profound intellect but whose time in office corresponded for much of the period with an international recession.

The second invitation was a luncheon to be given at Buckingham Palace by The Queen and The Duke of Edinburgh on Thursday 5 December 1968 and this was a magnificent occasion and was well attended by the invited team.

It started off quietly but with the best champagne being freely distributed to the team, things became a bit noisy but all in a spirit of happiness. I was in a conversation with Jeff Teale the shot putter and Howard Payne the hammer thrower plus a couple of female athletes who were listening when a male member of the catering staff offered tea and asked Jeff, "Earl Grey"? Jeff replied, "Don`t be daft you silly bugger, I am Jeff Teale from Pontefract!" All of us fell into a fit of laughter including the embarrassed waiter.

On another occasion after too much champagne , certain members of the team wanted the loo, so a group of us decided to find the gentlemen rest room and soon spotted a very smart man sitting on his own probably bored by this reception or there for a quiet smoke. I was impressed by his laced cuffed shirt which made him stand out. Before I could ask him where the male toilets were, someone just said, "Do you know where the bogs are?" He replied very politely, `"If you go to the end of the corridor, turn right and you will see a sign, so all is not lost?" It was rude to ask him in this manner and worse still, to find out that he was Angus Ogilvy later Sir Angus, best known as the husband of Princess Alexandra of Kent and a first cousin of The Queen.

All in all, a grand reception with a great climax to the end of the season in what was an Olympic year.

In honour of the British Olympic Team

The Prime Minister

requests the honour of the company of

Mr. W. R. Tancred

*at a Reception at Lancaster House, St. James's
on Saturday, 9th November, 1968, from 5.00 p.m. to 7.00 p.m.*

*Cars to approach Lancaster House
by way of Cleveland Row*

*An answer is requested to:
The Private Secretary,
10, Downing Street, s.w.1*

Reception at Lancaster House Prime Minister Harold Wilson

E R

*The Master of the Household
has received Her Majesty's commands to invite*

Mr. William Tancred

*to a Luncheon to be given at Buckingham Palace
by The Queen and The Duke of Edinburgh
on Thursday 5th December, 1968 at 1 p.m.*

*The reply should be addressed to
The Master of the Household, Buckingham Palace*

Dress: Lounge Suit

Reception at Buckingham Palace for the 1968 Olympic Games team

At Loughborough, the term was coming to an end and I remember a group of us visiting the girls at their residence at Somerton House. We were all looking forward to Christmas, chatting along in a friendly manner and when 11pm arrived, all the boys had to leave the premises quickly. I stayed longer, enjoying the girls banter, when I was warned that Paddy Brown, my Education tutor and Warden at this site was approaching the door and if caught, punishment, with possible suspension could be handed out. As I opened the door, he was three yards away, I wished him, "A merry Christmas Mr Brown" to which he replied ,"I'll give you merry Christmas Mr Tancred, please see me in my study tomorrow morning without fail".

I reported the next morning to his office and waited a few minutes before 9am when suddenly a stern faced Mr Brown told me to come in and sit down opposite his desk. As we both sat down, he asked if I wanted coffee or tea before any proceedings were to take place. I declined and wanted to get this incident over. "Well Mr Tancred, let me warn you. These girls are only after one thing and that is your body, so in future tread carefully. A man of your status would undoubtedly be a good catch for any one of these girls. So have a Merry Christmas and I will see you next year!" I left with a smile on my face knowing quite well that the opposite was often the case with boys wanting the girls' bodies, especially the PE students!

January 1968 started really well with my athletics training making good progress and my studying going according to plan. The first thing I did was to make friends with the cook and catering staff at the refectory. I met the head cook, a Mrs Stanton when I first arrived and she knew I had been in the Armed Forces because after each helping I would say, "Thank you".

Other students were not quite in the same benevolent frame of mind but she spotted other ex-servicemen who did the same as I when receiving food. By being this friendly, I managed to get extra rations albeit potatoes!

Other lecturers who were committed and very supportive to our group included Alan Guy, Colin Hardy, Rod Thorp, Rex Hazeldine and Derek Quant, all of them inspiring and a credit to the College. Having the quality of these lecturers provided me with the incentive to pursue my studies with vigour and enthusiasm.

On the athletics front I decided to compete indoors and entered the AAA national championships at RAF Cosford in January. I managed to win my first AAA indoor title with a throw of 56ft 9in/17.31m beating the young Geoffrey Capes who managed 54ft 1in/16.48m for 2nd place. Capes would later go on to be Britain's greatest shot putter, strongman and a professional Highland Games competitor of some distinction. In his prime, he stood 6ft 5in tall and weighed around 150kg. In retirement, he still coaches the event and is well known as a successful breeder of birds.

AAA Indoor shot champion 1969

After the AAA Indoor Championships, I represented Loughborough University in the first ever Midland Universities team championships in the University`s Recreational hanger at Derby Road. Despite the freezing conditions Loughborough provided most of the effective opposition and won the team competition. I managed to throw a personal indoor best of 57ft 1in/17.40m, so the strength gained from heavy weight training was starting to pay dividends.

I was looking forward to the outdoor season to start, so I entered all four throwing events but was warned by Basil Stamatakis that I had fierce competition from Ken Hill who reputed to have told him that he was a 55ft/16.79m plus shot putter, which he achieved at Pittsburgh University. Ken was on my course but I never saw him either in the weights area or on the track.

After successfully winning the trials for the javelin, hammer and discus events all `eyes` turned to the shot put in anticipation of a shock defeat for me. In round one, I managed a paltry 48ft/14.63m plus and now awaited Ken`s response. There was little to cheer as Ken fouled his first attempt, the implement only going around the 30ft/12.62m mark. In round 2, I managed to achieve a distance of 55ft/16.76m plus and awaited Ken`s effort. Again, his implement did not go beyond 30ft/12.62m. Basil Stamatakis was looking stern and gave Ken a look that said I don`t believe you are a shot putter! I fouled the next throw and to Basil Stamatakis`s horror, Ken asked him if he could use his `treasured` Loughborough track top as a cloth to clean the shot so that it would not be slippery. After doing this, he threw the dirty track top on the floor and proceeded to put the shot which again only travelled a paltry 30ft/12.62m or so.

Basil Stamatakis told Ken to return his track top but only after it was washed and ironed and recommended him to do another event which did not involve explosive strength and power coupled with a sound technique. He came over to me and congratulated my performances over the day and whispered, "Mr Hill could only shot putt over 55ft/16.76m not with a 16lbs ball but only with a ping pong!"

On the other hand Ken was a decent hardworking and likable student who went on to do well in his chosen career in Ireland but soon retired from active shot putting!

Duncan Case was the senior master at Gimson Hall and although a respected educational psychologist, liked athletics and the social life with energetic students. He was a very happy man who liked a joke and a beer or two. We occasionally had a few periods of relaxation with each other and a couple of other students in pubs around the town. However, one evening, he bragged in a pub that I could beat anyone over 40m in the street near the market place. Bets were taken, winner taking all and the landlord offering 10 pints to the winner. So on closing time, the pub emptied and Duncan was the starter with the landlord 40m away to see the winner.

What no one in the pub realised was that power athletes can accelerate quickly and keep up with many sprinters over short distances and I was no exception that night at 11.30pm. So after winning, Duncan, I and a couple of PE students had enough beer saved for a month. The only downside to this `drunken` challenge was that Paddy Brown, Head of the Education department and `my ally` at the Somerton house incident at Christmas, got to hear of it and kindly let me know when he saw me, stated, "Don`t forget you are a mature student and should set an example."

Just as Christmas was approaching a group of us decided to decorate our hall with a Christmas tree, so off we went to Charnwood Forest some two miles away from our place of residence and `collect` the `free` Christmas tree. The sight of seeing six students including the `mature` one carrying the tree on the path of the main Forest road must have raised a few eyebrows, especially as it was early morning!

The outdoor season started well with a match representing the AAA against Cambridge University in April at Milton road Cambridge. Concentrating on the shot I managed a personal best with a distance of 57ft 11in/17.65m.

In the British Isles Cup held in Grangemouth, I managed to break the Scottish `all-comers` record in the discus representing England with a distance of 173ft 1in/52.75m.

A discus throw of over 58m showing the final delivery (H Payne)

After this, it was the annual Loughborough Colleges past and present match against a strong AAA team that included Geoff Capes in the shot and John Hillier with John Watts in the discus event. The wind was not favourable, so the distances were down but I won the discus contest. The shot put was interesting. Although I threw further than Geoff Capes in feet and inches (56ft 6¾in) the metric conversion created a tie between us and as Geoff had a better second putt, he won the event. This is the first time someone had thrown further but lost the competition! Mr Stamatakis was furious.

The first full GB international was against Czechoslovakia in Brno and I was up against the great Ludvik Danek who could also `party` after competitions. Needless to say he threw over 200ft/61.00m again but I threw a respectful 187ft 11in/57.60m for 3rd place.

Athletics international vest badge

The team set off for the Banquet held in a village complex but on arrival food was not ready but wine was freely available. Ludvik again challenged me to down a yard glass but in my attempt much was spilled and Ludvik again won the `competition`. Young Geoff Capes wanted to be in the act and he too attempted to win a contest but these Czechs were made of sterner stuff. However, with nothing to eat, everyone were getting intoxicated and young Geoff getting out of control. Unfortunately for Geoff, Arthur Gold honorary secretary of the BAAB and senior official, saw him and called me over to say, "Capes is an utter disgrace, sort him out Bill". I went over, myself also under the influence, told Geoff what Arthur Gold had said. It made no difference and a fracas occurred.

Along with many athletes, I did not remember much after the banquet and I woke up in a ditch clutching my knife and fork to keep me company. I do know that I could not bear the smell of wine again for many years and even today, white wine is off the list. So much for a friendly night out with the boys!

Arthur Gold was a most influential sports administrator in athletics and one of the first and most vehement campaigners against the use of drugs in sport. He served on most of the major bodies in British and European athletics for many years in a voluntary capacity. Arthur Gold also led the British athletics teams at three Olympic Games and was Commandant of the English Commonwealth Games teams. Always immaculate in his dressing, extremely knowledgeable in the history of athletics, well respected he was finally knighted in 1994. He was married to Marion Godfrey who had been a secretary at the International military tribunal at Nuremberg.

After this international, I won my fourth AAA national title at the White City with a throw of 174ft 2in/53.08m, my brother Peter coming 2nd and Arthur McKenzie 3rd. It was the first time in a throwing event that two brothers finished 1st and 2nd. Also in these national championships I managed to come 2nd in the shot with a putt of 55ft 6in/16.90m which guaranteed my selection in both events against the mighty USA.

This fixture was unique for my family because in the discus event two brothers were thrown together to face the mighty Americans and of course, our father would be watching from the stands, inspiring us to perform well.

The British men's team were given a thorough trouncing, the Americans 131 points to 90 points, a losing margin of 41 points which came at the hands of what was in effect an American "B" team. The British girls faced with comparatively stronger opposition held on to their overnight lead to win by the narrowest possible margin, 67 points to 66 points.

The discus was won by Tim Vollmer with a throw of 196ft 2in/59.80m, Jon Cole 2nd with 194ft 8in/59.34m, myself 3rd a throw of 189ft 6in/57.76m which equalled the UK National record and Peter 4th with a great personal best throw of 183ft 5in/55.90m Our father in the stands was jubilant as we performed at our very best.

The day before both Jeff Teale and I were against the world leaders in the shot put, Randy Matson at 6ft 7in tall and Neil Steinhauer, another giant of a man. Matson was the Olympic shot champion at Mexico City and was the first man to throw the shot over 70ft/21.33m. Also, in 1967 he threw the discus to within 3in/8cm of the (then) world record. Steinhauer was always in Matson's shadow but had a personal best of 68ft 11in/21.0m, so the competition would be between these two shot put giants.

So while warming up, they were sending the shot close to the 70ft/21.33m mark whilst Jeff and I struggled to reach the 55ft/16.76m line. As soon as the competition started, Matson threw over 68 ft/20.72m but to our embarrassment the officials did not have a tape to reach this distance! Hence there was a delay while officials were searching for a longer tape to accommodate this prodigious distance. No one thought these distances were feasible and certainly not on British soil!

Matson won the contest closely followed by Steinhauer and way behind, Jeff Teale and myself with 54ft 9in/16.68m. On reflection, I was glad that my main event was the discus because to perform at the American`s level you had to be big, strong, fast and athletic.

The next GB international was to be held in Verona against Italy and Czechoslovakia. Both Danek (Czechoslovakia) and the Italian wonder boy Silvano Simeon had thrown over 202ft/61.57m, so at best I could come 3rd. Danek did indeed win with Simoen 2nd and myself 3rd beating the other Italian Armando De Vincentiis with a throw 181ft 3in/55.24m. Simoen was not big in stature but had an effective technique coupled with a peculiar walk with both feet spreading outwards and appearing to look like Benitto Mussolini, the Italian leader of the fascist Party, who eventually in 1945 was executed near Lake Como by the Italian Communists.

Another appearance was made for the shot put event gaining 4th place with a throw of 55ft 1in/16.78m. I suppose an advantage in competing in both these throwing events in Italy was that each competitor after their event would receive a case of wine to take home. Unfortunately for me, Arthur Gold asked me to give one case to a member of the team who had been a reserve and therefore not given any wine. Similarly, when arriving back home, my only case of wine disappeared as my father took a liking to the wine cask.

In Verona, we had the opportunity to see a first class opera performance in the evening which was magnificent and a great experience to us who had never before seen a high profile performance on stage.

After Verona the next fixture was at the White City in a match against France. I always looked forward to competing against the French because I had a real chance of winning! As it turned out this time I was not lucky in that I finished 2nd with a throw of 176ft 2in/53.70m and 4th in the shot event with a modest 54ft 2in/16.51m. As usual after this contest, the evening proceedings would involve much wine tasting particularly with the French who were eager participants. Sore heads were the order of the day when all the heavy throwers met up the next morning for cups of black coffee!

My course at Loughborough was fine and I appeared to be doing well. Importantly,

I was improving my understanding of sports training principles by attending first rate lectures and other workshops organised by the British Amateur Athletics Federation. Furthermore, although proficient in the theory and practice of weight training, I was beginning to get to grips with its science application.

Sports psychology was a real interest and having the College near the University gave me an opportunity to explore its merits first hand, to attend classes and speak to informed lecturers on the campus. I was interested in goal setting, performance anxiety control, peaking and visualisation for example. It was the question of developing the right mental attitude. The difference between the good club runner and champions physically, is not that great. It is their mental attitude where the difference occurs. So with this in mind, I began to read more books on this subject and broaden my education.

At the end of the summer term, first year exams were passed, my throwing had improved and importantly, my interest in `academic` subjects was expanding.

The major 1969 European Athletics Championships in Athens had now arrived so it was off to Greece (September 16-21) and compete against the best Europeans. New events for these Championships were the women`s 1500m and the women`s 4 x 400m relay event. Jurgen May the former East German 1500m runner was not allowed to compete for his new country West Germany because IAAF rules required him to live there for at least 3 years as he had already competed for East Germany in the 1966 European Championships.

Due to this ban, West German officials withdrew their athletes from all individual events and decided to enter only the relay events as a symbolic gesture not to be disrespectful to the organising country. The other incident at these championships was the disqualification of the Dutch decathlete Edward de Noorlander for using amphetamines which resulted in being the first disqualification for doping in athletics.

Great Britain won six gold medals through John Whetton (1500m), Ian Stewart (5,000m), Ron Hill (marathon), Paul Nihill (20km walk) with Lillian Board (800m) and the women`s 4 x 400m relay (Rosemary Stirling, Pat Lowe, Janet Simpson and Lillian Board).

Both Peter (brother) and myself failed to qualify for the finals. The winner was the East German Hartmut Losch (202ft 9in/61.82m), Ricky Bruch of Sweden (200ft 4in/61.08m) and East German Lother Milde 3rd (194ft 7in/59.34m). In the shot put there was no surprise as the East Germans took the first three places.

1969 European Athletics Team. My brother Peter and I are at the far left protecting sprinter Barry Kelly! (BAAB).

It is interesting to add that on many occasions members of the press attended with the team on away fixtures and a few sat amongst us during the plane journey and mutual respect developed. Many of them offered support and advice and to me this was most welcomed. The Guardian correspondent John Rodda always provided valuable information, Neil Allen of the Times always supported the throwers and was most informative on what our opponents had achieved, Terry O`Connor of the Daily Mail wanted to test you with his firm hand shake and if beaten which was very often, then an arm wrestle would be the order of the day with the winner buying the pint in the after match banquet, and Frank Taylor of the Daily Mirror.

Frank Taylor was a small, stocky and ebullient man and before entering journalism served in the RAF and in Egypt, took part in athletics. It was these two things that we had in common when first sitting with each other at the back of a plane journey overseas. His stories were captivating. However, it soon became apparent to me that he was the sports journalist and the only one to have survived the Manchester United devastating air disaster that took place on the 6 February 1958.

He told me that he owed his life to two things. The first being that he always sat on his own rather than with other journalists and secondly, that he was hauled from the plane wreckage by a very brave photographer called Peter Howard. His injuries to his right leg and left arm were so severe that surgeons did consider amputating either or both of them. In the event, he was left with only 50% movement in the left arm and his right leg was 3in shorter than the

129

left. Even today, I cannot imagine how I would have felt to fly again after this terrible experience.

The one journalist who the `heavies` throwers detested was Desmond Hackett who I believe wrote for the Daily Express. A smartly dressed man, thin but looking older than his true age most probably due to his love of spirits. He obviously did not like the throws and any reporting reflected this message. One particular report of his stated that Great Britain failed to qualify for the finals of a European competition due to the `Extra Baggage throwers`! I am sure he did not realise the hard and discipline training that went on to make the national team compared with better funded athletes with far superior facilities and importantly, competing against many steroid induced performers.

On reading Hackett`s report Jeff Teale was livid and on the next trip approached the journalist to state his case. Jeff informed him the front room of his father`s house in Kippax, near Leeds was made into a weights room, many of the weights used were of sleepers from the pit and his stop –board used to prevent fouling, was a kerb at the local car park pub! I informed him that I too used to train on a footpath, with chalk circles and throw into a field with grass almost 2ft tall. Furthermore, many times I trained in the back garden with weights during the winter. Hackett then admitted that, "I did not know how enthusiastic you throwers were and the Sports Council needs to spend money to improve facilities!" So with some tact and truthful exchanges, his reporting became kinder to the throwers and in addition, the `extra baggage` description disappeared and I think eventually he left athletics reporting.

The long season continued with an international against West Germany gaining my 21st cap, coming 3rd with a respectable throw of 182ft 10in/55.74 m discus throw and 54ft 7in/16.42m for 4th place in the shot. The West German discus throwers were Dirk Wipperman who won the event and Klaus –Peter Hennig who narrowly beat me for 2nd place. The shot putters were the giant (6ft 8in tall) Heinfried Birlenbach and an extremely muscular Ralf Reichenbach.

Another full international this time against Finland, took place at the White City on October 8/9 1969. Already a very long season most of the team treated it as a friendly encounter. The Finish discus thrower Penti Kahma thought differently and threw over 190ft/58.00m to take 1st place. Managing 2nd place with a throw of 178ft 2in/54.32m was pleasing as I was experimenting with a new technique in trying to get more range, hence remaining longer in contact with the discus before releasing it over a braced left leg, in the final phases of the throw.

Kahma was not a big man for a world class thrower. Slim, muscular yet he possessed explosive power and was a good model for smaller men to emulate. After all, he was the surprise winner at the 1974 European Championships in Rome.

To round off the season, I was placed 4th in the shot event with a distance of 53ft 11in/16.42m, the 6th full international for this event.

With the experience of competing internationally, seeing various techniques and the sheer enjoyment of competing and training made me more determined to do well. After all, although an amateur, what a fantastic life to be an international athlete and placed in a wonderful institution for sport, Loughborough College. With a new PE Centre built, a weights room and elected as Athletics Club Captain, 1970 should be better on all fronts.

Making the cover of the annual Loughborough Colleges versus the AAA (D Lee)

When I arrived back at College, just before the Christmas recess my life took a turn as I met my future wife Angela (Moore). She was in her third year and studying to be a primary school teacher with her home being in Bridport, Dorset.

Interestingly whilst I stayed with Angela's parents in Bridport, I happened to use the school's (Colfox) playing fields one afternoon to train with the discus when I was approached by a man with his dog. He mentioned that years ago in British India he had a friend who used to throw very long distances with the implement. "What was his name?" I enquired. "Adrian Tancred" came the reply from the dog walker. Startled I said, "Well I am his eldest son Bill." He replied, "He was better looking." I paused and then answered, "But I can throw further." We carried on with our conversation for a few minutes and then he said his name was Des Laws and he taught at Angela's school. Such a coincidence as my father and Des were extremely good friends in India and my mother had many photographs of them together.

My father throwing the discus in India

Another coincidence relating to Angela was the friendship of my father with Ken Bloomfield who lived in Bridport Avenue in Ipswich. Maybe all of this was meant to happen?

At home, I was lucky not to seek a part-time job to earn `pocket money` as my grant in those days was sufficient for my meagre needs. I got a generous grant as a mature student from Ipswich Borough Council`s Education department which included maintenance as well as tuition fees. A large cheque would arrive at the beginning of term and I would safely put it into the Loughborough Lloyds bank. I don`t remember ever being in debt. What I do know is that had it been today, I could not afford to go either to College or University and therefore, would have had stay in the Army. Also, my parents could not support me financially, so I was extremely lucky to go to college in the late 60`s.

My first priority at the start of the new term was to meet Angela and catch up with all our Christmas news and discuss plans for this year. I wanted to go to the USA on a sports scholarship and study for a Masters degree after my course here in Loughborough finished. Also training for the impending Commonwealth Games in Edinburgh would take up much of my `free` time but Angela was fully supportive and understanding.

I entered the AAA Indoor championships and was beaten by shot put rival Jeff Teale who threw 56ft 5in/17.19m against my 54ft 2in/16.50m effort with Cardiff`s representative John Walters 3rd at 51ft 5in/15.68m. This performance gave me another indoor international cap against the mighty East Germans.

Needless to say, the East Germans outclassed both me and Jeff with outstanding distances that would have been the world best at the time. The winner was the young Udo Beyer who would go on to win the 1976 Olympic Montreal shot put event. At a height of 1.94m, he weighed 130kg and even for a shot putter, Beyer was exceptionally strong. His personal best was a most impressive 74ft 3in/22.64m set in 1986.

All his siblings were fantastic athletes and at the Moscow 1980 Olympics, Udo was with his sister Gisela and his brother Hans-Georg, all of them reaching the finals of their respective disciplines. Hans-Georg won the gold medal with his Handball team, Udo was 3rd in the shot put and Gisela 4th in the discus event. Not to be undone, another sister Gudrun, was the physical therapist for her national team at the 1992 Barcelona Olympic Games. Udo eventually became the National team captain for many years and was a well-respected athlete both in his country and around the world.

The other shot putter Heinz-Jochim Rothenberg did not achieve the results of his compatriot but was good enough to finish eleventh in the men`s final at the Munich Olympics 1972.

At Loughborough College there was the usual inter collegiate and club competitions and as Captain of the Athletics Club, I represented them in all the fixtures. In the weights room, the lifting was going well and I had a companion on most evenings, the hammer thrower Jim Whitehead who later on in his athletics career represented Great Britain. We set an example that anyone entering the weights room was there to train and not talk about their personal lives and who they fancied at College! This soon `caught on` and everyone knew this code of practice was to their benefit. It was a good club and everyone supported each other in motivating one another.

On the 2 May in Cambridge during the match against Cambridge University Angela and I got engaged with a view of getting married in September, as I intended to study in the States after Loughborough. It was symbolic at the time because as I asked Angela to marry me Concorde flew above us. To our friends and family this was a whirlwind romance but as I said at the time, "If you are certain why wait? "

My lovely wife Angela in full bloom!

The first outdoor international before the Commonwealth Games was again against East Germany and although suffering from a shoulder strain, I still took part but finished 4th with a poor distance which did not do my confidence any favours or impress the England selectors. The top two, Hartmut Losch was the 1969 European discus champion with Detlef Thorith, the 1966 European champion. So in fine tradition, these were the athletes to emulate but rumours were spreading about the illegal use of performance drugs used by many of the East German athletes.

After this poor performance I rested for a week before commencing full training again and was eager to defend my AAA national discus title and impress the England selectors so that I could be chosen for the Games.

To my disappointment we heard that Les Mills of New Zealand would be taking part in what was our National Championships but with him competing, it might be difficult to win this prestigious national title again. It turned out successfully for me albeit rather close for comfort as I won my 5th AAA title with a throw of 176ft 9in/53.88m, Les Mills (NZ) 2nd with a throw of 175ft 10in/53.60m and John Watts gaining 3rd place with 175ft 6in/53.50m. This was pleasing as Les Mills was one of the favourites to win in Edinburgh.

4. LEAVING LOUGHBOROUGH COLLEGE, GETTING MARRIED AND WORK

Soon after this competition, I successfully passed my teacher training course and much to my disappointment it was time to leave Loughborough College. I had really enjoyed studying there and felt very settled.

The next phase was to compete in my second Commonwealth Games in the beautiful city of Edinburgh during the 16 July until 25 July.

The village was in my opinion good with the food offered first class. The atmosphere as usual at these Games was friendly and it was great to see so many Commonwealth athletes from the past.

These Games were for the first time ever in track and field athletics, to feature events in metric units rather than imperial units. It was also the first Commonwealth Games that HM Queen Elizabeth II attended in her capacity as the Head of the Commonwealth.

I was looking forward to the competition and on arriving in the new Meadowbank stadium the wind was blowing in the right direction. I could not wait to start to take advantage of the prevailing wind because I noted at times it levelled off and at times swirling to the detriment of throwing long distances.

In round two of the competition, I unleashed the discus for a new Games record and seasonal best with a throw of 185ft 11in/56.68m which put me in the gold medal position. However, 3 rounds later this distance was improved by the eventual winner George Puce from Canada with a throw of 193ft 6in/59.02m with Les Mills of New Zealand 2nd with a throw of 189ft 8in/57.84m. Both these men had previously thrown much further so I was delighted to be close and importantly, win my first medal in a Major Championships.

Throwing at Crystal Palace, London (Mark Shearman)

As a result of this performance, many telegrams and phone calls were received which was very humbling and pleasing, particularly from my parents, immediate family members, Ken Bloomfield and of course, my lovely future wife Angela.

I managed to see other Competitors in action including the great Lynn Davies in the long jump with a certain Allan Wells raking the pit, who eventually became the 100m 1980 Moscow Olympic champion.

Weight lifting has always been an interest so I went and watched little Precious McKenzie win the Bantamweight gold medal adding to the gold medal he won at the last British Empire and Commonwealth Games. He was an engaging man with a diminutive stature at 4ft 9in/1.45m who went on to represent New Zealand in future Games. The great Louis Martin who won the Mid-Heavyweight title was seen performing so it was a great privilege to see him in action. He was a bronze medallist at the 1960 Rome Olympics and went one better in Tokyo four years later achieving a silver medal. He is undoubtedly, Britain`s greatest Olympic medallist in weightlifting. In the Super-Heavyweight contest Ray Rigby from Australia won the gold medal and interestingly at the 1974 Commonwealth Games, he finished 6th in the shot put event.

The closing ceremony was a wonderful occasion and a great show was put on by the organisers of these Games. It was a joyous occasion and at one of the receptions, the Prime Minister Edward Heath paid a visit only a month after he was elected. A group of us had the honour to speak to him and by all accounts he was a Burnley Football Club supporter and was in full praise for this Lancashire team. As soon as this brief conversation with us had finished, he was swiftly off to do some dancing and we all noted his swift footwork as he laughed throughout the dance.

I too would be laughing as my marriage to Angela was imminent. Before the big day there was another two Great Britain internationals to contend with. The first being a European cup semi- final in which I finished 4th in my event with a throw of 171ft 9in/52.36m but sadly, Britain's men failed to qualify for the final in Stockholm in which the East Germans won easily. The last invitation against Poland I declined as my marriage to Angela was on the same weekend! A couple of weeks before our wedding though, I competed at the World Student Games in Turin, Italy and just missed out in making the finals which mainly consisted of East European internationals with the Hungarian Janos Muranyi winning the competition with a throw of 197ft 4in/60.16m.

Also around this time I had heard from Indiana University in the USA that there was a major administration query that the authorities there could not understand the two year mature student course at Loughborough having the necessary 'credits' to transfer me on to a Bachelor's degree programme at Indiana. There would be a delay in entrance, so our plans to start a new life in the States, was postponed but we thought we would look at this 'academic' adventure after our wedding.

The big day arrived and the wedding took place in Bridport, Dorset on the 12 September 1970. It was a wonderful day shared by all our families and friends and we had a wonderful reception in a hotel overlooking West Bay harbour. Brother Geoff was my best man and he took a delight to read out the many humorous congratulatory letters. Some were written by Duncan Case who had been my warden at Gimson hall in Loughborough.

Two of these I can remember can quite vividly which stated ' Look after Bill Angela, he likes his oats especially in the morning!' and the second, 'Don't waste a second you two, England needs some top class discus throwers, so start producing tonight!'. It brought a few smiling faces but I was not sure about my new father-in-law Jack!

After a wonderful reception in a hotel over- looking West Bay harbour with families and friends, Angela and I left for a short honeymoon before moving to Ipswich to start our new married life together before making a decision to relocate to the States and pursue further academic studies.

As the USA post-graduate acceptance at Indiana University did not materialise due to the Admissions Departments late query on the credits allocations for a two year mature students course at Loughborough College, I was left to get a temporary job with a local British Sugar Beet factory in Sproughton road, Ipswich and live with my kind sister Maureen and her husband Bill, until we managed to get a flat on our own and a teaching post starting January 1971.

So my athletics training having stopped as I got involved in the shift working schedule of 6am to 2pm or 2pm to 10pm or 10pm to 6am which was not exactly the aim for both Angela and I, but it did provide a challenge coupled with a different type of experience and working pattern for me!

Most of the work involved unloading and storing the sugar beet onto trains for various delivery destinations. If you were fortunate or in some cases unfortunate, you worked in gangs near the furnace which over time was hard work with plenty of fluid loss which at the end of the shift entitled you to two pints of beer to replenish the sweat loss. I saved my entitlement for the end of the week so that I could `celebrate` the end of the shift cycle in style. I do remember the foreman with affection a certain Mr Pead, who lived near my sister in Bramford road and who was a firm supporter of athletics and Ipswich Town football club.

Performing the bench press in training for the Commonwealth Games 1970 (E Blackadder)

Just married!

This manual work finished after three months as I managed to get a teaching post at a school called Tower Ramparts in Ipswich and Angela at Springfield Junior School. Tower Ramparts stood in the centre of Ipswich until it was demolished in 1979 and the current Tower Ramparts Shopping Centre was built on this site opposite the bus station.

On my first day at the school I asked a senior pupil, "How many teachers are at the school?" He paused for a few seconds and answered, "Only half of them!"

The school had a reputation but it was a challenge. Facilities were poor and playing fields were at Sidegate Lane, some distance away from the school. George Denby was the head of the PE department and we were based near the storage room called the `Muscle Factory`, far away from the staff room. At first I was extremely impressed by the curriculum offered to the students at the school. On the first Wednesday lunch time certain boys turned up in boots, braces with knee high trousers and colourful shirts and when asked why they were dressed like this, they informed me, "Sir, we want to do horse riding as mentioned in the prospectus"! With no horses available in the Town centre, I informed them politely that we had no horses, so choose another sporting activity.

Another group arrived who were the `detention mob` who were to go to Pin Mill and clean the sailing boat for the headmaster! Pin Mill is a hamlet on the south bank of the tidal river Orwell, located on the outskirts of the village of Chelmondiston on the Shotley Peninsular.

My class had enrolled for Archery which was to take place at Sidegate Lane Playing fields some one mile away from the main site. This involved me walking with the group to the destination which only gave me time to deliver the safety procedures of this sport and then walk them back as that constituted the double period!

This curriculum looked good on paper but was flawed to the extreme. I felt sorry for the pupils but the headmaster assured me things would improve in the long run. Soon after this, the school provided sport and physical activity that was manageable with the facilities that existed. So many activities were therefore shelved.

I did enjoy teaching these pupils but initially they tested me and were disobedient to weaker staff. I remember a pupil who wanted `to beat me up` as he thought I was a tough guy who needed to be put down! He was the leader of this so called `tough` group at the school and in this role he arranged to meet me with members of his gang for a boxing contest at the Ipswich YMCA.

Myself with Peter doing a bench press with Geoff squatting at the YMCA in Ipswich (Archant)

141

He was not aware that I had started my training again and the YMCA had a few weights to accommodate my lifting schedules for athletics. More importantly, the `tough guy' pupil`s elder brother was my lifting companion, so you can imagine the face of this young man when asked by his elder brother why he was there and on being told, was given a real dressing down in front of his gang members and left with his tail between his legs. Furthermore, I had no trouble whatsoever again and all the pupils could not do enough for me, which included opening the doors when I entered a room and hands raised to ask a question in front of a bewildered headmaster who offered me a permanent position and a secondment to complete a degree programme if I stayed at the school for 3 years! I had certainly made my mark with both pupils and staff.

On a happy note, I did work with a student teacher Colin Culley who wanted to go to Loughborough College and was a keen athlete. On one lesson we informed the class of `ruffians` that the Health Inspector was arriving to inspect their feet. So I asked Colin to open the windows whilst asking the pupils to remove their shoes and place them neatly and quietly outside the classroom door. As Colin went outside to swap all the shoes with a different size, I proceeded to talk about cleanliness and feet care waiting for a nod from Colin that this was done and timing it perfectly, with the bell ringing for the class change over. It was fun to see them all trying to find their correct shoes with the break time rapidly diminishing and Colin and I laughing. This was virtually our last time at the school before departing to pastures new. I was not really surprised when this school was pulled down in 1979.

Weight training in the back garden. On the far left, is Colin Culley who was a student teacher with me at Tower Ramparts school in Ipswich and a promising thrower. In the middle is his father George.

At this time Angela and I had a flat at Cemetery road in Ipswich but despite having no car we managed to use local buses and to visit the beautiful towns and villages of Suffolk such as Aldburgh, Southwold, Bury St. Edmunds, Felixstowe, Woodbridge, Shotley and Kersey. We were also planning to return to Loughborough as I was accepted onto a Master`s programme in Human Biology at the University commencing in September.

Due to a lack of a committed training programme, my athletics took a `back seat` whilst pondering the best thing to do for my career in `civvy `street. I used the local YMCA for weight training and indoor work and at times used the old Ipswich Airport cellar for further weight training, if I was near my former home in Nacton Road. None of this was ideal for top class sport.

On one occasion, I along with brothers Geoff and Peter took our implements onto the local bus and sat on the top seats as we headed for the Ipswich Airport to train. As the bus approached the top of Bishops Hill to join Nacton Road, a 16lb shot rolled down the aisle and headed towards the bus conductor downstairs. He immediately pulled the wire to stop the bus in an emergency and shouted out, "Leave the bus as a bomb is on board!" After stopping, with all passengers and the driver off the bus, everyone realised the conductor`s error but we all thanked him for his swift action! For years afterwards the family have laughed about this amusing incident.

In the AAA National championships I managed to finish 3rd in the discus with a throw of 181ft 1in/55.20m, with my old foe and friend John Watts 2nd (189ft 11in/57.88m), the winner being the New Zealander Les Mills with a throw of 192ft 4in/85.62m.

Outside the athletics pavilion at Loughborough (D Readhead)

During the Eastern Counties Championships, taking advantage of the prevailing wind at HMS Ganges I broke my UK national discus record which I shared with John Watts with a throw of 190ft 6in/58.08m, easily beating Geoff Capes and my brother Peter. The track was next to the sea and there was a high bank to hold back the water. In the early 1990`s the sports field in which the track was located was excavated to a depth of one fathom and the sea let in to form what is now a thriving marina.

Such a performance enabled me to get selected for the Great Britain Team against France (3rd with a throw of 180ft 1in/54.88m) and another against West Germany, this time coming 4th in both the shot (53ft 9in/16.38m) and discus (179ft 5in/54.70m).

I suppose looking back my performances were pleasing as I had only been training since January with facilities much poorer than those provided at Loughborough. So to go back to University and the impending Olympic Games in Munich approaching, my mind was made up to really improve my discus and shot performances for 1972 and reach a world class standard in the former event.

Just before leaving to study at Loughborough University I received a lovely letter from Harold Abrahams who at the time was the Chairman of the British Amateur Athletics Board and an Olympic champion 100m gold medallist in 1924. He took an interest in the statistics of British athletes` full international representations. We often discussed Army physical training methods and throwing events. The letter contained all my full international appearances with distances thrown, positions and dates of the competition. Such a letter is treasured by me today.

His story and that of Eric Liddell was made into the film Chariots of Fire in 1981 which was a fact based story about them at the 1924 Olympic Games. Eric Liddell, a devout Scottish Christian who runs for the glory of god and Harold Abrahams, an English Jew who runs to overcome prejudice.

Winding up for a 60m plus throw (M Shearman)

5. LOUGHBOROUGH UNIVERSITY POST GRADUATE STUDIES, 1972 OLYMPIC GAMES AND INTERNATIONAL ATHLETICS

We moved back to Loughborough University to study Human Biology within the Masters programme. As I did not have a Bachelor`s degree my award would only be a diploma but it would allow me the following year in 1973, an opportunity to complete a master`s degree programme. On my course were Neil Armstrong who would eventually become Head of the School of Health, Exercise and Physical Activity at Exeter University, Dave Kellett, Kevin Sykes and a certain Peter Snell who like me, was pursuing the diploma route and was sponsored by the tobacco company Rothmans.

A protégé of the New Zealand athletics coach Arthur Lydiard, Snell is known for the three Olympic and two Commonwealth Games gold medals and the many world records set. For these achievements he was knighted and today lives in the USA. It was great to see this wonderful athlete again in Colorado in 1989 when I was on a Winston Churchill Fellowship and attending an athletics coaching convention. Both of us had achieved doctorates but not in human biology, Peter in exercise physiology from Washington State University and me from West Virginia University in Sports Management. We managed to `catch up`, talk about our initial induction in higher education post graduate studies at Loughborough and the personal tutors and lecturers who made a mark on us one way or the other.

Also attending this convention which enabled me to meet old rivals and friends were Jay Silvester, former world record holder who was now a Professor at Utah University, Meg Ritchie the British women`s discus record holder and Stuart Togher who had coached a number of UK hammer throwers including Chris Black, who finished a most credible 7th place at the 1976 Montreal Olympic Games with a distance of 240ft 2in/73.18m. He could not get a coaching post in the UK, so the Americans offered him one which was a shame because he was technically sound.

The course at Loughborough however, was very demanding with a full timetable and both Peter and I would `volunteer` for extra classes to be up to the standard of the others particularly with the experimental and laboratory work of the course. Our tutor Ernest Hamley, was an enthusiastic man who would often just talk about how to measure the intensity of exercise in the clinical setting and the relationship between heart rate and work (VO2) that needed to be understood, in order to prescribe exercise properly. This happened every week, so it must have been his pet speciality?

The computer lecturer would `ramble on` about how a computer is built but no teaching or lecturing provided. I was really lucky that Peter and I were in the same` boat` because all of this was alien to the both of us. We both knew that human biology in this form was not our destination but both of us approved and enjoyed modules relating to nutrition, physiology, anatomy, anthropology and population genetics.

My training was surprisingly going very well considering I was in the weights room at 7.30am prior to my 9am lectures. In the evenings, I would spend time performing discus and shot drills supplemented by plyometric training. Plyometrics also known as jump training are exercises in which muscles exert maximum force in short intervals of time with the aim of increasing power (speed and strength). The training focuses on learning to move from a muscle *extension* to a *contraction* in a rapid or explosive manner, such as specialised repeated jumps. This type of training is a highly effective form of power training. I might add that my training finished at 9pm most evenings!

I entered a couple of indoor competitions for the University and was approaching some of my best ever indoor distances. As a result, I decided to take part in the AAA National Indoor Championships at RAF Cosford in January 1972, the start of the Olympic year in the shot event. The winner was Geoff Capes with distance of 61ft 2in/18.65m myself coming 2nd defeating big Jeff Teale with a putt of 55ft 7in/16.94m to Jeff`s 55ft 3in/16.84m.

My weight lifting was going really well as I started to achieve many personal bests in the bench press, power clean, and in jump squats. So if I could stay injury free I was confident that 1972 would be a great year for me in both events.

The academic work was going as well as expected but one had to be really well organised, as I was attending a master`s programme, training hard for the Olympics and getting ready for fatherhood as Angela was expecting our first child in March which happened to be on the 27th when Nicola was born. It was an extremely emotional moment for both of us and I was glad that both Angela and Nicola were well and healthy.

What really changes when you become a parent? Everything does, instantly. When you are about to become a father for the first time, other men who have already blazed that trail are keen to share their experiences. You get those who tell you it`s the best thing that`s ever happened to them and there are those who talk knowledgeably of sleep patterns and of bottle feeding.

Then they are those who give you that knowing feeling, a peculiar expression somewhere between smug resignation and pity which seems to suggest `you don`t know what you have let yourself in for!` I was subjected to all of this but in retrospect only one person hit the nail on the head and told me the truth of fatherhood and he was now going to impart this profound piece of wisdom, like handing over a flaming torch , "it changes everything instantly", he said simply.

Some men find this responsibility easier than others whilst some embrace their new role and the changes to their routine, while others struggle with it. However, for most of us, in the end, something changes and we go from blokes to Dads.

Nicola was also a lovely girl who behaved so well that my sleep was not affected, so the plan was still intact and in my first outdoor competition, I managed to break my own UK national discus record with a throw of 193ft 2in/59.02m and the shot 59ft 8in/18.20m again a personal best. With my strength gains improving all the time and my technical work being consistent and fluid, I now knew I would make the Olympic team in two events if I stayed injury free.

On the 23 April during a rainy evening in Oxford representing the Southern Counties against Borough Road College and Oxford University with no wind but rain, I unleashed another UK national record with a throw of 194ft 3in/59.22m, 22 cm over the Olympic qualifying distance.

Further UK national records were broken with distances of 194ft 11in/59.42m and 195ft 6in/59.58m at the AAA versus Loughborough annual athletics match again in windless conditions and a personal best shot putt of 62ft 3in/18.97m at the end of May.

So it was no surprise that on the 7 June at Loughborough`s Athletics track in a match between Loughborough College and the Midland Counties, I broke not only the UK national record but also the All-Comers as well with a distance of 203ft 2in/61.94m, becoming the first UK athlete to break the 200ft 1in/61.0m barrier. This throw also ranked me 9th in the end of season world rankings for the event. It was a wonderful feeling to have broken this barrier as many throwers wanted to be the first, so up to this stage, this was my best performance ever as a discus thrower.

Front cover (my first) on the famous Athletics Weekly. In those days, it cost you 10p
(June 17 1972)

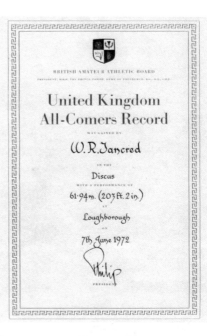

Certificates for breaking UK National and All-Comers Discus records

As a result, I was looking forward to face the Polish squad on the 19/20 June 1972. Facing two throwers who had thrown over 202ft 1in/61.60m the competition was just right. The match, jointly sponsored by *The Scotsman* and Malaysia Singapore Airlines, was the first full international to be staged in Scotland since Finland beat Great Britain in Glasgow 37 years ago.

Leszek Gajdzinski just beat me with a throw of 192ft 1in/58.54m to my 190ft 11in/58.20m which was a shame as I narrowly fouled an effort beyond the impressive 61m mark. However, in the shot put, I managed to go beyond the 60ft 0in/18.28m mark in international competition for the first time putting 60ft 6in/18.44m

In the AAA national championships I won my 6th title with a throw of 200ft 3in/61.06m beating John Hillier and my brother Peter in the process. In the shot event, the mighty Geoff Capes launched the 16lbs shot 63ft 10in/19.47m, beating Jeff Teale`s 61ft 10in/18.84m and myself in 3rd place with 59ft 10in/18.20m.

Further full internationals were against Greece and Holland in Athens with a winning throw of 191ft 11in (58.50m) and 4th placed shot put distance of 58ft 9in/17.81m. The next one took place in Helsinki against Finland and Spain. In this international I managed to be placed 2nd with a throw of 194ft 7in/59.30m. So with these competitions over, the anticipated invitation to compete in my second Olympic Games would now be welcomed.

The official letter dated 16 July 1972 signed by HRH Prince Philip The Duke of Edinburgh, arrived at my parents home inviting me to take part in both the discus and shot put events at the XXth Olympic Games in Munich. I was absolutely delighted and all the hard work had paid off.

BUCKINGHAM PALACE

16th July, 1972.

W.R.Tancred, Esq.

Dear Mr.Tancred,

I am delighted to inform you that you have been selected by the British Amateur Athletic Board to represent Great Britain and Northern Ireland in the XXth Olympic Games in Munich in the Discus. and Shot Put.

Many congratulations. I send you my best wishes for a happy and successful visit to Munich.

Yours sincerely

Philip

Selection letter to compete in both the discus and shot events at the 1972 Munich Olympic Games

Britain's Munich team and best performances

The 1972 British Athletics Olympic Games team with best performances and world bests (The Daily Telegraph)

Before flying off to Munich the British team assembled in London and most of the competitors optimistic that they were going to perform admirably and a few expecting to `startle` their global opponents. On arrival in the well organised and comfortable village I spent time `inspecting` the facilities and met up with old friends Jim Fox, Barry Lillywhite (Modern Pentathlon competitors) and Ron Bright (Coach) from my Army days at the Royal Military Academy, Sandhurst, including Robin Tait (New Zealand), Jay Silvester (USA) and Miklos Nemeth (Hungary) who went on to win the javelin event at the 1976 Montreal Olympics.

In the village, many fans were seen including celebrities who loved sport and the excitement that it brought to them. On one occasion we met Kenny Lynch the comedian, song writer and singer who had hits with songs like` Up on the Roof` and spoke with a cockney accent. He was a real gentleman with a sense of humour, who wished us the `very best of British`.

An opportunity arose to have a meal with the legendry Adi Dassler who was the founder of the German sportswear company Adidas and the younger brother of Rudolf Dassler, who founded the *Puma* Company after a rift between both of them. He was a great host and paid the bill. I suppose I was lucky to be invited being close at hand and furthermore, was sponsored by the shoe company which provided me with free throwing shoes and the occasional track suit. There is no such thing as a free lunch however, as part of the discussion over the meal was on how the discus shoe could be modified in order to prevent slipping in rainy conditions? My suggestion as a world class discus thrower was to exchange the sole of the hammer shoe with the sole of the current discus shoe. He took this on board and after the Olympics I was delivered three pairs of shoes modelled on my suggestion to practice with and provide feedback to his representative in Germany.

Adi Dassler made a point to attend every major sporting event in an effort to convince athletes to wear his shoes. He was a most successful businessman and a multi-millionaire.

A happy Bill Tancred after breaking another UK British discus record (Bill Potter – Camera Press London)

It was a wonderful Opening Ceremony and the British team were dressed immaculately in uniforms made by Hardy Amies, the fashion designer from Saville Row, London. He was also the official dressmaker to HM The Queen from 1952 to his eventual retirement in 1989. Furthermore, he dressed the 1966 English Football team and the previous 1968 British Olympic team of Mexico. Without any hesitation, he was one of the founding fathers of modern British menswear.

In the Munich Olympic Stadium and waiting for the other teams to appear. It`s a long wait!

It is interesting to note that when World War 2 intervened, Hardy Amies found himself in British Intelligence and later with the Special Operations Executive (SOE), organising sabotage and resistance in occupied countries.

When asked what he would like to have been remembered for as an epitaph he suggested something on the lines of making a lot of women happy for over 50 years!

The Games took place from 26 August until 11 September 1972. The Munich Olympic Games of 1972 was a great presentation of technical brilliance. The athletics stadium had phenomenal innovations in poles, cables and translucent plastic and could host over 80,000 spectators. All facilities, except the sailing were located in an area of one square mile so added much convenience.

Outside the Munich Olympic Stadium

However, the abiding memory is the violence of the Palestinian raid on the Israeli team and as such almost extinguished the Olympic spirit. On 5 September, eight Palestinian terrorists entered the Olympic village and captured eleven members of the Israeli Olympic team. Two of the hostages were able to wound two of their captors before being killed. The terrorists requested the release of 234

155

Palestinians that were being held in Israel.

The terrorists and their hostages were transferred by helicopter all clearly seen from our rooms in the village, to the military airport of Furstenfeldbruck ostensibly to board an aircraft destined for an Arab country. However, this did not happen as during the failed attempt to rescue all the remaining hostages, five of the terrorists were killed with three wounded.

The International Olympic Committee (IOC) decided that the Games should continue and on the following day, a memorial service was given for the victims, with flags flying at half- mast. The Games were suspended for one day. The decision of the IOC to carry on with the Games was very controversial considering what had taken place in a sporting venue.

This appalling attack instantly heightened security at subsequent Olympics beginning with the 1976 Winter Olympics in Innsbruck, Austria. Before all of this, any Olympic representative could bring someone into the village as long as accreditation had been given. Today, it is virtually impossible.

Even so I witnessed some truly outstanding performances and saw first-hand, the many global sports stars in the athletes village. I have always been interested in boxing and was delighted to see the great amateur heavyweight Teofilo Stevenson from Cuba, who subsequently won three gold medals in this division at the 1972, 1976 and 1980 Olympic Games. A very tall and athletic looking figure who impressed me with his training routine of foot and speed work. It was also sad to hear that he died of a heart attack when just 60 years of age.

Also seen regularly in the village was Mark Spitz who won seven gold medals while on the way to setting new world records for each of his seven gold medals. Spitz who was Jewish, was asked to leave Munich before the Closing Ceremony for his own protection, after fears arose that he would be an additional target of those responsible for the Munich atrocities. His record gold medal haul stood until 2008 when it was beaten by Michael Phelps from the USA who won eight gold medals in swimming.

Spitz was not the only one to leave Munich before the Closing Ceremony as the British team were asked after the massacre whether anyone from the team wanted to leave early. There were quite a few including myself, who after competing went home early.

Perhaps one of the `darlings` of the Games seen was of the Soviet gymnast Olga Korbut with her distinguished `pig tales`. She was certainly a media star after winning gold medals in the team competition, the *Balance Beam* and the *Floor Exercise* events.

One of the exciting and eagerly awaited contests was watching the clash between our David Bedford and the magical Finn Lasse Viren. Bedford usually ran in red socks with a distinctive moustache and hair cut. Although leading for many laps, he had no answer to Viren who upped the pace and left David to struggle in at 6th place. The Flying Finn went on to dominate both the 5,000m and 10,000m with his brilliant tactical method of resisting all attacks, to make sure that he was in front at all times. (This feat has now been achieved by our own Mo Farah).

Bedford affectionately known as `Bootsie` went on to dismantle the world 10,000m world record in 27m 30.8sec and held every UK record from 2,000m to 10,000m and the steeplechase. After retiring from athletics he owned a number of night clubs and became the Chairman of the London Marathon raising thousands of pounds for charity.

Russia produced an outstanding world class sprinter who had been discovered in a most bizarre way. Many years before Munich, Russian experts fed statistics into a computer (bodyweight, height, muscle power, leg stride and somatotype, all formulated as a mathematical equation).

The answer that came out was Valery Borzov who proved in Munich this to be correct. He won the 100m, the 200m and anchored the Soviet Union to a silver medal in the sprint relay. However, it was interesting to see the two top US sprinters and medal favourites in the 100m Ray Robinson and Eddie Hart missed their quarter finals heats by watching the TV in the village having been given the wrong starting time! Borszov went on to marry Lyudmilla Turischeva in 1977 who went on to be a nine time Olympic medallist.

For British fans, Mary Peters won the pentathlon by a mere 15 points but the whole stadium smiled with her, even though the partisan German crowd had two of their own girls who finished 2nd (Heide Rosendahl) and 3rd (Burglinde Pollack).

Heide Rosendahl was a phenomenal athlete who was very pretty and athletic. Two days before the pentathlon competition she had won the women`s long jump gold medal by a mere 1cm with a distance of 6.78m and at the end of the athletics events proved her outstanding versatility by helping the West Germany`s 4 x 100m relay squad to a gold medal and world record, holding off the East German sprints champion Renate Stecher in the process. (Stecher was the gold medallist in both the 100m and 200m at these Games).

Another outstanding performance observed was that of Frank Shorter of the USA. He was born in Munich and ran the marathon as if the city belonged to him. He put in an amazing burst of speed after 10k for at least another 5k, to `burn off` his rivals and then coasted home to win the gold medal. However, this ultimate achievement was marred by an imposter, West German student Norbert Sudhaus running into the stadium ahead of Shorter who was not bothered by the silence of the crowd who had been fooled into thinking that he was running for 2nd place. Shorter was extremely comfortable that he was going to win the gold medal because he knew no other runner had passed him in this gruelling event. However, the crowd were not impressed with the imposter!

His sporting successes along with other distance athletes, helped to create the *running boom* in the USA during the 1970`s. Sometimes it takes an event such as this to inspire people.

The men`s javelin event produced a shock winner, when world record holder Janis Lusis of Russia was beaten by Germany`s Klaus Wolferman by just 2cm. He proved that this performance was no fluke because in 1973 he broke the javelin world record set by Janis Lusis with a throw of 308ft 7in/94.08m.

If 2cm was close between 1st and 2nd place then the men`s shot put was even closer! Brian Oldfield of the USA was in magnificent form leading up to these Games using a new technique for putting the shot. It was similar to the discus style throw using a rotational spin before releasing the implement. Komar from Poland kept calm and beat the very large American thrower `Wee` George Woods by the shortest winning margin ever of 1cm!

Wladyslaw Komar became the surprised Olympic Champion and was a popular winner amongst fellow throwers who nick -named him `King Kong`. He stood 6ft 5in (1.95m) tall and weighed 125kg (276lbs) with a solid physique. Sadly, he along with team mate Tadeusz Slusarski (Pole vault gold medal at the 1976 Montreal Olympic Games) died in a car crash in 1998.

As I was selected for both the shot and discus events, I trained with many of my rivals particularly with the Americans Tim Vollmer, John Powell and the New Zealander Robin Tait, along with my team mate John Watts in the discus. In the shot put I trained with rivals Bruce Pirnie of Canada, Brian Oldfield USA and team mate Geoff Capes. So the training and preparation were going very well until what could have been a terrible injury to John Watts.

The Americans and both John and myself used the same circle to throw and on this occasion when John went to retrieve his discus some 60m metres away without looking, I threw the discus and with his back to the direction of my throw, he was hit on the shoulder which nearly knocked him out, with him requiring some 15 stitches on his ear and head. This was very upsetting to me and of course to poor John and was certainly not the best preparation for an Olympic competition.

Next morning the `tough man` turned up to train looking like a Sikh wearing a turban! So we trained together and during the session, I pulled my right deltoid muscle which had a negative impact on my throwing. With the discus qualifying date only two days away I was in trouble and not sure whether I would be able to compete, as I had difficulty in raising my right arm.

On the day I took part, putting all my effort to qualify on my first throw and although thinking I had not fouled the throw, the judge hesitated for 30 seconds before he raised his red flag to denote a foul throw. It was one of my biggest disappointments in athletics because the discus went well over the qualifying distance and landed on the 200ft/61m mark. To this day I am positive that he made a terrible mistake and I would have made the final. With the best throw of 187ft 10in/57.24m and finishing 19th it was a disaster and furthermore, the right shoulder was so badly damaged that I was in no fit state to compete in the shot.

Looking back it is a real shame because I could have been a shot and discus competitor at an Olympic Games. At least I can say to my grandchildren I was selected for both events and of Olympic standard in both. Deep down it was a bitter disappointment as I had high hopes in making the top six and was ranked 8th in the world rankings that season. There were no `Hawk-Eye` systems available in 1972 to help throwers or judges in these situations.

The event was won by Ludvik Danek of Czechoslovakia (211ft 3in/64.40m), 2nd place going to Jay Silvester of the USA (208ft 4in/63.50m) and 3rd to Ricky Bruch from Sweden (208ft 0in/63.40m).

After leaving Munich, it was back to Loughborough to see my family and seek a job as my course at the University had finished successfully with a Diploma in Human Biology. Angela and I decided to stay in this Midland town as we were settled and I secured a post at West Bridgford College of Further Education in Nottingham as a lecturer in Physical Education.

We managed to get our first house in Melbreak Avenue, Loughborough which was close to the University so training would be on hand and with a pre-1955 Morris Minor car, things could not have been better.

After all this, there was a further last full international to participate in and that was against France in Paris late September and with the shoulder rested with no training I accepted the invitation to compete. Surprisingly, I threw 192ft 3in/58.60m winning the event against the Frenchmen Alard and Petit, so completing the season on a better note and firmer footing for the 1973 season.

There were a number of girls who travelled out to Paris who were fond of the British athletes particularly the muscled throwers. I clearly remember a very well-endowed lady called Margarette who when asked where she came from in England responded, "Hangers" Lane, London. Very appropriate I thought! It was nice to have some supporters who liked the throwing events.

The banquet was a `boozy` affair with the shot putter and captain of the French team Yves Brouzet leading the wine drinking contest against myself and the other `heavy` throwers with the French national anthem being played every time the French drank. It soon became apparent to them that they had competition because we kept up with them and soon many of them dropped out and wanted another challenge!

The next morning the throwers were very quiet and boarded the bus to the airport having had a very happy ending to the season. Paris was indeed a first class city to play host to the British athletics team.

Representing Loughborough Colleges at Ashby Road in Loughborough

6. WEST BRIDGFORD COLLEGE OF FURTHER EDUCATION AND BREAKING DISCUS RECORDS

I was looking forward to starting my new teaching post at this College as this was a far cry from teaching in a school like Tower Ramparts in Ipswich. This Further Education College was slightly better as it shared the good outdoor facilities with the local senior School. The downside was that five a side football, table-tennis and the introduction of fitness testing and evaluation, became the main focus for these further education students. Although at half term and the end of school term, the facilities belonged to `us` which made up for the lost opportunities in pursuing other sports such as gym work, swimming, athletics, and basketball.

Looking back, this post was not mentally stimulating or tiring so my athletics training in the evening at Loughborough would certainly not suffer and I also considered seriously pursuing a master`s degree by research at the University due to its convenience and opportunity.

The introduction of Fitness testing and evaluation undoubtedly helped in my training preparation as I regularly took part in the practical work. Some of the students were also motivated to beat an Olympian in any test that they excelled in.

I delivered this programme for the promotion of physical activity and evaluating standards for 16-18 year old students. The tests were used for motivation, achievement, improvement, diagnosis, grading, classification and prediction. I measured body composition, cardiovascular endurance, strength and muscular endurance, flexibility testing, speed drills and agility testing.

More popular fitness test performances included the Beep test (20m multi-stage shuttle run), push up test, sprint test, sit-up test, sit and reach, skinfold tests, hand grip strength and the vertical jump.

The vertical jump was a great test of explosive power in which many top class throwers had in abundance. This test involved standing next to a wall and reaching up to full height to touch a point on a marker board with your fingertips. You than flexed your legs and jumped as high as possible making a mark with your fingertips holding the chalk. The difference between the two marks was then compared against a table showing explosive, elastic leg power. You were allowed three attempts to perform this test.

All this measurement and testing resulted from my Human Biology course at Loughborough University and my previous testing experiences from athletics training courses and in the Army Physical Training Corps.

Some of the students aspired to further their education and study physical education so I scheduled classes to teach PE and introduced sports studies during my two years working at this Institution, so after a `shaky` start, I felt that some special contribution had been made. In addition after several years, I managed to see a handful of these former students at Crystal Palace athletics stadium, informing me of their degree graduations and thanking me personally for helping them in their chosen careers which was very gratifying to say the least.

I was also reminded by them of an incident involving a certain student who regularly went swimming when most girls were taking part. On one day a blushing swimming female informed me that this student was enormously well endowed and was the `star` of the show every time he went by the side of the pool. Being inquisitive and jealous, I along with a small number of my male students entered the swimming pool to see this fabulous endowed student. Well within seconds, one of the boys noted that half of a football sock appeared outside his swimming trunk down his leg, so as to give the game away! Thereafter seeing his real manhood in the shower, he was nicked named `little piglet`!

The 1973 season started with the AAA Indoor Championships at RAF Cosford. Mike Winch winning with a distance of 61ft 3in/18.67m, with me 2nd at 58ft 9in/17.91m and my brother Peter 3rd with 51ft 8in/15.75m. Mike was a special athlete, not big in stature but explosive and technically very efficient. He was someone that other similar built athletes could aspire to and was very inspirational. He went on to become a silver medallist at both the 1974 and 1982 Commonwealth Games and is currently coaching talented UK throwers.

In the weights room, my personal strength gains were at the highest level thereby indicating that a promising outdoor season was on the cards. My fitness levels were on par with my Army physical training days, including many of my fitness testing results, plus having a consistent discus technical improvement.

Just before the outdoor season commenced the throwers had a training weekend at Crystal Palace National Stadium. One morning as we were having our usual large breakfast, Geoff Capes and John Watts spotted the meat delivery lorry parked outside our window with the rear of the door left wide open showing a number of butchered pigs hanging from the hooks in the delivery lorry. Without any fuss, both of them moved at lightning speed to take two of the pigs and brought them to the breakfast area. Well, the whole place was in a fit of laughter on seeing the poor delivery man rubbing his head in confusion at his `two runaway `pigs. Both Geoff and John waited several minutes before helping the poor man with the return of the prized two pigs.

On the same weekend in a London cafe the three of us spotted Rolf Harris walking down the street, so we ran out after him and again Geoff and John this time, lifted him up side by side with Harris shouting out, "Put me down fella's". On putting down a very frightened Rolf Harris, he said he had never met such large and strong men in his life and asked us who we were? On informing him that we were British shot and discus throwers he wished as well and hoped not to meet again especially in the dark! Geoff being a comedian asked him, "How was his Didgeridoo?" "Fine", said Rolf Harris. We did not know at the time that he would be jailed for being a paedophile and interestingly, created a working copy of the Aboriginal wind instrument during his classes at his former prison HMP Bullington in Oxfordshire!

The season got off to a flying start with a new UK national record at the Inter Counties Championships with a distance of 203ft 3in/61.96m adding just 5cm to the old record set in the previous year.

Other performances over the 196ft 10in/60.0m mark included (before the next UK National record was set) were 197ft 2in/60.08m at London Crystal Palace on 23 May; 197ft 7in/60.22m at Loughborough on the 6 June; 200ft 2in/61.04m at Loughborough on the 7 June; 201ft 8in/61.46m in the Southern Counties Championships at Crystal Palace and 197ft 11in/60.34m in the Great Britain international in Leipzig, East Germany where I came 2nd to the giant Pachale but beating Muller the second string East German and top ten ranked world discus thrower.

Siegfried Pachale went on to finish 5th at the 1976 Montreal Olympic Games and interestingly, his daughter Hanka represented her country in Volleyball at both the 1996 and 2000 Olympic Games. Pachale was an intelligent man who became a journalist in his career and spoke English eloquently.

On the 7 July at Loughborough another discus throw was dispatched to 203ft 2in/61.90m and following that match, the AAA National championships was won with a throw of 200ft 10in/61.22m at Crystal Palace making it my 7th National title. 2nd place went to my old rival John Hillier (190ft 7in/58.10m) and my brother Peter 3rd (177ft 10in/54.22m). In the shot event Capes was in fine form winning with a putt of 66ft 6in/20.27m, Winch 2nd with 64ft 1in/19.54m and myself collecting the bronze medal with a distance of 59ft 7in/18.14m.

There was another Full International match on the 18 July in Athens against Greece and Belgium with a throw of 199ft 6in/90.82m for 1st place which was achieved in windless conditions. This was very satisfying and this performance indicated to me that the British discus record would soon be beaten. As ever our hosts entertained us after the match with a trip to the Acropolis and on leaving this historical site a visit to a bar serving plenty of raki, ouzo and beer with lashings of delicious meze, including feta, ham, olives and tomatoes. Wonderful, generous and happy hosts!

The next match was a low key affair representing my club Wolverhampton and Bilston A C in a National League fixture on the 28 July. I used this competition as a training session and still produced a good result by throwing 198ft 11in/60.64m at Sale, Cheshire.

August was the plan in which to deliver the goods as I was both mentally and physically prepared. In gaining my 32 full international `cap` in Oslo representing Great Britain in the semi-final of the Europa Cup on the 5 August I managed to get 3rd place with a throw of 195ft 2in/59.46m in helping the team qualify for the final. This was a good result for the GB team as in the previous qualifying contest we failed to qualify, so things were looking up.

As soon as we touched down I was off to Portsmouth to compete again representing the AAA against the Armed Forces and the Southern Counties. Another throw of 201ft 10in/61.52m was dispatched to win the event but I was disappointed as a foul was around 207ft/63m would have been a new British discus record.

However, this disappointment did not last long because on 11 August at a Croydon Harrier Field Events meeting, a new UK national discus was set. In spite of the windless conditions, I managed to get all my throws beyond 196ft 10in/60.0m, the worst landing at exactly the distance (196ft 10in/60.0m) and the best landing 203ft 9in/62.10m, which upped my two months old UK record of 203ft 3in/61.96m set at the inter-counties in Warley. This was also a new UK All-Comers record.

The very next day I unleashed my second UK National discus record in 24 hours when the discus spun to 206ft 5in/62.92m, again at Crystal Palace (12 August). Another throw also broke the old record set the day before so I was in fine form. For setting the best performance at this athletics match I won a `dinner for two` at a Croydon restaurant which I donated to a thrower who needed double helpings! I then had to travel back to Loughborough and see my daughter Nicola and Angela who was expecting another child in November. This was a hectic but enjoyable life for me.

Front cover number two on the Athletics Weekly (August 25 1973)

The next international (27 August) was against Hungary who always had decent throwers and their number one and two was no exception. However, being in fine form I was not deterred at the slightest and relished the opportunity of meeting them at London`s Crystal Palace. It turned out to be a `ding dong` affair with each of us taking the lead. However, I finished a very close 2nd to Geza Fejer with a throw of 203ft 9in/62.04m and beating Jonos Farago in the process.

At the end of August, the Europa Cup finals took place in Edinburgh`s Meadowbank stadium. The discus contest took part in the rain so gripping the implement was made that much harder. Eventually Pentii Karma from Finland winning, Siegfried Pachale of East Germany 2nd and myself 3rd with a throw of 193ft 9in/59.06m, beating Pensikov of Russia, Hein-Neu of West Germany with the struggling Frenchman last in 6th place. It was a pleasing result and gratifying beating the Russian, West German and the French athletes.

The Soviets won the Europa Cup final with 82.5 points, East Germany 2nd with 78.5 points, West Germany 3rd with 79 points, Britain 70.5 points, Finland 65 points and France 6th with just 45 points.

In Bristol on 2 September, representing my club I produced another throw of 202ft 9in/61.78m and 202ft 5in/61.68m on the 14 September, this time in London Crystal Palace in a representative fixture showed the consistency but I wanted to go further as my training throws were around 213ft/65m.

Awarded my 35th full international cap I was ready to face Sweden and challenge Ricky Bruch the Munich bronze medallist in London at Crystal Palace on the 21 September. The wind was not favourable and both of us threw below our best with Bruch narrowly winning. I just failed to throw over 200ft/61m and had to contend with 2nd place with a throw of 199ft 9in/60.82m.

Throwing in the Europa Cup final finishing 3rd (H.Payne)

So I was off to Bristol on the 23 September to see if I could improve my record, yet again I missed out having thrown 201ft 5in/61.38m.

At the England Commonwealth Games trials at Crystal Palace on the 29 September, I booked my place in the team with a winning throw of 204 ft/62.18m and secured 3rd spot in the shot beating my old friend and rival Jeff Teale, who was so disappointed to miss out. So again I hoped to double up as I had done in the 1972 Munich Olympic Games of last year.

One last competition took place in Loughborough on the 13 October and at long last broke again my own UK national discus record with a distance of 209ft 11in/63.98m with a narrow foul of 216.6in/66.0m! I was happy and sad at the both time. Anyhow, that was the end of the competition for the year for me and now it was time to do some heavy intensity weight training for the forthcoming Commonwealth Games in Christchurch, New Zealand in January 1974.

It had been a very successful season, I had broken the UK discus record on three occasions, AAA champion for the seventh time, beaten some world class discus throwers and for sheer consistency, thrown the discus over 196ft 10in/60.0m in over 22 separate competitions and ranked 9th in the world. I was now the firm favourite to win the discus title in New Zealand.

On the left is cover number three on Athletics weekly and Athletics weekly cover number four is on the right, 7 September 1974.

West Bridgford College of further Education were very supportive in my quest to win the Commonwealth discus title and time tabled me, blocks of teaching time so that I had a couple of afternoons each week to train at Loughborough during daylight hours. Furthermore, they promised to release me on full pay at attend these Games from 24 January until 2 February 1974.

To make me even happier, Angela gave birth to another lovely girl named Andrea on the 4 November which was a great time for family celebrations. It would be a shame to leave them all in January and I was well aware that Angela would be extremely busy with no family around as we lived in Loughborough and I was to disappear for over three weeks. However, my thoughts were to win and thankfully Angela gave me full support.

I concentrated on strength and power work and due to the winter months I did less technical work. On reflection it hindered me as in New Zealand it was their summer, so I should have changed the emphasis of my training. As a result, I was more powerful but needed some warmer weather to `fine tune` my discus technique.

Today, athletes are sent to warm weather training camps in winter so that they are better prepared and more focused in producing top quality performances irrespective of summer or winter months.

My brother Geoff and I after taking a national discus training course at Loughborough

7. THE 1974 COMMONWEALTH GAMES CHRISTCHURCH, NEW ZEALAND

The Commonwealth Games excited me yet I knew that this was going to be a long season with these Games in January, the AAA in July and the European Championships in September along with full Internationals against East Germany, Poland and Canada, Czechoslovakia, Sweden, Norway and Belgium culminating with Finland. Therefore, training had to be meticulously planned.

The English team departed for the long journey some seven days before the start of the Commonwealth Games which was to take place from the 24 January until 2 February 1974. My companion on this long haul flight was the giant shot putter Geoff Capes who like me was a nervous flyer, so we had something in common as well as throwing. We kept ourselves amused with jokes, Geoff`s love of budgerigar breeding and my life in the Army.

Geoff Capes and myself flying to the 1974 Christchurch New Zealand Games

After the very long flight we quickly settled into the athletes village which was the student`s accommodation at Canterbury University and was surrounded by security guards and had a high profile police presence. After all, this was the first large scale international athletics event to follow the tragic deaths of the Israeli athletes at the 1972 Munich Olympic Games.

I started to throw in earnest in the warm, windy conditions not realising the strength of the sun and after an hour of training noticed how red I had become. In the weights room I felt very sluggish to say the least and on reflection, should have made a much more gentle start.

In the evening, Geoff and I went for a drink or two, impressed with drinking beer out of jugs. We appeared to be celebrities and the press were providing the drinks free as long as we provided information and stories. The next morning back in the UK, newspaper pictures of myself and Geoff were shown enjoying ourselves with headlines `Throwers training hard in preparation for the Commonwealth Games`!

I don`t think that our drinking cost us in terms of performance or results and quite frankly helped us to relax. We only drank lager, never spirits. Some of us enjoyed a drink, just like anybody else. I could always take my drink and would always train extremely hard the next day and sweat it out. Sometimes I would never drink alcohol for 2 months so as to stay focussed and remain fit to train hard. Looking back, when you are fit and comparatively young, you can cope with some drinking.

Anyway this was soon forgotten and we got back to full focus on doing our best. I entered a pre-Games warm up competition and threw 195ft 6in/59.60m beating all the main rivals in the process, so things were going well and now await the main competition in the Queen Elizabeth II Park Stadium on the 31 January.

Training at the Queen Elizabeth II Stadium in Christchurch, New Zealand

The Opening Ceremony had its usual excitement and the host nation was ecstatic when New Zealand were mentioned or seen. A *Maori* concert group also performed action songs and a haka before the teams marched past. The Games were also the last time that the entire immediate British Royal family visited New Zealand as a group. The Royal Yacht Britannia was the Royal residence during these Games.

At one of the functions prior to the Opening of the Games, Princess Anne who is now currently President of the British Olympic Association and her former husband Captain Mark Phillips paid us a visit in the Commonwealth village. I had told a few of the athletes that I personally knew Captain Phillips from my RMA Sandhurst days and if spoken to I would remind him. I think a couple did not believe me but on entering the room to the surprise of these two, Captain Phillips came over to me and wished me the best of luck. So with many supporters and well-wishers, I eagerly awaited my confrontation with Robin Tait of New Zealand, my main rival for the Commonwealth discus title.

The 1974 Commonwealth Games were also a milestone in New Zealand Television, making the introduction of *colour television* for the first time. However, due to the NZBC`s limited colour facilities, only athletics, boxing and swimming could be broadcast in colour. As a result, the discus would feature heavily as the host nation had a chance of securing a gold medal.

The day finally arrived and both John Hillier my English teammate and rival along with Chief Throws coach Wilf Paish travelled in style, chauffeur driven to the stadium. After a few warm ups, the competition commenced. All was going well until in the third round when Tait threw a personal best of 206ft 10in/63.08m to lead the competition and I responded with a throw of 195ft 5in/59.48m. Tait did not throw again as he and probably all of us were shocked that he threw such a distance. I again tried my best but could not go beyond the 196ft 10in/60.0m line, so I had to settle for 2nd place, the silver medal with a distance of 195ft 5in/59.48m and countryman John Hillier 3rd at 187ft 8in/57.22m.

After the event had finished we were ushered to doping control for testing. I, along with John Hillier, managed quite easily to provide the necessary urine sample and waited for the winner Robin Tait to appear. He had to drink large amounts of water but still had difficulties. Even to this day, I am not sure whether he fulfilled the necessary test. Although everyone was tested at these Games no reliable tests were available.

The medals were presented by Princess Anne in front of a capacity crowd with John Hillier and I either side of the grinning Kiwi. His chance had arrived and he went on to compete at 6 Commonwealth Games, an outstanding representation. He sadly died in 1984 aged only 43.

A very disappointed silver medallist as I was everyone's favourite to win the gold medal. That honour went to New Zealander Robin Tait with John Hillier 3rd. However, it was a pleasure to be presented with the medal by HRH Princess Anne at the victory ceremony.
(New Zealand Herald)

This defeat left me very disappointed and my chance to secure a gold medal had disappeared and today on reflection, it was my worst experience in athletics as I was the firm favourite. Had it been our summer, things could have been much different. To `shake` off this disappointment, I competed in the shot and finished in 4th place with a throw of 59ft 6in/18.13m with Geoff Capes 1st (68ft 1in/20.74m), Winch 2nd (63ft 6in/19.36m) and the Canadian Bruce Pirnie 3rd (61ft 3in/18.68m). It was another disappointment finishing 4th and missing out on the medals. Anyhow, I was determined that 1974 would still be a good season so continued to train and watch the other events and sports.

The 1974 discus Commonwealth silver medal

Other sports seen include seeing Neville Meade win the heavyweight boxing title and Precious McKenzie winning the flyweight weightlifting along with George Newton's gold medal performance in the Lightweight division and a silver medal by Andy Kerr in the Super- heavyweight division. I was really pleased that Andy had done well as he was also a promising shot and discus thrower in his youth.

In the track, the long awaited 1500m duel between John Walker of New Zealand and Filbert Bayi of Tanzania was upon us. It turned out to be a 'cracking' contest between two really world class athletes. In the end, it was heartbreak for New Zealand and John Walker as Filbert Bayi broke the world record with a time of 3min 32.16sec, Walker 2nd also inside the old world record with a time of 3min 32.52sec and 3rd place, going to the remarkable Kenyan Ben Jipcho, with a time of 3min 33.16sec Jipcho went on to win both the 5,000m and the 3,000m steeplechase gold medals, a phenomenal performance.

In a domestic confrontation, between England's David Travis and Charles Clover in the men's javelin, it turned out to be a thrilling competition and a shock defeat to the defending champion David Travis. Clover only 18 years of age unleashed the javelin to a distance of 278ft 6in/84.92m, a personal best of nearly 23ft/7m to Travis's silver medal position of 262ft 2in/79.92m. Such was Clover's outstanding performance, he never regained this form ever again. 'Charlie' Clover was discovered by my father Adrian who coached him when he was young. My father would say there is someone better than you in the javelin at the same age when I was introduced to this athletic javelin man who possessed all the attributes at the time to be a javelin star.

My parents on the left with Angela holding Andrea and me holding Nicola, with Charlie Clover and his family on the right side of the Mayor of Ipswich taken at a reception in the Ipswich Town Hall. (Archant)

The closing ceremony on the 2 February ended in fine fashion and enjoyed by everyone. In the evening, an elaborate banquet was held and many old faces were seen which included Peter Snell who introduced me to some of the All-Black legends such as Colin Meads who was known as `the enforcer` and was legendry for his hard play. He once played on with a broken arm in a game against South Africa when the team doctor cut his shirt and confirmed that he had indeed broken his arm, he famously remarked, "At least we won the bloody game". I was very impressed when we were introduced to one another with his very firm handshake!

It was also a pleasure to catch up with former Loughborough College students who had gone to New Zealand in the hope of having better opportunities in teaching and in improving their lives. I think they made excellent decisions because New Zealand is a wonderful country, the scenery stunning, the people generous and only having a population of 4.5 million. I was sorry to leave but I had a family to attend to and of course being an amateur sportsman, I had to return to work.

8. THE 1974 ATHLETICS SEASON - DISCUS RECORDS AND EUROPEAN CHAMPIONSHIPS

I soon returned to family life which was good and to see first-hand the two little girls growing up and taking part in family life. Work too was progressing and I soon `swept` into training at Loughborough College.

Due to the Commonwealth Games, I decided not to compete in any indoor meets as I wanted to concentrate on training with more family contact and visit my father and mother in Ipswich when it was possible.

My first outdoor competition took part at London`s Crystal Palace on the 8 May and I registered a creditable 201ft 6in/61.42m in a Southern Counties fixture which pleased me as I also just fouled a throw around 207ft/63m so knowing full well that this year would be athletically good.

However, the next outdoor meet took place at HMS Ganges Shotley for the Suffolk AAA championships on 18 May for what was my best ever double. In almost the opening event of an exciting afternoon`s athletics, with my first throw shattering the County record which I had set up in 1966 by over seven metres. The distance of 203ft 11in/62.16m was a great start but it was when I stepped into the shot circle some 30mins later that had the enthusiastic crowd roaring in approval with a tremendous throw of 63ft 9in/19.43m. This smashed my old record and was a personal best. It was a great start to the season.

My personal best shot put of 63ft 9in/19.43m at Shotley (Archant)

175

On the 2 June at Crystal Palace another throw of 204ft 7in/62.36m was registered and then in Cleckheaton, on the 8 June in an invitational match, I managed another 196 10in/60.0m plus throw, this time 199ft 1in/60.66m and beating all my British opponents easily, again with no help from the wind and in rainy conditions.

Following this on the 12 June, with not a helpful wind, I threw a distance of 205ft 5in/62.64m in a Loughborough fixture but better still, again at Loughborough four days later, I threw close to my UK National record a distance of 208ft 4in/63.50m and as a result, I was looking forward to competing in the first full British international fixture against the mighty East Germans on the 19 June at London`s Crystal Palace.

It was the same story, although getting closer to these giants of throwing I finished in 3rd place with a distance of 195ft 10in/59.70m, collecting my 39th full international cap in the process.

The next international was against Canada and Poland in Warsaw, Poland on the 30 June. In favourable conditions I managed to win this competition with a discus throw of 199ft 3in/60.74m just missing the 200ft/61m mark. After the match there were the usual banquet and free beer drinking which always turns out to be a competition amongst the `heavy` throwers. After a good night it was time to pack the bags and head off to the airport and fly back to London.

At Loughborough on the 7 July in a representative match, I got off to a flying start with the first round and best throw of 205ft 3in/62.54m which put me in a positive mind to defend my national AAA title against the best British throwers and John Powell of the USA. Powell won the competition and the AAA national title, although an American with a distance of 203ft 7in/62.06m, I came 2nd and the first Briton home with 196ft 11in/60.02m and John Hillier 3rd at 190ft 3in/57.99m.

John Powell would go on to set a world discus record of 226ft 6in/69.08m in 1975 and represented the USA Olympic team in 1972 (4th), 1976 (bronze), 1980 (USA boycott) and 1984 (bronze). I had admired Powell`s technique as it was smooth and fluid and made throwing long distances look easy. He was also a very nice man and I had the pleasure of staying in his condominium in Cupertino, San Jose, California during 1976 training with the elite USA discus throwers.

On the 20 July at Loughborough in a representative invitation, I broke the UK national discus record again for the 17th time with a distance of 211ft 3in/64.40m which indicated that I was in the best form of my life and furthermore, knew the discus could go further judging by the superior warm –up throws over 215ft 3in/65.0m. Luckily, another competition was arranged for me by my coach for the next day at Loughborough in the hope of breaking the British record again.

So on the 21 July at 3pm, I managed to take advantage of a gentle head wind and went even further with a throw of 213ft 1in/64.94m, just missing out in breaking the 213ft 3in/65.0m distance. Another foul throw of 216ft 6in/66.0m plus would have been my best ever discus result. This last distance would have been the best I had achieved in my long discus career. All the necessary official recognition was complete but unfortunately there were no graded I field event official at the meet, so this performance of 213ft 1in/64.94m was not ratified as a UK record but was good enough for the world rankings.

The next British international took place in Edinburgh on the 27 July against Czechoslovakia and the world discus leader and friend, the great Ludvik Danek. It was billed as one of the star attractions as I and Ludvik were in great form.

After a great tussle with a chance of either of us winning, Ludvik Danek won the close encounter but my registered throw of 204ft 10in/62.44m for 2nd place, made him aware that I was on `his heels`! I soon departed and left Ludvik and his colleagues to start and finish the wine tasting sessions, much to his surprise as I departed to Middlesborough for an invitational throws meet organised some few months previously and I had indicated that I would compete and not let the organisers down.

Again, I despatched the implement in poor and rainy conditions a distance of 202ft 9in/61.80m to win the competition and a prize of a splendid picnic hamper which we as a family could use on our infrequent days out. In today`s athletics the prize would have been money.

So with this performance and the one in Edinburgh against the mighty Danek under my belt, It was off to magical Stockholm on the 31 July, collecting another full international cap against Sweden and my old foe Ricky Bruch, the 1972 Olympic Games bronze medallist. The venue was the old 1912 Olympic stadium, which is one of the smallest athletics stadiums used ever in a summer Olympics. Amazingly, possibly to its compactness, 83 world records have been set in this stadium.

Stockholm is the cultural, media, political and economic centre of Sweden, cosmopolitan with both classical and modern architecture with a captivating old town, *Gamla Stan.* An island with wonderful waterfront views with the northern part of the old town dominated by the *Royal Palace* and the *Swedish Parliament.* The remainder of the island is a collection of beautiful old buildings and narrow streets that are cobbled.

I was to represent Great Britain in both the shot and discus events and on the first day warming up, I heard an almighty cheer with the words, "Come on Bill Tancred" from a section of the stadium to my right. I looked across and saw about 20 Royal Navy sailors with their full uniforms on. On closer inspection, I recognised the leader of my fan club to be my old Felixstowe school friend

Graham Vine. His serving ship had docked in Stockholm for a few days and for relaxation, came to the stadium to give me and the British team support. What a wonderful surprise and gesture.

The encounter with the eccentric Ricky Bruch dressed as an Englishman with a bowler hat and umbrella was close with him just beating me as I threw 203ft 6in/62.02m for 2nd place. In the shot put the next day, I managed to come 2nd with a putt of 60ft 3in/18.36m which was a remarkable result as I had little sleep but plenty of `grog` socialising with Graham and his Navy mates. This was a very satisfying trip and athletics competition with the surprise meeting of my school friend Graham Vine. Even today, when we meet up we both mention this wonderful meeting.

Soon after this encounter I travelled to Woodford Green, Essex for a representative match and threw an official UK National record of 211ft 0in/64.32m. This record of mine lasted for over 25 years, one of the longest in British athletics history!

Prior to the European Championship in Rome, an invitational international took place. The venue was the Bislett stadium in Norway and I registered a throw of 201ft 5in/61.38m for a new stadium record, beating the previous record set by the former world record holder Jay Silvester of the USA. The memory of this stadium has certainly a warm place in my heart.

The stadium is the best known sporting venue in Norway and it has seen over 70 world athletics and numerous skating records set there. In fact when Seb Coe set those magical 3 world athletics records in 1979, two were set at this stadium, the 800m in a time of 1min 42.33sec and the mile in 3min 48.95sec. A couple of weeks later in Zurich he broke the 1500m world record. These performances all within 41 days by Seb Coe were fantastic.

In the international match again at the Bislett Stadium, between Great Britain, Norway and the Benelux Countries I got off to a good start and although the wind was not favourable, I managed to win the contest with a throw of 199ft 6in/60.80m and furthermore, produced my best ever international shot performance by launching the missile (16lbs shot) 62ft 4in/19.00m.

David Moorcroft former 5000m world record holder, myself in the middle and a young Seb later Lord Coe, photographed by Mark Pidsley at a Loughborough versus AAA athletics match. It was interesting to note that I was asked did I mind having these two athletes on either side of me! Both Coe and Moorcroft broke world records in the Bislett stadium, Oslo.

Shortly after this fixture, the European Athletics championship took place in the 1960 Rome Olympic stadium between the 2 and 8 September. As soon as I arrived in Rome, John Hillier, Geoff Capes and I, headed towards the training facilities to see what was available and how we could prepare for these championships.

In the discus training area, when I first arrived they thought I was an Italian discus thrower being dark and sun tanned. However, to prove my nationality, speaking English, straight away they knew differently and furthermore, I was recognised by some of the other throwers I had met on the `circuit` and on International duty.

To qualify for the discus finals 22 throwers had to throw the required 190ft 3in/58.0m having only three attempts. So if unsuccessful on your first throw, you had to wait nearly 30 minutes for your second attempt. I fouled my first throw and on the second managed only 188ft 2in/57.36m, some 64cms short of the qualifying mark. To make matters worse, I fouled my third attempt so failing disappointingly to qualify. Having such high hopes made this performance that much more upsetting. I also had a number of dedicated fans who came to Rome to support me, including my brother Peter which made me feel even worse. My teammate John Hillier also failed to qualify with a mark of 181ft 4in/55.58m.

The eventual winner Finland's Pentii Kahma threw 208ft 8in/63.62m, 2nd Ludvik Danek with 205ft 11in/62.76m and 3rd Ricky Bruch at 203ft 5in/62.0m. What was frustrating I had beaten 4th placed Pachale (East Germany), 6th placed Penzikov (Russia) and 7th placed De Vincentis before, so these were disappointing Championships for me personally.

Despite this I managed to see some outstanding performances which included Geoff Capes's bronze medal distance of 66ft 3in/20.21m, Ralf Reichenbach of West Germany, the silver medal with 66ft 10in/20.38m and the winner Hartmut Briesenick from East Germany with a putt of 67ft 5in/20.56m. A brilliant performance by Geoff who beat some outstanding shot putters from Europe, particularly from the East.

The men's 100m was won by the Soviet sprinter Valeriy Borzov with a time of 10.27sec to defeat the wonderful majestic Italian Pietro Mennea who was timed at 10.34sec. However, Mennea went on to win the 200m final with a time of 20.60sec and the Italian stadium erupted in delight. This was not the only performance that he would be remembered for because he went on to break the world record in this event at the altitude 1979 World Student Games in Mexico and won the Gold medal at the 1980 Moscow Olympic Games. After retiring from athletics, he became a successful lawyer and sports agent. Aged just 60 he died after a long battle with cancer.

Great Britain had plenty to celebrate as Alan Pascoe won the 400m hurdles, Ian Thompson the marathon, 4 x 400m men's relay and Brendon Foster in the 5000m. Foster's time of 13mins 17.2sec outsmarted the flying Finn Lasse Viren who came 3rd and Jos Hermens (Netherlands) 4th in a time of 13mins 25.6sec.

In retirement Foster went on to become UK Managing Director of Nike International Ltd, Athletics commentator to the BBC and Founder of the 'Great North Run'. Hermens became a successful coach and agent whilst Viren went into politics holding a seat in the Finnish Parliament.

Frenchman Guy Drut won the 110 hurdles with a time of 13.40secs who later on won the 1976 Montreal Olympic gold medal. This tall, athletic and debonair high hurdler in retirement from competitive athletics became a politician and a successful businessman. It is the former for which he is now remembered because as a politician, he had been a Minister of Youth Affairs and Sport in the conservative government of Alain Juppe from 1995 until 1997.

Unfortunately for him, in 2005 he was convicted by the French Courts for accepting fictitious employment as political patronage which resulted in a suspended 15 months sentence. The IOC also suspended him, so in reaching the `top heights` he `dropped down `again which was a real shame as he was a great hurdler and very friendly person.

On a sadder note, I watched the brilliant Baron Malinowski from Poland win the 3000m steeplechase and then later on went on to win a silver medal at the 1976 Montreal Olympics and then in the 1980 Moscow Olympics, he claimed the gold medal he desperately wanted. He sadly died in a car crash in Poland just aged 30 years. I spoke to him in Rome and found him very personable, happy and a `man`s man.

To complete the viewing it would be remiss of me not to mention the multi-talented Polish athlete Irena Szewinska who won both the 100m and 200m women`s sprints events. She was a phenomenal female athlete who between 1964 and 1980 competed in five Olympic Games winning seven medals, three of them Gold and broke six world records. It is interesting to note that she is the only athlete male or female to have held world records in the 100m, 200m and 400m. She has also served as a member of the IOC with distinction and been the Head of the Polish Athletics Federation for many years.

Another interesting person I came into contact regularly was the East German discus thrower Wolfgang Schmidt who stood 6ft 6in tall and weighed 115kg. No fat, pure muscle, he was blond and good looking. Having finished a disappointing 8th in the Championships he would come into our accommodation block and talk nervously to us saying he was constantly being watched by the *Deutsche Volkspolizes* (German People`s Police). He was paranoid that members of his team were informers and worked for the *Stasi* the State Security. The Stasi infiltrated almost every aspect of GDR life. In some cases, spouses even spied on each other. He wanted to know more about our lives in the West particularly Britain and the USA. All this worry, must have affected his discus performances at these Championships.

Wolfgang Schmidt (1), Muller (2), Tancred (3) and Hillier (4) GDR v GB International. (DDR press)

In 1976 he won a silver medal at the 1976 Montreal Olympic Games and in 1978, broke the world discus record with a throw of 233ft 5in/71.16m.

However, he made different headlines in 1982 due to his failed attempt to escape from East Germany. He was always under surveillance by the Deutsche Volkspolize and who eventually uncovered his plan of escape to the West, interestingly aided by his discus rivals Ricky Bruch (Sweden) and Alwin Wagner (West Germany). As a result of his actions and intended escape, he was sentenced to an eighteen months prison sentence in the latter part of 1982. Luckily for him he just served one year of his sentence but was `forced` into coaching with travel restrictions. In the early part of 1988, he was granted permission to leave the East and therefore, headed for West Germany to continue his athletics as a competitor.

In the inaugural match between East and West Germany Jurgen Schult (the current world discus record holder), having won the discus throw competition, refused to shake hands with Wolfgang Schmidt which was disappointing to say the least.

After retiring from competitive athletics, Schmidt later moved to California, USA to become a successful stockbroker and management consultant. He was a very likable and intelligent man.

THE DRUG PROBLEM

During our `secret` meetings in Rome and in the various internationals that we had against each other, Schmidt mentioned the drug situation in East Germany years before the files were opened in 1990, indicating that East Germany did indeed run a systematic and state-controlled performance enhancing doping programme officially known as *State Plan 14.25.* Also, the GDR athletes who were due to compete internationally were told when to stop taking their pills beforehand and tested to make sure no illegal traces remained in their bodies. If by any chance they showed up positive, they were told to withdraw because of a feigned injury.

Many former athletes today suffer from serious health problems related to steroid consumption. These are the forgotten victims of drug abuse in sport. For over three decades, East Germans competed for their country in various sports at the highest level, winning gold medals, breaking world records and by doing this, demonstrated to the world the communist superiority.

Most of these victims received Oral-Turinabol which is an anabolic steroid containing testosterone. This drug had astonishing powers in that it accelerated muscle build and helped the recovery process that much quicker. However, it had significant side effects which proved to be catastrophic in that it caused infertility in women, produced embarrassing hair growth, developed breast and testicular cancers and gave heart problems. It is estimated that over 900 East German athletes have developed serious ailments due to this ill-advised and dangerous State programme.

A very public face of the doping scandal is that of the female shot putter Andreas Krieger who due to this programme, took so many male hormones that she decided to have a sex change.

It is also worth noting that some of the world records set by the East Germans athletes still stand today while they used these banned drugs, which makes a mockery of the records set. You do feel sorry that athletes who are `clean` deserve to be better recognised because the competition has been unfair, corrupt and is utter cheating.

More alarming, the premature deaths of a number of world class athletes should be a warning to anyone contemplating using these performance enhancing drugs. I am not suggesting that they took this route but if their bodies were abused with anabolic steroids then there is strong circumstantial evidence. Some of these athletes listed below did not live beyond 50 years and include:-

☐ Former world discus record holder Ben Plunkett (USA) Age 48

- 1974 Commonwealth discus champion Robin Tait (NZ)
  Age 43

- 1964 Olympic Games hammer bronze medallist Uwe Beyer (WG)
  Age 48

- 1976 Olympic Games hammer silver medallist Aleksey Spiridonov
  (USSR)
  Age 46

- Detlef Gertenberg Hammer champion (GDR)
  Age 35

- Hartmut Losch 1969 European discus champion (GDR)
  Age 50

- 1984 Olympic hammer champion Juha Tiainen (Finland)
  Age 47

- Ralf Reichenbach 1974 European silver medallist (WG)
  Age 47

- Florence Griffth Joyner World record holder 100m/200m (USA)
  Age 38

- Rositha Hellman a 66m plus javelin thrower (GDR)
  Age 42

- Tevetanka Khristova discus bronze/silver 1988/1992 Olympic Games
  (BUL)
  Age 46

- German Skurygin 50km Walk silver medallist 2003 World
  championships (USSR)
  Age 45

So it appears that if athletes take drugs their lives could be at risk or they will suffer in later life with serious health issues and major psychological problems.

It is worth noting that in the late 1990`s criminal cases were brought against Manfred Ewald, the former East German doctor and Dr Manfred Hoppner, a former team medical consultant, both of whom were subsequently given suspended sentences.

After these European Championships there was another British international against Finland on the 25th September to complete a very long and tiring season. It was treated like a training session for some of the team including myself as there were no targets to aim for but just personal pride. As a consequence, I threw 186ft 6in/56.86m for 3rd place but going better in the shot with a distance of 60ft 7in/18.44m for a close 2nd place.

With the season finally over I managed to get into the top ten World rankings list which was rather pleasing considering what I and other clean athletes were against. The 1974 World discus rankings list were as follows:-

1.	BRUCH (Sweden))	68.16m/223ft 7in
2.	POWELL (USA)	68.08m/223ft 4in
3.	Van REENEN (S. Africa)	68.04m/223ft 3in
4.	DANEK (Czechoslovakia)	67.18m/220ft 4in
5.	KAHMA (Finland)	66.52m/218ft 5in
6.	PACHALE (East Germany)	65.64m/215ft 3in
7.	PENSIKOV (USSR)	65.22m/214ft 0in
8.	WILKINS (USA)	65.14m/213ft 8in
9.	**TANCRED (UK)**	**64.94m/213ft 1in**
10.	MULLER (East Germany)	64.94m/213ft 1in

POST GRADUATE REGISTRATION FOR PART-TIME RESEARCH STUDY AT

LOUGHBOROUGH UNIVERSITY

It was time to relax and catch up with family life and start to prepare myself for a career advancement. To do this I needed to have a Master`s degree. So while at West Bridgford, I decided to visit Loughborough University to seek the help and support from the then Principal John Kane.

I had several meetings with John who eventually asked me to write a few chapters on my proposed thesis and when completed, make another appointment before registering for a part-time research degree. When this day arrived, I went into his Loughborough College office and was not only greeted by John but also another older man called Joe who had come to visit John as well.

We all started talking about athletics, swiftly to cricket and then basketball in which the older visitor took a delight in expressing his love of this game. It was only after leaving the office that John mentioned that I had been talking to Joe Jagger, the father of the Rolling Stones, Mick Jagger.

He had been a lecturer in Physical Education at St. Mary's College, Twickenham in the late 60's and early 70's. Basil `Joe` Jagger was a leading figure nationally in the development of outdoor pursuits and credited with popularising basketball in Britain in its infancy and organising courses on how to teach and coach the sport.

He is fondly remembered as a very professional teacher and coach who always put his students first and who devoted his working life to promote physical education and sports participation.

Meanwhile John Kane during his academic life had various posts to include St. Mary's College, Twickenham (at the time a colleague with Joe Jagger), and Principal of West London Institute of Higher Education from 1976 until his retirement in 1995.

It was soon after this meeting (December 1974) that I registered to pursue an MA research degree by part-time study in the Department of Education at Loughborough University, which certainly proved to be an eventful year one way or the other.

9. TRENT POLYTECHNIC, NEW ZEALAND AND SOUTH AFRICA INVITES AND GB ATHLETICS 1975

I registered for a higher degree but I was also thinking of finding another new job as two years was enough time spent at West Bridgford College of Further Education. I had been shortlisted for several local authority positions such as a Director of Leisure and Recreation but was assured that these positions might interfere with my athletics, so I concentrated on Higher Education Institutions.

I decided to miss the AAA Indoor championships again as I was given an invitation to tour New Zealand at the end of January and this gave me another opportunity to beat the New Zealand star Robin Tait. During the long flight I mingled with the small British contingent that included Ian Chipchase (1974 Commonwealth hammer champion), Andrea Lynch (British women`s 100m sprint record holder), Kevin Shepperd (Javelin) with Bill Sykes (Team Manager) and Merea Hartman as the Leader of the tour.

During the flight, it was a pleasure to talk informally to Marea Hartman as I found her having a happy disposition and a genuine fondness for athletics. We shared a drink or two discussing our respective lives and occupations. She informed me that for over 30 years she had been a Personnel Officer at the paper manufacturers in Bowaters.

In her athletics career, she was one of the longest serving and most influential people along with Arthur Gold (Chairman of the British Olympic Association) in athletics. She was the honorary treasurer to the BAAB and Chairman from 1988 until 1991. For this stellar contribution she was awarded a DBE (Damehood) for services to Sport in the 1994 New Years Honours List.

When we eventually arrived in Christchurch, New Zealand on the 20 January we were ushered to our accommodation block to get some well-earned rest before the tour began. It began with a low key discus event in Dunedin which housed the School of PE, Sport and Exercise Science and had (and still has) an international reputation.

Tait won these encounter, Dick Dreacher of the USA 2nd and myself 3rd, all throwing around the 190ft 3in/58.0m mark. I was not worried about this as I wanted to beat Tait and the American in the first New Zealand Games in Christchurch, the venue of last year`s Commonwealth Games when I was beaten surprisingly by the big New Zealander Tait.

It turned out to be a bitter sweet victory as I won the Inaugural event beating both my rivals clearly but not over the 196ft 10in/60.0m mark but who cared! In the shot I was placed 1st so had a good double on New Zealand soil.

The last contest took place in wonderful Auckland and this time I had to settle for 2nd place behind the American Dreacher who had in his career thrown over 213ft 3in/65.0m. As it was a friendly tour, many celebrations were performed together including the usual sightseeing, arranged by our magnificent hosts. Memories of a fine climate, beautiful harbour and friendly people still remain with me.

Bill Sykes (team manager), Ian Chipchase (hammer), Kevin Shepperd (javelin), Ann Wilson (long jump), myself, Bernie Plain (middle distance), Frank Clements (800m), Marea Hartman (Leader) and kneeling, Andrea Lynch (Sprints) and John Davies (steeplechase). All of us were attending the first New Zealand Games (Green & Hahn photograph)

Soon it was back to the UK and the cold February months of training and preparing for the next long overseas invitation to South Africa in March.

This time I would have to throw against the world record holder, the massive gentle giant, John Van Reenen. Having never visited South Africa before, I wanted to go to compete even though the issues of apartheid remained. I felt that politics should not play a part in sport. Interestingly, I received two letters from people asking me to decline the invitation but I proceeded to go.

Sport has long been an important part of life in South Africa and any boycotting of Games or international events/teams, had a profound effect on the whole population, perhaps more so than any trade embargoes did.

Apartheid reforms in the 1980`s failed to quell the mounting opposition and in 1990 President de Klerk began negotiations to end apartheid, culminating in multi-racial democratic elections in 1994, which was won by the African National Congress under Nelson Mandela.

The small invited team arrived in Johannesburg and met by the very warm welcoming official of the South African Athletics Federation and a few athletes. Our leader was Robert Stinson, a well respected official of the British Amateur Athletics Board. After a brief couple of days of rest we were thrown into competition at various venues to include Pretoria, Durban, Port Elizabeth and Cape Town.

John van Reenen was in tremendous form having set the world discus record at a meet in Stellenbosch on the 14 March with a throw of 224ft 8in/68.48m. His international competitive exposure had been curtailed due the ban on South Africa from International Games and Events as a result of the Apartheid regime at the time.

John won all four contests but his winning margins were nowhere near his world record distance. In the main competition, the South African Championships in Port Elizabeth, I came a close 2nd to van Reenen with a throw of 198ft 7in/60.54m, a pleasing result as I beat the world ranking Hein-Dereck Neu from West Germany and this was an excellent start to an early season.

It was not all competitions and training as our hosts including `Biblical` John took us everywhere ranging from a fantastic meal and view in the Cape Town Revolving restaurant, a trip to Addo Elephant National Park situated about 72km by road from beautiful Port Elizabeth. The Park was the third largest in South Africa, offering a wide range of game viewing and outdoor activities. In addition, we travelled to the Cape of Good Hope at the top of the Cape Peninsula, some 50 plus kilometres from Cape Town including breathe taking views from the Table Mountain overlooking the City of Cape Town.

I had a personal invitation to accompany `Biblical` John as he was known due to his appearance of a beard and manner, to attend Stellenbosch, the heart of the wine land, historic mansions and its famous University. We managed to go to a winery, one of the best in the region and sampled a few glasses. John had known the owner who loved athletics, rugby and `English` jokes and as the night or early morning approached, he presented me with a bottle dated 1852 as a token of friendship and great comradeship. Being a poor connoisseur of wine, a few years later I opened the bottle at a family dinner and on being told by an informative son-in-law that it must have been very valuable, I could have cried in my beer!

John van Reenen, in athletics retirement went on to be a very successful Graphic artist with his art being sold in the USA and all over South Africa. It was not the last time that I would face John. This was scheduled for the 1 August at the AAA National Championships in London.

This short trip also helped in fostering friendships with athletes from other countries such as the very friendly Belgian Ivo Van Damme who enjoyed a laugh and enjoyed the throwers company. After this tour, he was destined for great things and did not let anyone down for in the 1976 Montreal Olympic Games he achieved silver medals in both the men`s 800m and 1500m. Sadly, on the 29 December 1976 he was killed in a car accident aged just 22 years. His early death was a great loss to his family, friends and to the world of athletics.

Another athlete, this time from Britain, included the gutsy Yorkshireman and fireman Walter Wilkinson who liked a joke and was a good teammate on this trip. Walter was a class miler with a personal best of 3mins 56.6secs set in 1971. Such was his love of running that he continued on into his late 50`s.

There is a lovely story that was relayed back to me from Walter, concerning a train journey when Walter was driving from Leeds to London St. Pancras involving Seb Coe. Both of them were due to run in an international meet and when the trained arrived at its destination, Seb saw Walter and said, "Hi Walter, had I known you were on the train, I would have sat next to you". To which Walter replied, "Don`t be a daft bugger, I was the train driver!" Seb was gobsmacked.

Our team leader for this trip was Bob (Robert) Stinson, who in his time acted as The International Amateur Athletics Federation (IAAF) Honorary Treasurer for over 20 years and had similar positions with the British Amateur Athletics Board (BAAB). On our return to the UK, somehow the plane needed refuelling with a couple of passengers disembarking in Luanda in Angola.

We were all concerned and slightly nervous due to the large military presence in the airport. In the transit area Bob confided to me `stick together so as to cause no problems` as we waited anxiously to hear the announcement to board the plane.

After a military coup in Portugal which toppled a long standing authoritarian regime on 25 April 1974, the new powers to be decided to divest the country of its expensive colonial empire. Angola being one, so with its impending independence, it led to the Angolan civil war in 1975 and when we arrived, things were not settled, hence the armed guards at the airport. At one time there were 11 separatist movements involved in this Angolan Civil War.

We were relieved to leave and a few drinks on the plane back home helped all of us including Bob to relax. Bob was indeed a happy man on the plane as team leader he was bringing all the athletes back to London safely.

He was one of the last great Oxbridge athletics administrators and enormous credit should be given to him, as he helped to set-up athletes` trust funds and importantly, laid down the framework for the sport of athletics from amateur to the eventual professionalism.

I do remember a funny incident involving Bob due to the claiming of expenses by some of the British team at a match in London. I went to see him at his desk and provided him with my travelling expenses to compete for Great Britain. I put down that I had travelled from Penzance to London. "I thought you came from Ipswich Bill", remarked Bob. "Yes I do Bob, you have a marvellous memory. The reason I am claiming from Penzance is that I went and stayed with my coach who lives there", I replied.

He looked bewildered and was lost for words for a few seconds and then proceeded to pay my travelling expenses. The very next day at breakfast, Bob said quietly, "Bill your coach in Penzance must be very good because half the team have him down as their coach as well! Let`s hope he moves back to Ipswich very shortly". "Yes Bob, he is due to move back next week", I replied meekly. To me he was a most honourable man with a love of athletics and fairness but many called him `Stingy` Stinson.

Back in Loughborough it was time to adjust my training with the an emphasis on getting more powerful as I had little time in doing this type of training due to my long tours of New Zealand and South Africa.

It also gave me a chance to get to know my little girls as I had been away much of the time in their small lives and with Angela, we had the opportunity of being a family again. Looking back, we had a nice semi-detached house in Melbreak Road, Loughborough and as an amateur in those days, drove a pre-1955 `split-screened` Morris Minor. It was a lovely car and we used drive it all the way to Dorset to see Angela`s parents and family and to Suffolk to do the same with my family. The four of us just managed to fit in.

During May, I was offered a Senior Lectureship at Trent Polytechnic who was associated with Nottingham College of Education at the time. The College had on the staff some very high calibre lecturers and athletes in John Whetton (1969 1500m European champion including being `king of the Boards` as the 1966, 1967 and 1968 1500m European Indoor champion; Janette Roscoe (1972 Olympic 400m specialist) and Colin Rains, the Head of the Creative Arts Department in which all of us belonged. Other lecturers who graced this Department were Brian Head-Rapson who was an international rugby referee and Peter Shaw an England basketball coach.

I accepted the position due to Colin`s encouragement in athletics and it gave me an opportunity to work in higher education. So after two years plus, I left West Bridgford to work nearby in Clifton, Nottingham as the Physical Education and Sport Organiser.

The athletics domestic season was `up and running` and after a couple of low key fixtures, the annual AAA versus Loughborough Colleges competition commenced on 5 June with a winning throw of 204ft 9in/62.42m beating my major rivals in the process. This performance and others including 198ft 3in/60.44m and 202ft 1in/61.58m helped me gain the GB versus East Germany fixture in Dresden on the 21/22 June.

I had a good battle against the two East Germans Pachale and Muller and although just beaten by Pachale, managed to defeat the dejected Muller with a throw of 200ft 2in/61.05m. This was very pleasing to `split` this pair with Capes doing the same in the shot. All of a sudden the throwers from Great Britain were becoming prominent internationally.

At the next international, the Europa Cup semi-final in London, I finished 3rd with a distance of 194ft 0in/59.14m and gained my 44th international cap. The British men`s team were now heading to Nice, France for the finals on the 17/18 August.

However, before this fixture the long awaited clash against the South African John van Reenen was eagerly awaited. I was in excellent training form and fancied my chances in these championships and had a good record of being placed in the first three from 1964 to 1974 at the AAA`s National championships

Sadly, I badly injured my left heel which curtailed my throwing for a while. It was a bad injury because I relied on this heel to drive across the discus circle and gain the necessary momentum so as to arrive into a good and effective power position to deliver the discus. With the enforced throwing rest, the heel improved slightly so that I could compete again, albeit carefully. In a match at Crystal Palace a comfortable 198ft 3in/60.44m winning throw was registered so I was confident to face the giant South African.

20 July was a lovely day as Angela gave birth to another girl Joanna making me a proud father again. A big, healthy baby and now I really am going to be surrounded by women in the Tancred household. Who knows, any one of my lovely girls could be a budding athlete?

The AAA national championships took place on the 1 August at Crystal Palace, London and what a exciting battle we had against each other. First John took the lead, then I, then John again before in the fourth round, I released a throw of 204ft 1in/62.22m to take the lead. This was unfortunately not the winning throw as van Reenen`s final throw of 204ft 3in/62.26m agonisingly deprived me of an eighth title by just 4cm or two inches! It was the ninth occasion on which I was the highest placed Briton in the discus. It would prove to be the last time that I would ever compete in these AAA National championships although I would compete indoors in 1976, which will be mentioned later.

As the best placed Briton, I received a blue wind- proofed jacket with the sponsor`s name Nationwide written (4 x 2in) across the left breast side. However, the following week at the same venue in a Southern Counties fixture whilst warming up, Mike Farrell the British Amateur Athletics Board track official came screaming over to me and yelled, "Take that top off at once, you are contravening the AAA rules!" I angrily replied, "I won this as a prize in last week`s AAA National championships". "I don`t care if that was the case because as it stands you are breaking the amateur code", he replied again. So to keep within the `rules`, I removed the Nationwide Building Society top. The sport of athletics at the time still did not permit advertising. Needless to say after this short rules confrontation my winning throw was just below 193ft 6in/59.0m.

After this in training, my heel started to play up again and I had to see a sports medicine specialist at the Derby Infirmary called Dr Cochran who eventually administered a cortisone injection in the heel. A cortisone injection has to be on the right spot if it is to be successful, if not the injury and pain persists. I was warned that this was a temporary measure and could have some side effects. At the time, this appeared to be the only option available to me.

I went into the Europa Cup final in Nice, France fit but mentally worried about the injured heel and how it would react to stiff competition. With the first throw, I turned to throw and felt `a stiff tear` around the heel and knew it would hamper further throws and damage the injury further. As a result, I finished a poor 7th place with a distance of only 187ft 7in/57.18m so gaining only 2 points for the men`s team. Overall the team finished in 4th place and the women 7th.

At the banquet, the delightful French wine was very tasty and some of the team consumed more bottles than they should but everyone was happy and relaxed. At this venue, there were a number of athletics supporters who wanted to `mingle in` at the party including a past Loughborough College friend Keith Meredith, a 200m runner. I invited him on the condition that he should pretend to be a French sprinter who had retired from the sport through injury. So he entered as a Frenchman who could not speak a word of English so no interrogations could be made by anyone! After a `boozy` hour, John Le Masurier our chief coach, asked me, "Who is that chap talking to our athletes?" I replied, "I think he is a retired French sprinter" He went over with me and speaking in French asked the French sprinter what was his name. A very startled and quickly sobered Keith replied in a poor French accent, "Roger Druffian" John looked puzzled, turned round to me and a couple of athletes and said," Never heard of him and he`s pissed!" So this fixture ended with a laugh but I had a worrying injury to contend with.

On my return, I had another cortisone injection by Dr Cochran but was warned that this would be the last injection otherwise permanent damage could arise. So with careful technical training I managed to throw quite well in training and was ready to face a strong Soviet team on 24 August in London. A throw of 196ft 4in/59.84m secured 3rd place with the heel not bothering too much and the Russians just managing to go over that distance. It was also my 50th international cap.

I was looking forward to the end of the season, firstly to rest the injured heel and secondly, have some quality time with the family. Trent Polytechnic was also giving me plenty of satisfaction and enjoyment in lecturing the students. On the academic side, my Master`s research degree performed on a part-time basis was also going according to plan with its deadline in coursework approaching.

One interesting group of `mature` students at the Polytechnic were the players from Nottingham Forest football club who were` persuaded` by a certain Brian Clough, the team manager, to study for a certificate of administration in sport on a limited part–time basis. They included midfielders Ian Bowyer, Paul Richardson and Ian Branfoot from Lincoln City FC who wanted to go into management when his career finished (He became one of Reading`s FC most successful managers). There were also a few lesser known players who had to attend the course.

On one particular late afternoon I noticed that all the players both senior and juniors were very attentive to what I was saying to them as normally Bowyer would `fool `around with his clowning antics to the laughter of the young players. On turning round Brian Clough had entered the gymnasium at the main site of Trent Polytechnic dressed in his usual green top and black track suit bottoms and just stood there listening to me lecturing.

On finishing he came up to me and said ,"Good afternoon , I am Brian Clough the manager of these so called footballers and if anyone misbehaves or goes absent, please let me know. Thank you" and then he left! He was one of the most successful football managers ever and as a player, gained two England caps and was a prolific goal scorer with Middlesborough FC, scoring 251 league goals from 274 starts. Injury stopped his playing days at a young age of 29. Unfortunately in retirement he fought alcoholism and ill-health and died at the age of 69. He is also remembered for his quotes such as the one on the appointment of Sven Goran Eriksson as England manager, "At last England have appointed a manager who speaks English better than his players!" He seemed to be a real great character and an outstanding football manager with excellent man-management skills.

The last season`s international took place at the end of September and although coming 2nd with a throw of 191ft 5in/58.24m, I was relatively pleased as my training towards the latter part of August and September was performed carefully and not with such high intensity due to the heel injury.

Importantly, I had qualified on three occasions for next season's 1976 Montreal Olympics and this put me in a positive mind that I could make my third Olympics.

So with the season over, it was a short break before possibly my last season at International level athletics due to career aspirations and prolonged injury problems.

10. THE END IS NEAR IN INTERNATIONAL ATHLETICS

From October to December 1975 I went into training extremely determined to break my British discus record and make the team for the Montreal Olympics for what could be my last season due to the points mentioned above. I had the necessary motivation and desire so with `fingers crossed` no injuries to hamper these aspirations.

During these months, as Angela had said, the weights room was like my second home as I was spending so much time getting more powerful and strong. With pop music blearing out, training was most enjoyable particularly hearing the tapes by the Four Tops, Rolling Stones and Bryan Ferry. I was also practising throwing a discus 1kg heavier than an official 2kg one. In addition, I was also aiming to put on more bodyweight, so my food intake increased including my daily milk consumption.

The 1976 Season

I entered the AAA National Indoor championships at RAF Cosford in the middle of January winning the shot event for the 2nd time in my career with a distance of 59ft 1in/18.01m, Peter my brother 2nd at 57ft 5in/17.49m and Bob Dale 3rd with a distance of 56ft 2in/17.13m. Having been placed 1st and 2nd in the shot competition, both my brother Peter and I were selected to represent Britain against the mighty East Germans at RAF Cosford on the 31 January. This was the first time that two brothers in the shot put event, represented Britain in a full international. We also achieved this distinction in the discus event at the 1969 European Athletics Championships all those years earlier.

The mighty Udo Beyer easily won the competition from his countryman Heinz-Joachim Rothenburg, with me coming 3rd (60ft 3in/18.35m) and Peter in 4th place. Beyer would go on to become the 1976 Montreal Olympic shot put champion whilst Rothenburg failed to make his national team for these Olympics. He did compete in the Munich Olympics where he finished in 11th position.

Both Peter and I were chosen to compete in the GB international against Canada on 5 March in Montreal as a `show piece` for their forthcoming Olympic Games. I did ponder whether to accept this invitation or not as it meant another long haul flight before the outdoor season had commenced. In the end, I decided to go and gain another international vest.

After a brief rest from the long flight we were in competition against two good Canadian shot put specialists Bishop Dolegiewicz and Bruce Pirnie who had beaten me to 3rd place at the 1974 Commonwealth Games. To add `spice` to the competition the multi-talented Mac Wilkins made a guest appearance and was warming up with throws over 68ft 0in/20.42m.

Mac Wilkins was a phenomenal all-round thrower who would become the 1977 USA National indoor shot put champion with a putt of 69ft 2in/21.06m. In the discus he became the 1976 Montreal Olympic gold medallist defeating East Germany's Wolfgang Schmidt by over 4ft/1.22m with a throw of 221ft 5in/67.50m. In the Los Angeles 1984 Olympics he won silver, after missing the boycotted 1980 Moscow Olympics and gained 5th place in the 1988 Seoul, Korea Olympic Games. He also broke the world discus record on four occasions. Wilkins was a tremendous athletic individual, who also looked the part.

Both Peter and I were beaten by the Canadian pair, my distance for 3rd place being 58ft 8in/17.89m with Mac Wilkins dominating the event with a put close to 68ft/20.72m. This international did involve a long journey but it did provide experience in competing in Montreal who was to hold the 1976 Olympics and the indoor crowd were enthusiastic and very loud.

On returning to Loughborough where I was residing, taking advantage of the University's splendid facilities, I increased my strength by working harder in the weights room and throwing heavier implements than the standard ones, to increase the power of moving across the circle to the detriment of speed for which I was famed. Looking back this was a terrible mistake on my part.

However, I was fortunate to be given an opportunity to travel to San Jose, USA for three weeks to train with John Powell the former world record holder at De Anza College which had superb throwing and weight facilities. On arrival at the airport I was met by John's girlfriend as he was still on duty as a police officer, so she took me to his condominium in Cupertino not far from San Jose.

She then said I could sleep in the spare room which had a water bed and was the rage in California at the time. Apparently, it was ideal for healthy living and helped the body to relax and importantly, provided maximum body support. So off to bed I went looking forward to a good night's sleep. After two hours or so, I was woken up to the words, "Who is this Englishman sleeping in my bed?" I looked up and saw this giant of a man who turned out to be Brian Oldfield, the outstanding American shot putter and friend of John, who had unexpectedly arrived earlier than planned from Atlanta, Georgia.

So I had to move to the lounge and sleep on the sofa and thought what have I done to deserve this? However, early in the morning his booming voice was heard again when he shouted, "Bill Tancred wake up, I made you your breakfast". I quickly went to the kitchen and was pleasantly surprised that he had prepared eggs and toast with a cup of delicious coffee for me. What a change of personality!

We exchanged pleasantries and got on extremely well and he said, "I hate Geoff Capes and he has no chance at the forthcoming Olympics because he's just fat!"

I replied, "He's our best shot putter and could make the final". "Well, I saw him last week here in San Jose, gripped him by the waist and could hold 2 to 3 inches of fat. What's more, he has the bruises to show anyone where this fat lies".

So I was always wary of him just in case he 'went for me'. On another occasion Brian invited me along with a shot putter from Kentucky by the name of Jesse Stuart to go for a drink after training. I accepted and sat at the back of Brian's spacious car and within minutes both were smoking a 'joint' with all the windows of the car closed. After several minutes they spotted a police patrol car and opened all windows to clean the air in case the car was stopped. I thought this would be some news back home if caught because both of them would have said, "It's the English guy who did the smoking of the joint!" It was the last time I ever went out with these two 'high spirited' shot putters!

Brian Oldfield is credited with making the rotational style popular around the globe and with this discus style shot putting, set both indoor and outdoor world records for the event. Unfortunately for him due to being a professional none of his world records were ever ratified. Sadly today, he is seen in a wheelchair and when standing needs a cane, all due to the severe training methods of his youth.

Jesse Stuart was also a large man with plenty of hair on his head and chin so in appearance looked wild but on knowing him he was a pleasant individual. As a shot putter he had a best throw of 68ft 11in/21.02m and failed to make the USA team for the Olympics.

I did manage to have competition in Sacramento on the 3 April which was called The Sacramento Relays and threw 192ft 2in/58.84m coming 2nd to Ken Stadal who was aiming to make the USA Olympic team. It was a steady performance and I came close in this encounter to beat a very good and talented thrower.

My last meeting on this three week training course was at San Jose on the 17 April and most of the USA top discus throwers took part including John Powell, Mac Wilkins, Ken Stadal and shot putter Brian Oldfield. The conditions were not perfect for discus throwing so performances were down. However, I managed to finish 3rd with a throw of 198ft 8in/60.56m which was over the British Olympic standard now making it four times that I had beaten the Olympic qualifying standard, so I was optimistic in making my third Olympics. Furthermore, all the USA throwers commented, "Bill we will see you in Montreal for the Games!" So with those comments and my throwing I was confident in making the team if no injuries occurred.

It was interesting that this 'Discus Club' in San Jose, all the throwers had discus names on the number plates of their cars -discobolus, disque, Mr Discus, discus spinner and the 65 metre man. They were a friendly group of young men aspiring to represent their country at an Olympic Games. I noticed however the fierce rivalry between the two former world record holders John Powell and

Mac Wilkins. No wonder, because they both made their Olympic team and importantly, Wilkins winning the gold medal with a distance of 221ft 5in/67.50m and Powell 3rd at 215ft 7in/65.70m! So it was a great honour to train and compete with these world discus stars from the US.

At this meet I was introduced by John Powell to Bruce Jenner who subsequently became the 1976 Olympic decathlon champion at the Montreal Games with a world record. I found him to be in great shape and looked a fit and mobile athlete. Very confident and wanted all the media attention that was available at this meet. After winning the Olympic decathlon he was voted the top USA amateur athlete of 1976 and after retiring from the sport, worked in TV and films and was considered for the role of Superman but lost out to Christopher Reeve for the part.

The big shock for many people including all athletes is that Jenner revealed her identity as a woman in April 2015 and publicly announced a name change from Bruce to Caitlyn. Today, she is a very successful business women and a dollar millionaire.

No sooner had I arrived in London from San Jose, within a week on the 1 May gaining my 54th full international appearance, I competed in both the shot and discus events against the mighty East Germans and Yugoslavia in Split. In the shot I finished 5th with a putt of 59ft 1in/18.01m and was placed 4th in my main speciality the discus, gaining 4th place with a throw of 189ft 3in/57.68m and in the process injuring my left heel again. This was worry as another international was fast approaching on the 22 May against Russia in Kiev, so with rest and physiotherapy treatment, I hoped to make the trip and gain my 55 international cap for Great Britain.

On arriving in Kiev, although not fully fit I was asked to throw the javelin against the mighty Janis Lusis who was a former world record holder and Olympic champion in the event. I had not thrown the javelin for years but competed to gain a point for the GB Team. Having known Lusis from previous internationals as I was warming up he spoke to me saying, "Bill are you the secret weapon from England?" I replied, "Janis, wait and see!" It was no need for him to worry as I just performed a token throw for the point using virtually a standing throw which landed at 157ft 3in/46.90.m.

After that performance it was the shot put coming 6th with a throw of 51ft 2in/15.90m which left me in a poor position to compete in my favoured event injured and unable to throw. As a result, I finished 4th with a credible 190ft 5in/58.04m having competed internationally in three throwing events and injuring myself in the process all for the good of team points!

Needless to say, I did not enjoy the after match dinner and although having a few beers with colleagues from the British team and vodka with the Russian throwers, I wanted to go home and seek medical treatment on the injured heal. I did not know at the time whether this would be the end of my international career or not.

Back in Loughborough, I had intensive physiotherapy treatment for two weeks and trained lightly and adjusted my technique somewhat so as not to damage the heel further. Also, I gave up heavy lifting and concentrated on speed work including just short quality discus throwing.

I attended the Olympic trials at Crystal Palace on the 5 June hoping for just one throw that would in effect be good enough to qualify. Needless to say, this did not happen and I was beaten by my brother Peter who was in fine form and for the first time ever, by Mike Cushion which meant I took 3rd place throwing just under the qualifying mark (193ft 6in/59.00m) with a throw of 192ft 3in/58.58m. Had both Cushion and I had qualified that afternoon, we would both have joined my brother Peter on the plane to Montreal.

The selectors had indicated that the `door was not closed` and athletes could still be selected if qualifying throws could be accomplished in the remaining three weeks before the team left for Montreal. As a result, on the 17 June at Loughborough v AAA match, I won the event with a throw of 200ft 9in/61.20m well over the Olympic qualifying distance, then at the Harvey Hadden stadium Nottingham on the 22 June I dispatched the discus to 201ft 1in/61.30m, again over the qualifying mark.

Still no words from the selectors but on enquiring there was still time before `the door would be closed`. So I made another frantic dash on the 29 June, this time to Aldersley stadium in Wolverhampton, the home of my former club Wolverhampton and Bilston. Taking advantage of the prevailing wind, I dispatched the discus beyond the qualifying mark yet again to 202ft 7in/61.78m.

In a final desperate attempt on the 3 July in a club competition in Warley where in 1973 I set a new British record, I threw a personal best for the season of 203ft 1in/62.14m, so I peaked at the right time and within the time scale advocated by the selectors.

To my great disappointment, I was told that my selection was not forthcoming due to a hammer thrower who had caused some problems with certain officials of the British Amateur athletics Board. Obviously, as he too was trying to qualify which he did, made certain selectors more determined not to pick us. Had this not been the case then I would have made my third Olympics.

Other athletes affected by this quite frankly authoritative and appalling decision were Alan Lerwill who took over Lynn Davies as Britain`s best long jumper who on hearing his non-selection quit the sport, Dave Ottley the young javelin thrower who went on to win a silver medal at the 1984 boycotted Los Angeles Olympic

Games and Barry Williams the leading British hammer thrower, who often courted controversy. All were field event athletes and to make matters worse, Alan Pascoe the Commonwealth champion ran his first 400m hurdles race at Crystal Palace and was immediately named for the event in Montreal!

In a space of three weeks I had thrown the discus over 200ft/61m four times and during the qualifying period of the whole year a further five 196ft 10in/60m plus throws were achieved, so I felt totally aggrieved. I had given such long service to the British athletics team and even recently in the match against Russia, when injured, competed for team points! As a result, like Alan Lewill, I at the age of 33 retired from the sport feeling let down and dispirited. To put my performances in perspective in 1976, my qualifying distances would have qualified me for the 2012 London Olympics! Today it appears just one qualification makes the Olympic team. To this day, I know I should have been a triple Olympian.

A caption from Colin Hart of The Daily Herald

I have had a wonderful career in athletics, met so many great people in the sport and a few `plonkers`, travelled to some beautiful countries and achieved so much as an ordinary Olympian and have many fond memories.

Looking back as a throwing athlete, had I had more mental training in my preparation and better periodising of the training year, my performances would have been improved somewhat. The term periodisation has been defined as a method by which training is divided into small, easy to manage segments, typically referred to as phases in training, enabling the coach to effectively plan and manage a training programme. In addition, periodisation structures the training phases to target sport specific abilities allowing athletes to focus on what they must do to improve performance and consequently better adapt to a higher level of practice. The use of periodisation can be seen in two major aspects of the training programme: the programmes cycles (units) and the programmes phases (templates). It`s the key to successfully peak for an event and helps in reducing injury risks.

To represent Great Britain 55 times, be ranked in the world`s top 10 twice, breaking the British discus record on 19 occasions, the last one standing 25 years and winning medals at two Commonwealth Games has been very satisfying. As Angela my wife says, "It`s such a pity that it all ended leaving such a sour taste, so undeserved, so undervalued and so wrong".

Blazer badge for representing Great Britain in Athletics

ATHLETICS CAREER STATISTICS

Personal bests:

- 100 yards 10.3 sec (1965)
- Decathlon 6015 points (1965)
- Shot Put 19.43m/63ft 9in (1974)
- Discus throw 64.94m/213ft 1in (1964)
- Javelin throw 64.10m/210ft 3in (1976)
- Hammer throw 57.10m/187ft 4in (1968)
- Bench Press 225 Kg/496lbs (1974)

Listed below are all competitions at 58.00m and over for the discus event (Peter Matthews):

64.94 (I)Loughborough 21 Jul 74	61.04 (I)Loughborough 7 Jun 73	58.70 (I)Loughborough 15 Jun 72
64.40 (I)Loughborough 20 Jul 74	61.02 (5)Dresden,GDR 22 Jun 75	58.70 (I)Edinburgh 16 Jun 73
64.32 (I)Woodford 10 Aug 74	60.86 (I)London(CP) 28 Jun 75	58.60 (I)Paris(C),FRA 1 Oct 72
63.98 (I)Loughborough 13 Oct 73	60.82 (2)London(CP) 21 Sep 73	58.58 (3)London(CP) 5 Jun 76
63.50 (I)Loughborough 16 Jun 74	60.80 (I)Athens,GRE 18 Jul 73	58.54 (2)Sacramento,USA 3 Apr 76
62.92 (I)London(CP) 12 Aug 73	60.80 (I)Oslo,NOR 21 Aug 73	58.38 (3)Cape Town,SA 31 Mar 75
62.64 (I)Loughborough 12 Jun 74	60.74 (I)Warsaw,POL 30 Jun 74	58.30 (I)London(CP) 5 Sep 75
62.54 (I)Loughborough 7 Jul 74	60.66 (I)Cleckheaton 8 Jun 74	58.26 (I)Athens,GRE 27 Jun 77
62.44 (2)Edinburgh 27 Jul 74	60.64 (I)Sale 28 Jul 73	58.26 (3)Pretoria,SA 22 Mar 75
62.42 (I)Loughborough 5 Jun 75	60.62 (I)London(CP) 11 Aug 74	58.24 (2)Edinburgh 14 Sep 75
62.36 (I)London(CP) 2 Jun 74	60.58 (I)Portsmouth 14 Aug 74	58.22 (I)London(WI.) 14 Jun 75
62.22 (2)London(CP) 1 Aug 75	60.58 (I)London(CP) 25 May 75	58.20 (2)Edinburgh 17 Jun 72
62.18 (I)London(CP) 29 Sep 73	60.56 (I)San Jose,USA 17 Apr 76	58.18 (I)London(CP) 30 Nov 73
62.16 (I)Shotley Gate 18 May 74	60.54 (2)Fort Elizabeth 25 Mar 75	58.12 (3)Christchurch 28 Jan 75
62.14 (I)Warley 3 Jul 76	60.44 (I)London(CP) 1 Jun 75	58.04 (4)Kiev,USSR 23 May 76
62.10 (I)London(CP) 11 Aug 73	60.36 (2)London(CP) 26 May 74	58.00 (I)Shotley Gate 1 May 71
62.04 (2)London(CP) 27 Aug 73	60.34 (2)Leipzig,GDR 30 Jun 73	
62.02 (I)Stockholm,SWE 31 Jul 74	60.26 (I)Bristol 22 Sep 74	
61.98 (I)London(CP) 22 Jun 74	60.22 (I)Loughborough 6 Jun 74	
61.96 (1)Warley 27 May 73	60.08 (I)London(CP) 23 May 73	
61.94 (I)London 7 Jun 72	60.02 (2)London(CP) 12 Jul 74	
61.90 (I)Loughborough 7 Jul 73	60.02 (I)Loughborough 9 Jul 74	
61.80 (I)Middlesbrough 28 Jul 74	59.98 (I)London(CP) 6 Jan 74	
61.78 (I)Wolverhampton 29 Jun 76	59.98 (2)Carshalton 9 May 76	
61.74 (I)Bristol 2 Sep 73	59.96 (I)London(CP) 6 Oct 73	
61.72 (I)London(CP) 3 Jun 73	59.94 (I)Bristol 1 Sep 73	
61.68 (2)London(CP) 14 Sep 73	59.86 (I)Leicester 19 May 73	
61.58 (I)London(CP) 11 Jun 75	59.84 (3)London(CP) 25 Aug 75	
61.52 (I)Portsmouth 8 Aug 73	59.80 (I)Loughborough 3 Jun 72	
61.52 (I)London(CP) 22 May 74	59.78 (I)Loughborough 14 May 75	
61.46 (I)London(CP) 5 Aug 72	59.70 (3)London(CP) 20 Jun 74	
61.46 (I)London(CP) 23 Jun 73	59.60 (I)Christchurch 20 Jan 74	
61.42 (I)London(CP) 8 May 74	59.58 (I)London(CP) 10 May 72	
61.38 (I)Oslo,NOR 23 Aug 73	59.54 (I)Kirkby 29 Apr 73	
61.38 (I)Bristol 23 Jun 73	59.48 (2)Christchurch 31 Jan 74	
61.30 (I)Nottingham 22 Jun 76	59.46 (3)Oslo,NOR 5 Aug 73	
61.22 (I)London(CP) 13 Jul 73	59.42 (I)Wolverhampton 29 Jul 72	
61.20 (I)Loughborough 17 Jun 76	59.38 (I)Edinburgh 5 Jul 75	
61.06 (I)London(CP) 14 Jul 72	59.36 (3)San Jose,USA 17 Apr 76	
61.06 (I)Derby 3 Sep 73	59.30 (2)Helsinki,ITA 25 Jul 72	
	59.28 (I)Wolverhampton 26 Jul 75	
	59.26 (I)Loughborough 1 Jun 72	
	59.22 (I)Oxford 26 Apr 72	
	59.22 (I)Edinburgh 11 May 74	
	59.18 (I)Loughborough 18 Jul 72	
	59.18 (I)London(CP) 31 May 75	
	59.16 (I)Loughborough 10 Apr 72	
	59.16 (I)London(HL) 2 Jun 73	
	59.14 (3)London(CP) 13 Jul 75	
	59.10 (I)Middlesbrough 29 Jul 73	
	59.08 (I)Wolverhampton 8 Jun 75	
	59.06 (2)London(CP) 15 Sep 72	
	59.06 (3)Edinburgh 9 Sep 73	
	59.02 (I)Loughborough 7 Apr 72	
	58.98 (I)Twickenham 15 Jul 73	
	58.98 (3)Christchurch 25 Jan 74	
	58.96 (I)Loughborough 16 May 73	

AAA NATIONAL SHOT PUT RESULTS:

Outdoors:

- 1969 - 2nd
- 1972 - 3rd
- 1973 - 3rd
- 1972 - 2nd
- 1973 - 2nd

Indoors:

- 1968 – 2nd
- 1969 – 1st
- 1970 – 2nd
- 1976 – 1st

AAA NATIONAL JUNIOR JAVELIN RESULTS:

- 1960 - 3rd

RECORD IN MAJOR DOMESTIC CHAMPIONSHIPS AT DISCUS (compiled by Peter Matthews):

Year	A A A	CAU	Area (M Midland, S South)
1964	3 - 47.12	4 - 46.62	2 - 47.78 S
1965	3 - 48.62	2 - 47.76	1 - 49.30 S
1966	1 - 51.76	2 - 49.96	
1967	1 - 51.74	1 - 50.78	1 - 50.42 S
1968	1 - 53.06	-	1 - 53.80 S
1969	1 - 53,.08	-	-
1970	1 - 53.88	1 - 51.98	1 - 55.06 M
1971	3 - 55.20	3 - 52.98	1 - 55.40 M
1972	1 - 61.06		1 - 56.70 M
1973	1 - 61.22	1 - 61.96	1 - 61.46 S
1974	2 - 60.02	2 - 60.36	
1975	2 - 62.22	1 - 60.58	1 - 60.86 S

COMMONWEALTH GAMES
1966 - 9th 48.88, 1970 - 3rd 56.68, 1974 2nd 59.48

UK RECORDS:
1968 - 57.26
1969 - 57.76
1971 - 58.00u
1972 - 57.96, 59.02, 59.16u, 59.22, 59.42 & 59.58, 59.80u, 60.56 & 61.94
1973 - 61.96, 62.10, 62.92, 63.98
1974 - 64.40u, 64.94u, 64.32

GREAT BRITAIN INTERNATIONAL APPEARANCES 1964 - 1976

INTERNATIONAL APPEARANCES 1964-1976   *— Compiled by Peter Matthews*

No	Year	Event	Code	Pos	Mark
※	1964	A v Benelux		3	50.26
1		Poland		4	47.44
2	1965	Poland		4	47.28
.8		W Germany		3	50.96
4	1966	USSR		3	51.90
5		Sweden		4	50.00
6		France & Finland		3	52.88
7	1967	Europa Cup SF		4	51.40
8		Hungary		3	53.94
9		Poland		3	53.46
10		USA		3	53.20
11		W Germany		3	52.16
12	1968	W Germany	SP	3	16.38
13		Poland		4	54.48
14		Olympics		dnq	51.74
15	1969	Czechoslovakia		3	57.26
			SP	4	16.67
16		USA		3	57.76
			SP	5	16.75
17		Italy & Czech		4	55.26
			SP	5	16.50
18		France		2	53.68
19		European Ch		dnq	53.30
			SP	4	16.63
20		W Germany		3	55.72
			SP	4	16.42
21		Finland		2	54.32
22	1970	GDR i	SP	4	16.27
23		GDR		4	51.26
24		Europa Cup SF		4	52.36
25	1971	France		3	54.88
26		W Germany		4	54.70
27	1972	Poland		2	58.20

No	Year	Event	Code	Pos	Mark
	1972	Poland	SP	3	17.81
28		Greece & Neth		1	58.26
29		Finland & Spain		2	59.30
30		France		1	58.60
31		Olympics		19	57.24
32	1973	GDR		2	60.34
33		Greece & Belgium		1	60.80
34		Europa Cup SF		3	59.46
35		Hungary		2	62.04
36		Europa Cup F		3	59.06
37		Sweden		2	60.82
38	1974	GDR		3	59.70
39		Poland & Canada		1	60.74
40		Czechoslovakia		2	62.44
			SP	4	18.35
41		Sweden		1	62.02
			SP	2	19.00
42		Norway & Belgium		1	60.80
43		European Ch		18 dnq	57.36
			SP	4	18.46
44		Finland		3	56.84
45	1975	GDR		3	61.02
46		Europa Cup SF		3	59.14
47		Europa Cup		7	57.18
48		USSR		3	59.84
49		Sweden		2	58.24
50	1976	GDR i	SP	3	18.45
51		Canada i	SP	3	17.89
		GDR	SP	5	18.01
52		Yugoslavia		4	57.68
			JT	6	46.90
			SP	6	15.58
53		USSR		4	58.04

54 European Championships 1966 dnq 57.48

An oil painting by Gerry Blood

When the British team left for Montreal I along with my family, headed for Bridport, Dorset to see Angela`s family where her father Jack had a small farm which proved to be very attractive to our three girls. I did manage to see some of the Olympic Games on the TV but my heart was not in it. From Bridport we made another long journey to Ipswich to see my parents in our old Morris Minor which had a small engine but carried five people in the car. The journeys were also longer in those days because of the necessary toilet or `pit` stops for young girls and of course, there were many slower roads to travel on.

They were happy and carefree days and I was able to devote more time for the girls to appreciate their dad. We spent many days on the beach, visiting zoos and catching up with friends and old acquaintances. From then on my life took on an air of normality away from juggling so many balls in the air i.e. studying, career progression, training twice a day and life with my family. Today life as an athlete is very different, for a start they are paid and train full time with medical and sports science assistance.

Andrea (3 years), Nicola (5 years) and Joanna (2 years) in the late 70s

During the winter months I was spending time writing up my Master`s thesis and seeing my knowledgeable tutors Margaret Hughes and Professor Len Cantor, the head of the University`s Education department and Pro-Vice Chancellor at

Loughborough University. Professor Cantor was fully supportive in my research and passionate about teaching. Many hours were spent with him discussing various teaching methods used in schools and the Army. He was one mentor who made me really interested in academia and I am truly really grateful for that.

So one major chapter finished and another commenced. I decided to get better qualified and pursued my studies part-time as if in training for some major competition ahead and in my case, completing my Master's degree by research by early next year (1977).

11.   A NEW CHALLENGE

In late February 1977, I submitted my completed thesis to the Department of Education and waited the call for a Viva in about three weeks' time. The Viva would be an academic discussion and an opportunity to show that I possessed a thorough understanding of my topic and defend my own research ideas to the examiner.

My thesis for a Master of Arts of Loughborough University was entitled `A comparison of the learning and performance effects of two techniques for teaching an athletic throwing skill to adolescent boys` and my external examiner being Dr. James Oliver from Birmingham University on 3 April 1977.

Dr Oliver at the time was a respected sport pedagogy expert and had published several research papers which were invaluable in terms of theoretical and practical guidance for studying to become an effective physical education teacher or coach.

The oral examination took just over one hour and was a refreshing experience especially as I passed on condition that I corrected only a few minor errors. So with an MA degree, I felt that I could move on to better things in the Education sector.

Although retired from active athletics I still used the weight room at Loughborough, so kept in shape and when asked by my old friend and discus rival John Watts to accompany him to Scotland for a few Highland Games, I jumped at the chance.

John was an accomplished Highland Games performer and had the right physique to do well. So we met up and travelled the long distance to Pitlochry recreation ground in John`s car laden with his highland shoes, throwing equipment and kilt. I arrived carrying just my track suit and discus shoes and no kilt.

We met the Chieftan who seemed jolly and asked both John and myself if we wanted a few `wee drams` to warm up before the competition commenced! He instructed me to wear a kilt and call myself MacTancred and told both of us to return to the marquee after the close of the Heavy events to collect our prize money and have a few more `wee drams` to celebrate!

The Heavy events included five events:

☐   Putting the stone. (It weighed 16lbs but varied in shape, so it was difficult to hold in the neck to put).

☐   Throwing the hammer. (A shafted hammer and no turning allowed. Also one needed shoes that had 6in spikes protruding in front of the boot)

☐ Throwing the weight for distance (The weight is an iron sphere of 28lbs on a chain with a handle on the end which measures 18 inches overall. Most effective if you can use three turns before delivery)

☐ Tossing the Caber. (This event involves a tree trunk weighing around 150lbs and 18 feet long and generally tapering about 9in thick at one end to about 5in the other. A perfect throw is one which goes straight over, with the light end landing 12 o`clock precisely).

☐ Throwing the weight overhead. (Using a 56lbs weight, the competitor has to throw the weight over the bar at the highest height to win the event).

I was appalling in the caber, slightly better in throwing the weight overhead and throwing the hammer but having no prize money for my efforts. However, I did manage to do well in throwing the weight for distance and putting the stone using my experience in throwing the shot and discus as a thrower. So with the paltry prize money gained, I gave it to John for his petrol money! John did perform quite well and seemed pleased.

We did go to see the Chieftan at the end and left the marquee in an alcoholic haze. It was the only time that I had competed at such an event and made my way back home leaving John to `further his Highland Games career`!

On returning home I was considering studying Sports Management at the doctoral level and in order to do this, I needed to have financial help in supporting both my young family and pay all the necessary fees while pursuing this higher level course.

With Angela`s approval and support, I sought out grant awarding bodies such as the Research Councils and the British Council in the UK and also a few United States Universities that offered sports management programmes for Scholarships and Graduate Assistantships. Sports Management in the mid-seventies did not exist in the UK, so it appeared that USA was the best option.

I also approached the Director (Chief Executive) at Trent Polytechnic for help and guidance. He supported the idea on the condition that I would come back and lecture on a forthcoming new Creative Arts degree course and provide information on the module *Administration and Sport*. He would also provide me with a return airline ticket and keep my job open for my two year leave of absence. I thought this fair given the circumstances.

I was attracted to West Virginia University at Morgantown, as it appeared to have a good sports management programme which on completion would be very useful to me and the UK, if any institution would like to introduce this new and exciting academic discipline.

In order to enter West Virginia University I had to take what was called a *Miller Analogies test* which is a standard test used primarily for graduate school admissions in the USA. It consisted of 100 questions and must be completed in 50 minutes. The tests were implemented to measure an individual`s logical and analytical reasoning through the use of partial analogies and was conducted in London.

With the successful outcome of this, and having previous Loughborough College and University degree and Diploma certificates plus three academic references, I was accepted onto the Doctoral (PhD) programme at West Virginia University. It remained to be seen whether any successful grants applications were received.

Well the `sun` must have been shinning on me as I received a letter informing me to attend an interview in Swindon at the Economic and Social Science Research Council centre for a possible NATO Scholarship. Without any hesitation, I travelled to Swindon for the interview.

In the waiting room I met 5 other possible recipients of this prestigious award who were much younger and furthermore, interested in scientific areas of study and nothing related to sport. So on first appearance, I did not feel that I would be granted an award.

The interview lasted just over an hour which was conducted by four `celebrated` scientists, one of whom was the chair and a young happy looking secretary. I was `grilled` and felt that my discussions, aspirations, country needs of both sports management and sports science were necessary, if we were to compete with other nations who were offering such programmes to their students at the post-graduate level. I left feeling that I had a good interview and impressed my learned interview panel.

Two weeks later, I received a letter informing me that I was successful and a full NATO Scholarship for two years would be honoured by the Economic and Social Science Research Council on the condition that I return to the UK on the completion of the programme.

Everything now was going to plan and I would be going to the United States next year (1978) to study for the PhD in Sports Management. The only downside was that I was going to leave Angela and the three girls during this period but I promised them I would be coming home briefly each semester. One factor in this choice was that American children started school one year later than in England. Andrea who was 5 years old would have been affected by this.

USA BOUND TO WEST VIRGINIA UNIVERSITY

School of
Physical Education

I left my family in August leaving the Loughborough home to fly from London Heathrow to Pittsburgh and then get a connection to Morgantown. It was a sad occasion to leave the family for so long but I felt this was my only chance to make a success in my academic career particularly as I retired from active athletics participation.

I was very fortunate that in the waiting area prior to boarding the plane I sat next to Stan Smith the 1972 Wimbledon tennis champion who beat Ilie Nastase in that final.

He seemed a very modest man considering his status as one of the best tennis players in the world and had a military appearance due to his upright stance and trademark moustache. We spoke at length about fitness training for tennis and athletics and aspirations for the future for both of us.

To non-tennis players his Adidas tennis shoe is extremely popular for casual wear and is not used today by top class tennis players but it has sold more than 30 million pairs world- wide as it is a stylish brand. In fact, I wear his shoes today but pay for them!

We landed in Pittsburgh some 6 hours later and I just managed to get the connection to Morgantown. To my horror, as I am an extremely bad `flyer`, the plane had just six seats for passengers and I just wanted to be back home in my comfortable and safe surroundings. Anyhow, with much closing of eyes and clenched fists, I managed the flight and landed safely at Morgantown airport.

After clearing customs and immigration details, I preceded to go to the arrival area to await being collected and taken to my accommodation block called Glenlock Hall. I waited for some time before being told that the airport was closing as it was 12pm! No one was there from the International students Office which was planned earlier and I thought that this was America and not some distant outpost in some developing country.

Luckily, a kind black man said he had a caravan close to the Campus and that I could stay the night with him. Even with his generous demeanour I slept with my eyes open! The morning could not come quickly enough but this kind man showed me where to go and register.

After registration I went to see my tutors at the wonderful Coliseum which holds around 18,000 spectators and is a multi-purpose arena. The facilities were excellent and the Coliseum which opened in 1970 is primarily used for academic studies, conferences, basketball events, degree ceremonies and music events. Interestingly, the late John Denver played there and his song *Take Me Home Country Roads* is the West Virginia theme song and therefore, has a prominent status as an iconic symbol of West Virginia.

My mentors were Professor Bill Alsop and the Dean of the School of Physical Activity and Sports Science, Professor Bill Douglas. They made me very welcomed and judging by their comments, thought British students to be hard working and industrious. They were also aware that I was away from my family so needed not to waste time. To them, I was likened to an American veteran who knew exactly what he needed regarding qualifications to better himself in `civvy street`. Soon I became known as the `Hustler`.

For my doctoral programme I had to undertake several course modules which included:- Sport Marketing, Management of Sports Facilities, Resources Development, Finance, Legal Principles applied to Sport Management, Professional Sport, Media Relations, Research Methodology and an Advanced Internship that involved working with the Director of Athletics (Sport). All good sports management aspects, theoretical and practical based but with the American system, the student had to achieve an A grade in all the modules to pass.

Once the coursework was passed the student needed to have a PhD Oral and a General Examination (called a Comprehensive) to pass before proceeding to undertake the doctoral dissertation, which required a great deal of communication with the advisor and committee members.

When upon completion of the dissertation, the candidate appears before the doctoral committee for purpose of orally defending the study. Successful defence of the dissertation results in awarding of the degree.

With this doctoral programme agreed I made sure that I would undertake as many modules as possible within each semester so as not to waste time. Such was my commitment, my nickname changed from `hustler` to that of `the work horse`.

Luckily for me, I met two good friends in Ken Sissons and Rick Phalunas who were pursuing the same course and as the campus was wide spread, they provided the cars to transport me to the various lecture theatres. I was also grateful as my back was just starting to flare up and restricted any long walking, so today on reflection they were great friends and good company.

On the other hand, the hall of residence named Glenlock Hall was mostly filled up with undergraduates who liked `partying` as if it was an Olympic sport. Weekends were the worst as it appeared that some did not want to sleep at all and the poor Hall representatives who were paid a small stipend could not control them. There was also many issues of drug related problems so as a 36 year old `student`, it was hard to stay there, hence my determination to work hard and as quickly as possible. I was approached many times by the owner of these halls a certain Joe Fredlock, who was very friendly and wanted me to act as the `Chief Policeman` whilst he was away most days and nights! I was on a full grant so I declined this offer.

It was not all work and play because on home games I use to watch the University football team called the *Mountaineers* at the Old Mountaineer field which held more spectators at the time than Nottingham Forest who were the European Cup winners in 1979. At the start of the game the usual cheer leaders would be in action and at some games a `frisby dog` would entertain the large crowd. The dog had this name as it chased a thrown frisby and on catching it in its mouth, returned it to the frisby thrower. All of these `antics` made the game that more exciting.

If the local team had a touchdown or a field goal the mascot dressed as a mountaineer would fire his rifle to celebrate the scoring.

During Saturday nights, again when the home team were playing I use to head for the Coliseum with Ken Sissons to watch the basketball matches which captivated over 18.000 spectators. The standard of play was outstanding and the matches most enjoyable and worth every dollar to watch.

I also had the chance to see the West Virginia State, courtesy of my Dean who wanted a strong man albeit with a bad back to move his furniture from one part of the State to the other, using the U-Haul truck and trailer. After all, who was I to refuse what effectively was my boss!

Ken Sissons did take me for what was a long drive to Maryland which boarders Virginia, West Virginia and Washington D.C. It is one of the original colonies and one of the smallest in terms of area. As far as I can remember, we visited a park and a museum before entering a fast food restaurant for a big yet cheap meal.

It would also be appropriate to mention that on the staff at the School of Physical Activity and Sports Science was Ed Etzel, an Associate Professor in Sport Behaviour.

We shared many coffee`s together and seemed to get on well due to our backgrounds of being Olympians and former Army personnel. He actually was not an ordinary Olympian but won the gold medal at the 1984 Olympic Games in Los Angeles in the Men`s English Match Rifle event. He is an avid fitness enthusiast, animal lover, a rock and blues DJ on the local radio, golfer, an accomplished cook, water colour painter and a Vietnam War veteran. Such was the man.

Another fine professional who at the time of my studies was Dana Brooks who provided me with support and guidance on the American Education system whilst he too was doing his doctoral work. Today, he is the Dean of the School.

Of course in many Institutions and Businesses you get the `talkers` or crudely the `bull-shitters`, West Virginia University`s School had its fair share.

I did manage to make it home every semester to see my lovely wife and wonderful girls who were growing up fast and it was always difficult to leave them. I managed to pass all the necessary coursework and comprehensive examinations within my target time scale and importantly, had the approval by my Doctoral committee to do my dissertation in England after presenting to the doctoral committee, a prospectus of the dissertation which all five of them approved unanimously.

Rick Phalunas drove me to Pittsburgh Airport from Morgantown in his Triumph Sports car and congratulated me on completing my coursework so quickly, as he was only half way from completing his coursework yet we started at the same time. I thanked him for all is help and friendship and said we would meet again when I had to return to defend my dissertation in due course at the University.

I proceeded to queue and check in and as I got closer to the checking- in desk, I heard a disgruntled passenger shouting and raving to the male checking-in staff. When it was over and my turn I said, "You were very calm when that man shouted some verbal abuse to you". " Yes Sir" he replied, "He is going to London but his baggage is going to Tokyo!" We both had a laugh but I would have loved to have seen the irate passenger`s face when he landed in London with no baggage to accompany him!

As I settled in my seat on the British Airways aircraft I was asked to make my acquaintances with the Flight steward on the tannoy system. I did this immediately and was told that the PhD course members had paid for a number of drinks to celebrate my achievements. Obviously Rick had known of my flight details and timing. I thought that to be a great touch. It was certainly a happy flight back to Heathrow.

At Heathrow, I was met by Angela and the girls with lots of hugs and kisses being exchanged and a solid handshake from my brother Geoff, who had driven them from Loughborough to meet me. It was a most pleasant drive back with everyone catching up with news, events and schoolwork. It was time for holidays as a family again.

12.   BACK SURGERY

I was having back problems for a number of years which started I suppose, by slipping with a barbell over my head on one winter`s night, training in our back garden in Ipswich when I was 18 years old. Within a few days it was fine but every so often, it flared up again. I did hurt it again, this time quite severely whilst attending my physical training course in Aldershot and on a few occasions, attended the Osteopath clinic run by the well respected and knowledgeable back expert Mr Coulsting in Camberley, Surrey. He kept me in shape and I was pain free after a couple of days and then able to train with vigour and intensity.

In those days to develop explosive power I used what is termed plyometric training and jump squats, the latter jumping for 10 repetitions with 200 kilos on my back! Performing this type of exercise 4 times a week for 10 years did not help the back! Plyometrics which is still used today by top class athletes, is known as *jump training* and are exercises in which the muscles exert maximum force in short intervals of time with the aim of increasing power (strength x speed).

I did see Mr Coulsting again but on this occasion nothing helped and he appeared very old and frail and suggested surgery as the remedy.

I went to see the Sports Medicine specialist Mr John Williams at Farnham hospital in Surrey for consultation and advice. He suggested having a myelogram which was a type of *radiographic* examination which hopefully, could find the cause of the pain. So a special x-ray dye was placed into my spinal sac and Mr Williams awaited the results on the x-ray. It was confirmed that a disc was indeed pressing on the nerve which therefore suggested that surgery was the best solution.

Having surgery was the last resort so in talking to another consultant, he suggested having a few epidurals which could help with the pain. An epidural would mean an injection of local anaesthetic or other pain relieving medicines into the space that surrounds the spinal cord, numbing temporarily the nerve.

My first number of epidurals was carried out by Dr. Mike Hutson who was an Orthopaedic medicine specialist specialising in chronic back pain. Furthermore, he was interested in sport particularly cricket and was team doctor to Nottingham Forrest football team. After these epidurals and waiting a month, he suggested seeing Mr John Webb who was a leading spinal surgeon based in Nottingham and had operated on several top sports stars in the past.

On seeing him, he recommended having a laminectomy, which was a surgical procedure that removed a portion of the vertebral bone called the lamina.

After the operation in 1980 which was performed by Mr Webb in the Harlow Wood Orthopaedic Hospital at Mansfield, I was allowed home after a few days to recuperate and perform very light exercises, then returned to work within 3 weeks.

Although never the same again because of stiffness and slight rotational restrictions, I was pain free and could still keep fit by doing daily exercises such as walking, cycling and light multi-gym activities, so I am very grateful to the surgeon.

However, after just 3 weeks rehabilitation I returned to work, although not fully fit but with a new term starting thought it best to prepare for the new academic year.

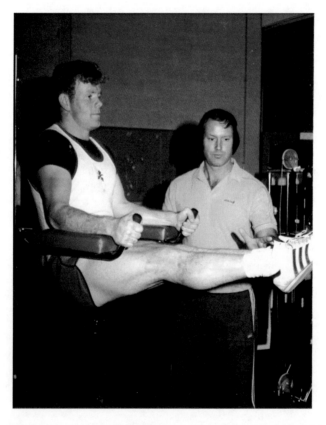

An Army Physical Training Corps Instructor in the multi-gym showing his abdominal strength.

13. COACHING ATHLETICS: BRITISH AMATEUR ATHLETICS BOARD 1980 – 1989; ENGLAND ATHLETICS 1986 – 1989; THE INTERNATIONAL AMATEUR ATHLETICS FEDERATION 1980 – 1996 AND 2007 - 2008

Later on in the year, I was approached by both the British Amateur Athletics Board`s Coaching team to become the National Discus Event Coach under the very talented Chief Coach Frank Dick and Max Jones, who had the responsibility for the British Throwing events. The tenure was for four years and although I had missed the opportunity to compete in what would have been my third Olympic Games, I accepted this invitation to help discus throwers and coaches in the UK to improve their performances. This invitation started in January 1980 and I was looking forward to a new career as a coach albeit on a part-time basis.

Coaching under Frank Dick and the other National Athletics Coaches included the highly respected coaches Wilf Paish, Malcolm Arnold, John Anderson and Carl Johnson. This was an exciting venture for me as I was always interested in Coach Education.

Frank Dick coached Daley Thompson to the decathlon gold medals in both the 1980 and 1984 Olympic Games and is probably Britain`s greatest all round athlete ever. Frank has also created training programmes for many individual sports stars to include tennis player Boris Becker and golfer Justin Rose and his expertise derives from his meticulous detailed research and the knowledge gained from the practical experience and achievement in sports coaching.

Such was Frank`s global recognition that on one occasion on a coaching course in Spain, a journalist asked a few of us, "Have you seen your (Senor) Dick this morning?" "I did thank you very much" was the reply from one of the junior coaches! Today, he is in demand as a motivational speaker in business and in the sports industry.

Wilf Paish was a throwers` friend who was nicknamed `Fighting` Harada after the Japanese World Flyweight and Bantamweight champion due to his same stature (5ft 3in) and resemblance. Wilf was a most talented athletics coach having trained javelin thrower Tessa Sanderson to her gold medal in the 1980 Moscow Olympics, Peter Elliott silver medallist in 1500m at Seoul 1988, my old discus rival John Watts and on occasions advised me on the technical aspects of discus throwing.

Although small, he was a large character who shared a joke and was very confident in his ability as a coach. I use to spend many hours with him during my time as an athlete and now in coaching during athletics trips and his home in Guiseley, near Leeds in Yorkshire. He was also a fantastic cook and host and loved to be associated with the heavy throwers. Away from athletics, he was a successful part-time stamp dealer.

Malcolm Arnold a graduate of Loughborough College coached John Aki-Bua, when he was the Chief Coach to the Uganda National Athletics team, to win the 1972 Munich Olympic Games gold medal with a world record time of 47.82sec in the 400m hurdles beating David Hemery who was our defending Olympic champion who finished 3rd.

I met Aki-Bua at Crystal Palace National Sports Centre a few times and found him to be a very modest and unassuming person. Always happy to see you and he had a great physique for this event. Tragically he died in Uganda at a very young age of 47 and was given a State funeral.

Malcolm is also famed as the coach to Colin Jackson the former world record holder in the 110m hurdles and Jason Gardener the sprint relay gold medallist from the 2004 Olympic Games.

Max Jones who was responsible for the throws was extremely cordial and hard working. In addition, he wanted to improve all throwers so that they had the opportunity to compete in major competitions. He spent much time in researching talent identification and one of the major findings was his compilation and scoring of the Quadrathlon Test.

This test could be used by coaches to see how their athletes reacted to the training schedules set by them. The test consisted of the 30m sprint, an overhead shot put throw, standing long jump and the standing triple jump.

He coached a number of international athletes to include discus Olympian Paul Mardle and strongman John Alderson in the shot to name just two.

Carl Johnson from the North East was another influential coach and was responsible for the Coach Education syllabus and delivery for athletics coaches in the UK. He had a wealth of experience in teaching and coaching athletes and we had things in common due to our interest in teaching throwing events in the correct manner. Similarly, we `bounced off` each other the merits of different types of weight training and lifting, so that athletes would not only become stronger, more powerful but importantly, remain injury free. He was also the former coach to Meg Ritchie, still the current British discus record holder, Paul Dickenson hammer Olympian and BBC TV commentator , Jonathon Edwards the world record holder and 2000 Olympic triple jump champion and Ian Chipchase, the 1974 Commonwealth hammer champion.

John Anderson was another influential coach who had coached the runner David Moorcroft and the sprint hurdler William Sharman to name just two athletes and at one time, was Scotland`s national athletics coach. He was a very experienced and knowledgeable coach and a delight to work with.

Feedback after the training session.

Demonstrating the shot put. (IAAF Photograph}

Working with these professional and very talented coaches, one could not fail to become a good coach, so in this company coaching progress was made although I had a good start in being an accomplished all—round thrower and an Army Physical Training Corps instructor and a qualified teacher from Loughborough College.

There are many roles and coaching styles that are effective in today`s competitive sport ranging from a motivator, friend, scientist, authoritarian, technical, teacher and personable. After all, the coach is an educator and director of people who are striving for a goal being therefore, guides them intelligently towards their goal.

As the national discus event coach I also had to organise the periodic training camps and provide training schedules for the leading men and women discus throwers to include their coaches.

On other occasions, I attended meetings with the Director of Coaching and his National Coaching staff for updates, coaching progress, athletes' problems or advancements and presentations on coaching and training theory.

FROM THE INTRODUCTION TO COACHING THEORY MANUAL
(permission from IAAF)

Planning the Training Programme

One of the most important responsibilities of the coach is planning the athlete's training programme. Planning is a long term process since elite athletes may not reach their full performance capabilities until 24 years of age or older.

In this long term planning the coach usually looks at what the athlete wants to achieve for a particular year and divides this year into a number of periods. For younger, inexperienced athletes performance targets may need to occur at more frequent intervals, such as the immediate season ahead. This is because young athletes are often unable to work towards objectives that they think of as being too distant.

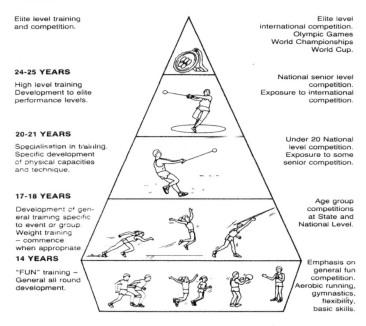

Elite level training and competition.

Elite level international competition. Olympic Games World Championships World Cup.

24-25 YEARS

High level training Development to elite performance levels.

National senior level competition. Exposure to international competition.

20-21 YEARS

Specialisation in training. Specific development of physical capacities and technique.

Under 20 National level competition. Exposure to some senior competition.

17-18 YEARS

Development of general training specific to event or group. Weight training – commence when appropriate.

Age group competitions at State and National Level.

14 YEARS

"FUN" training – General all round development.

Emphasis on general fun competition. Aerobic running, gymnastics, flexibility, basic skills.

Training at any time must be seen as part of the long term plan

I found these meetings to be very valuable and they provided an opportunity to know all the other National Event Coaches and discuss various training theory and practices. We also attended European Coaches Congresses organised by the European Coaching Federation such at Aix-les-Bains in the south east of France, 66 miles from Lyon. All the coaches were exposed to top class presentations from European athletics specialists and much socialising was done in the process trying out the various wines and champagne which was on offer!

223

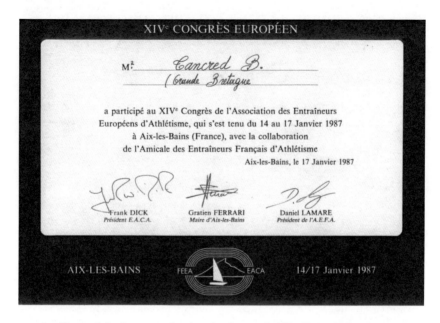

Certificate of the European Coaches Conference held in Aix-Les-Bains, France.

I thoroughly enjoyed working with the National Coaches and when the 4 years contract came to an end, Max Jones wanted to extend the coaching commitment for another 3 years, which I duly accepted. I felt at this stage that my coaching and advice was well received by all and perhaps my main attribute was in *motivating* the athlete and coach who were working with me. Due to my lack of high level sport psychology experience when I was competing, I took a real step to learn this `art` to benefit not only these athletes and coaches but also in my physical education career.

Therefore, I researched many articles, journals and books on the subject linking them to my throwing competitive experiences. Over time I became quite knowledgeable in this science and was able to introduce many of factors that influence performance and how these factors may be controlled by the use of mental skills. These benefits interestingly, extend far beyond the world of athletics. These skills are of great benefit to coaches and athletes in everyday life. Most athletes and coaches recognise that physical development alone is no guarantee of success in athletics. The athlete must have a positive mind and psychological preparation is as important as physical conditioning. Having both produces the excellent performance.

As the National Event discus Coach, I was also selected as one of the British Athletics Team Coaches` in internationals against France in 1985 and in 1986, against Bulgaria who had in their team the very large and evil looking Velko Velev in the discus throw. He married Faina Melnyk the 1972 women`s Olympic discus champion from Russia. I remember him well because we all received some `pocket money` or a daily allowance from our Board and poor Max Jones dropped his paper money on the floor and walked a few paces, turned round to pick up the money to see Velev move like lightening to pick it up and put it into his tracksuit pocket. Who said throwers were slow to react? Max was too afraid to ask for his money back and the look of the Bulgarian discus thrower was one of full joy!

On another occasion, when the National Event Coaches were asking the prospective coaches to give presentations to one-and-all, one football coach asked could he present a football formation instead of a tactical running hypothesis? We had no objection so he preceded to enlighten the group. He commented, "Everyone is aware of the 4-4-2, 4-4-2 diamond, 4-3-3 and 3-5-3 formations. Well sometimes these are not so successful so I have been implementing 6-3-1 formation to my teams". So we asked, "How successful have you been with this unusual formation?" To which he replied, "We lost the bloody lot by not scoring and letting in far too many goals"! The whole class broke into laughter. So coaching can be fun!

I also had the opportunity to be the throws coach for the England team against Czechoslovakia in Gateshead in 1987 which was stimulating to see. Of particular interest was seeing Paul Mardle our talented discus thrower against Imrich Bugar, the Czech silver medallist at the 1980 Olympic Games. Bugar made it look simple as he had a very effective technique that showed no effort. He eventually had a best ever throw in San Jose with a distance of 71.26m/233ft 9in which is still his country`s national record.

This was the first time that I really missed the `buzz` of competing because I wanted to compete instead of coaching by the sidelines. With Bugar`s distance this thinking soon disappeared. At the venue was Andy Norman who at the time was probably the most powerful man in Athletics. In fact, it was he who invited me to become the England coach on that day.

I knew Andy well as he came from Ipswich when we both belonged to Ipswich Harriers our local club who at the time, were based on the current Ipswich Town FC training pitch. As a junior he specialised in the 400m and 800m events and when he reached senior level he joined the Metropolitan Police. After leaving the Police, he became the British Athletics Federation`s Promotion Director and thereafter, a leading agent to many top stars.

He had a tremendous influence in International athletics and persuaded most of the leaders in the governing bodies in world athletics to allow athletes to go professional, after years of `shamateurism`, which allowed under-the-table-payments to athletes and breaking the amateur rules in the process. He managed or influenced nearly all the British athletics stars to include Foster, Coe, Pascoe, Cram, Backley and Fatima Whitebread, who later became his second wife.

Due to his power and ego he was often bombastic and seen as a bully and eventually fell from grace. There was no doubt whatsoever, that he changed the face of British athletics. To me, we got on fine and whenever possible, he would invite me to coach throughout England as a throws coach or mentor.

GREAT BRITAIN TEAM THROWS COACH

☐ Great Britain v France 1985

☐ Great Britain v Bulgaria 1986

☐ England v Czechoslovakia 1987

COACHING ATHLETICS - INTERNATIONAL AMATEUR ATHLETICS FEDERATION (IAAF)

1980 - 1996 AND 2007 - 2008

In March 1980, I happened to be at Loughborough College`s athletics track when I came across Jim Alford who was a former British National Athletics Coach and now the co-ordinator of the Development of Athletics for the IAAF, the world`s governing body. Jim was a wonderful, gentle man who shared a joke or two and was very knowledgeable in both the theory and practice of athletics.

He had an impressive athletics career having won the mile at the 1938 British Empire and Commonwealth Games and ran for Britain on a number of occasions with his active running career being short due to World War II. He was a Squadron Leader in the RAF and still had time to stay fit and well.

Part of his responsibility was the organisation of athletic coaching courses, mostly in less developed countries of Africa and Asia. After seeing me coach, he invited me with the approval of both Jozef Sir and Bjorn Wangermann, the leading figures for the IAAF Development programme to join the IAAF Coaches team. This was a prestigious appointment as a very few British coaches were ever approached or appointed. Needless to say, I jumped at the chance and Jim became my `father figure` in coaching.

I had to go to London in Knightsbridge and meet some of the team including John Holt and presented a short paper on Coaching Throwing Events in Athletics. John Holt at the time was the Secretary General of the IAAF and within one week, I had met three very important people connected with International Coaching Development and I was keen to `get on board`.

Within one month I was invited to attend a course in London and meet other coaches from abroad including meeting up with Jim Alford again and the

Director Bjorn Wangermann. I think they were all impressed in what I had to say but more so with my presentational skills learnt from the Army Physical Training Corps and Loughborough College, the Teacher Training Institution.

IAAF Cyprus course introductions by the President of the Cypriot AAA (IAAF - Char Savvides)

My first IAAF course was conducted in Cyprus during May 1980 arriving in Larnaca and taken to a five star hotel called Golden Bay. I was accompanied by Jim Alford who was responsible for the hurdles and sprint events while I undertook the throws. To my surprise Mike Elia my fellow student from Loughborough College days greeted us with his friend Costas Loucaides, a well-respected coach in the island.

As this was an 18 day course, the first day was to check the facilities and agree the time –table with the Cypriot organisers. Later on, I had the afternoon with Mike and Costas spending most of the time swimming and speeding along the coast in their speedboat! In the evening, some of the dignitaries were met and all of us were treated to a Meze. I was so hungry that I filled my dish so high to the amazement of my very friendly hosts, thinking it would be the only dish. To my utter surprise many more `small dishes` with many different courses were put on the table to consume. How embarrassing as I was full- up after only two dishes but the hosts thought it very funny and it was a good way to start the IAAF Course.

The lecturing and coaching got off to an excellent start and then we set off to Nicosia for another group, who at meal times were keen on fish dishes to include

227

Calamari (fried squid) and Afelia, which was made from pork, potatoes and mushrooms with plenty of Keo beer to `wash it down`!

Although the students were interested in the theoretical aspects of coaching they were not fond of the practical work—maybe the sun was too hot or they were not enthusiastic at all apart from examination time, as most were PE teachers and were given time off to attend this course.

Jim and I then travelled to Paphos which in 1980 was very small in terms of development and hotels. Today, this small habour has slowly and steadily emerged as an attractive tourist destination. Our splendid hotel, used for the theoretical components of the course was opposite the Paphos castle, one of the most famous landmarks of the town.

We had a very large group at this venue and all the participants worked hard to achieve their coaching certificates. At the end of the course, we were both presented with Cypriot flags and brass plate ornaments as an appreciation of our coaching and lecturing these past 18 days.

This was not the last time that Jim and I visited Cyprus because on the 5-15 September 1984, both of us took an Olympic Solidarity/IAAF Intermediate coaching course on the Island. Pre-course arrangements were not without their problems! The lecturer nominated to cover the hurdles and high jump events was forced to withdraw at the last moment. However, I was quite willing to undertake the first week on the throwing events alone and after many vain attempts to find a suitable substitute for the hurdles and high jump events at short notice, Jim Alford volunteered to cover these events during the second week.

My session on the throws and weight training, during the first four days, took place at Nicosia, which had good facilities for lecturing and a stadium with a synthetic track and run-ups for the practical sessions. The stadium used was the Makarios named after Makarios 111, the Ethnarch of Cyprus, Archbishop and first President of Cyprus, who survived four assassination attempts and a 1974 coup. Today, it has a seated capacity of 16,000 spectators and used by top soccer clubs and international athletics.

The owner of the hotel and a number of others nearby, was the leader of the community and during his youth was involved with EOKA (National Organisation of Cypriot Fighters) uprising in 1954 and served under Colonel George Grivas to begin a querrilla campaign aimed at driving out the British and gain its independence. I told him that I was a British army veteran and he had no objections in our political differences judging by his laughter of jokes and providing me with free Keo beer `on the house`.

With the 55 participants, I found their theoretical knowledge well up to the required standard and they were at all times enthusiastic and willing to learn. Again, as in the last course some four years back, practical work was not their forte!

Jim Alford arrived in Cyprus on the 9 September and was picked up at Lanaca airport by my Cypriot friends Mike Elia and Coustas Loucaides and taken straight to the hotel in Larnaca for a meal and a good rest before taking over the course the next day. At the end of Jim`s lecture, we managed to observe their coaching abilities which were part of the course at an international match at the National Stadium. It was a pleasing experience as Cyprus won the competition.

An interesting observer to the course was Mr Costas Hadjandreou, Chief Inspector for Cyprus Physical Education who after every lecture wanted your notes including any athletics and weight training books that we had because he wanted to `file them`? We were warned by both Mike and Costas that he would possibly translate the handouts into Greek and publicise that it was his work! You find them everywhere.

All in all, a most memorable and pleasant course backed up by friendly enthusiastic coaches, athletes and officials.

A most interesting IAAF development course in Singapore during July 1985 for Asian coaches also involved influential administrators such as Dr Muthiah from the Indian Sports Institute and Chi Cheng, the highly respected Chairman of the Chinese Taipei Olympic Games. She had also represented the Republic of China (as Taiwan), winning a bronze medal in the women`s 80m hurdles in the 1968 Mexico Olympics. This performance made her the first Asian women to win a track and field medal in a post-war Olympic Games. Also attending was Maurice Nicholas, Secretary of the Asian AAA. With these three highly regarded officials attending, all the coaches worked extremely hard to impress them and pass the course with `flying colours`!

The high standard IAAF throws course in Singapore. On the front row at the far left is me, the centre two are of Maurice Nicholas (Singapore AAA Secretary), next to him is Jim Alford (IAAF Coach Co-ordinator), further along in the long dress is Chi Cheng (Chairman of the Chinese Taipei Olympic Games) and on the far right is Dr Muthiah (Director of the Indian Sports Institute) (IAAF photograph)

Later on during September another IAAF Coaching and Lecturing assignment took me to Sliema in Malta for another 10 day throwing events course. We used the local schools facilities and what is now the Malta National Athletics Stadium for the necessary course requirements. Twenty participants, many of them not built to even lift a 16lb shot let alone putting it, so we had to improvise using tennis balls for shot putting demonstrations! Eventually through the good contacts of `Joe` Zammit the course organiser, we managed to get some light shots to continue the course.

The two Sports administrators were very hospitable and on my two days off took me to the Navy Museums of Valletta and Mdina, `The silent City`, which was fascinating to visit for its timeless atmosphere as well as its cultural and religious treasures. Also, in one of Valletta`s top hotels, I was treated to a number of thirst quenching Gin and Tonic`s prior to a lavish meal at the closing ceremony dinner.

The IAAF Malta AAA course in Valetta. Standing on the far right is 'Joe' Zammit, Maltese AAA Secretary. (IAAF Photograph).

Malaya was the next invite albeit 6 days to complete the course and was to be conducted in a local school and also at the Merdeka stadium at Kuala Lumpur on behalf of the Malaysian Athletics Federation. The Federation wanted to develop, produce and manage decent throwers who would represent their country at major championships with possible success.

The stadium hosted the fight between the `Greatest` Muhammad Ali and Joe Bugner in July 1995 and having a capacity of 110,000, it sold out to the Michael Jackson concert in October 1996.

As usual the participants were hard working and a delight to coach and lecture. An opportunity was offered to see Chinatown, the markets and enjoying a delightful authentic dinner in a Malay restaurant.

As the Singapore course was so successful, an invitation arose for me to undertake a throwing IAAF course in Taipei, Taiwan in March 1988. Taiwan is located some 100 miles off the coast of China and has had at times, a difficult relationship with them. The course was held in the large Keelung stadium and attended by a huge number of budding coaches obviously marshalled to attend by Chi Cheng and her husband James Wong, who was also a participant on the course! On a worthy note the Keelung district was famous as a top steel manufacturing area, ranked fourth in the world for its export business.

Every word spoken by me was recorded and demonstrations filmed by the entire course participants who after each lecture wanted additional handouts! A strange feeling of being `watched` all the time which included my eating habits!

On one particular lecture, the hall was filled with nearly 80 people attending to listen to what I was to say about `Techniques in Discus throwing`. I started off enthusiastically and within 3 minutes noticed six or seven attendees in the front row falling sleep. This was unfamiliar to me so soon into a lecture that I `clapped my hands` to awaken them and everyone in the lecture hall clapped loudly and enthusiastically as if I had performed a `miracle!` I do not remember anyone else ever falling asleep again.

Chi Cheng was a wonderful host along with the Taiwan athletics officials and for the last night, a dinner was arranged for me and the coaches to attend at the wonderful 5 star Grand Hotel near Yuanshan which was rated in 1968, as one of the best in the world.

I did coach again in Singapore and met a New Zealand Coach by the name of Kerry Hill who later on became New Zealand`s Athletics Director of Coaching. We conducted a Level 1 IAAF course to the coaches of the Singapore AAA`s from the 7 to 21 December 1992. On this occasion, the facilities were excellent and were part of the Teacher Training College of some repute and had a former Loughborough College Lecturer from the past, Dr Paul Robinson, heading it. Also, Maurice Nicholas the secretary of the Asian AAA was a regular attendee and infrequently by Loh Lin Kok, a solicitor by occupation and a somewhat `karaoke` singer in the evening!

In the evenings, he instructed both Kerry and I to attend a seafood restaurant but before we could eat, we had to `sing for our supper`. Karaoke was the rage then and I would only sing if some Tiger beer was available to prevent stage fright! Loh Lin Kok drank the brandy and proceeded to sing on the stage as if a seasoned professional, followed by myself and I got better as the night progressed. This `activity` was continued for most nights and at one stage we sang a duet to the Beatles song `Hey Jude don`t make it bad, Take a sad song and make it better.....`. He was a good host and later on in life, became the President of the Singapore AAA.

Maurice on the other hand was a very quiet man, hugely respected by the IAAF and loved the British and it`s music. He and his wife often played tapes of the 1960`s pop music in their car. He was indeed passionate about athletics and a person who could not do enough for you.

The students worked very hard, were extremely good at theory work and tried their utmost in the practical demonstrations. It was one of the best IAAF courses that I conducted for the IAAF.

1.   African Regional IAAF Athletics Centre-Nairobi

There were three IAAF Regional Athletics Centres in which I coached and lectured in athletics which included the African Regional Centre in Nairobi, the Indian Sports Institute in Patiala and the Asian Regional Centre in Jakarta, Indonesia.

The African Centre was held in the Moi International Stadium which was multi-purpose and had the necessary facilities to conduct the Level 2 course for the more advanced coach.

Our hotel was the excellent Safari Park close to the stadium and Jim Alford was the other IAAF coach. Interestingly, the Director of the Centre was John Valzean who originated from Ipswich, so we had a lot in common. After coming to Kenya as a physical education teacher he devoted his life to athletics and has coached and motivated many Kenyan top athletes including Kipchoge Keino, the gold medallist at the Mexico 1968 Olympic Games in the 1500m and the 3,000m steeplechase, in the Munich 1972 Olympic Games.

This was an outstanding course as it involved some of the best Kenyan and African coaches who were knowledgeable and importantly, wanted to learn all about the throwing techniques. It is interesting to state that Julius Yego became the first Kenyan field event athlete to win a medal at the 2015 world athletics championships with a victory in the javelin. This was quite a remarkable change from the successes of track events so at long last, it shows that Kenya could be a force in throwing.

We also met Ron Pickering again and his BBC TV crew who were making a documentary about the success of Kenyan athletes and how courses such as the IAAF would undoubtedly raise standards in the field events. Had he lived he would have seen the great strides made by the Kenyans in the throws as seen at the 2015 World championships and other competitions globally. Such improvements, makes everything seem worthwhile.

On our two days off, we set off on a Masai Mara Safari, one of the 'bucket list' to do and I was not disappointed. The huge protected landscape is one of the top wildlife destinations in Africa and Kenya's major conservation area. I was very lucky to see what are called the Big 5 namely the lion, leopard, elephant, buffalo and rhino including gazelles, giraffes, zebras and wildebeest.

We did have a scare however, when the small 6 seated partially open truck, got stuck in the mud and with Jim and four female tourists on board meant that our knowledgeable and brave driver, 'volunteered' to get help. This left us alone with no protection. We must have been immobile for about 50 minutes or so when a herd of elephants moved in convoy some 30 metres in front of us, so with everyone's co-operation, I told our group to keep quiet and stay very still, so as not to disturb these very large animals. Everyone was relieved when they departed and within 10 minutes, our brave driver assisted by a helper arrived with two shovels to dig the car tyre out of the mud. On arrival at a base camp we immediately ordered some drinks to relax from this ordeal.

Another interesting tour arranged for the group was to see the Masai tribe and their `living quarters`. Their `houses` are small, circular and built by the women using mud, grass, wood, and cow dung. The men on the other hand, build the fences and sheds for the animals. They adore their cattle and interestingly, their wealth is measured by the number of cattle and children they possess. They even put on a tribal show for us and we paid them a few Kenyan pennies for their efforts and real friendliness.

2. The National IAAF Indian Institute of Sport-Patiala

To give it its proper name the Netaji Subhas National Institute of Sport is Asia`s largest Sports Institute housed in the palatial monumental building and sprawling lawns built by the Maharaja of Patiala, reported to have been married only five times and sired scores of children but was said to only have loved cricket! The Institute is known today as the Mecca of Indian Sports and has produced coaches of the highest distinction who have significantly contributed to the success of their sports National Teams and individual achievements in world- wide competitions.

Netaji Subhas National Institute of Sport, Patiala, INDIA.

(Photograph courtesy of the IAAF)

I was slightly apprehensive to go when I was selected in 1987 to coach on this course but with encouragement from both parents, I opted to travel there. The

234

long flight to New Delhi was made and on arriving outside the airport, I had a real culture shock. So many people were crowded outside and everything appeared congested yet it was only 6am! People and cattle roaming the streets, with many people looking so poor but after meeting my driver and escort, I was taken to a decent hotel for the weekend stay and rest.

After breakfast, we headed for the long car journey to Chandigarh via Panipal, Karnal and Ambala which happened to be the birthplace of my father. Stopping at a railway crossing, we were approached by two beggars seeking money with their eyelids turned `inside out`, to feign blindness. Our guide told me not to give them a rupee or coins otherwise more beggars would arrive like flies. We proceeded on to Chandigarh, which was 275km from New Delhi and a car journey of 5 hours. After, a short break, we headed to the Indian Sports Institute in Patiala, another 90 minutes journey, ending a very long and tiring day.

After a good night`s sleep, I was met by the Director and shown the facilities and provided with the course syllabus for the throwing events.

Dr Muthiah the Director of the Regional Centre was supported by very well respected and senior coaches which included Ken Bosen, who were already well qualified but wanted additional `tips` from our IAAF Level 2 course. Importantly, the students were enthusiastic and knowledgeable and to strengthen the course, were able to provide excellent demonstrators to enhance the course.

One such throwing demonstrator was a certain Praveen Kumar, who stood 6ft 7in tall and won a silver medal at the 1966 Commonwealth Games in the hammer event as a very young man. He also had supposedly thrown the discus over 210ft 0in/64.0m and therefore, was an excellent man to participate on this course. At one time Kumar was banned for two years for taking anabolic steroids.

After retirement, he became a very successful actor, mostly playing the henchman or villain due to his height and made over 50 films before concentrating in politics.

The only `downside` to this Indian adventure was that I succumbed to` Deli Belly` and was laid low for two days which evidently, was the same fate achieved by the other international coaches! The course on the whole was successful but due to the short illness, I was ready for home and this time, flew from Chandigarh to New Delhi and then to London, making the journey time slightly less.

My next major international coaching input took place in Jakarta, Indonesia when it appeared no one else wanted to go so I was asked to fill the vacancy!

3 Asian IAAF Regional Athletics Development Centre - Jakarta

This Level 1 course commenced in November 2007 and my other coach included the Frenchman and now a resident New Zealander Didier Poppe, a world renowned throws coach. He is also the coach to both Jacko Gill, world junior men's shot putter and the 2012 London Olympic champion women's shot put gold medallist, Valerie Adams. Working with Didier would give me the chance to work alongside one of the best coaches in the world and would undoubtedly enhance my coaching credentials at international level.

At Jakarta Airport I was met by a driver who had been sent to pick me up on behalf of the IAAF Centre. Apparently he needed to collect another passenger and instructed me in 'pigeon' English to wait. I must have waited at least an hour, then went looking for him but could not see him anywhere. So in a slight panic as I did not have any Indonesian contacts, I tracked down a policeman who said he would help in an hour! However, by sheer chance, I recognised the 'bloody' driver in the bar 'chatting and drinking' with his two friends! I immediately asked him to take me to the hotel urgently. I think he knew that I was upset, so instantly we travelled without any words spoken to one another. I arrived tired and given a room at the 4-star Century Park Hotel which was in walking distance to the track.

The next morning at breakfast, I heard that the driver was 'sacked' due to his frequent mishaps and liking for Bintang beer! At the time, I thought that was good news so feeling in better spirits I met the other major officials including Didier.

The newly appointed Director was named Ria Lumintuarso who seemed very friendly and knowledgeable on a range of athletics statistics including about myself as a discus performer! That was good to know and he and his team showed us around the Atlet synthetic track called the Senayan Madya stadium which had a seat capacity of 25,000. It had sufficient seminar rooms, the latest video equipment and all the necessary throwing implements.

The course participants came from around 16 different countries from Asia including two very bright Pakistani coaches who would do anything to be 1st and 2nd on all the tests given even to the point that on the final day, both Didier and I were presented with a wonderful colourful ornamental plate to show their appreciation of us!

In the Century Park hotel, security was of the highest order after a couple of explosions down town, so on entry, our training bags including ourselves were searched and checked by the security staff. However, anyone could enter from the back of the hotel with no security staff on duty! Their security system had a lot to be desired.

However, there was no trouble and the 15 day course went smoothly and according to IAAF plans.

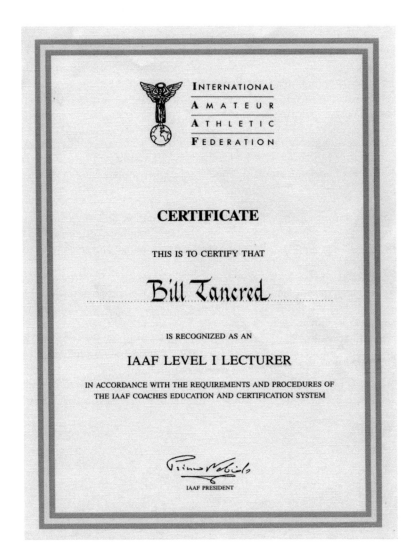

INTERNATIONAL AMATEUR ATHLETIC FEDERATION

CERTIFICATE

THIS IS TO CERTIFY THAT

Bill Tancred

IS RECOGNIZED AS AN

IAAF LEVEL I LECTURER

IN ACCORDANCE WITH THE REQUIREMENTS AND PROCEDURES OF
THE IAAF COACHES EDUCATION AND CERTIFICATION SYSTEM

IAAF PRESIDENT

EUROPEAN COACHES SEMINARS, WORKSHOPS AND CURRICULUUM DEVELOPMENT

There were a number of seminars and workshops held in Germany, France, Spain, Portugal and the UK, the venues being Loughborough and London. Two are worth mentioning in more detail. The first in Cologne, Germany was attended to gain a Level 2 IAAF Lecturer and Coach Certificate. The sports facilities were the most impressive at the time. Attending the course with me was Wilf Paish, the former National Athletics Coach from Guiesley with Briton`s Peter Thompson directing the proceedings and the workshop.

The German Port's University is the largest sports University in Europe and has many departments to include Applied Movement Sciences, Humanities and Social Sciences, Medicine and Natural Sciences, all of them offering various types of degrees in a range of subjects to the 5,000 plus students. In addition, the facilities were second to none and catered for the performer, coach, sports scientist, sports medicine specialist and managers of sports teams.

The London venue was most impressive and the Course was conducted by the then Director of the IAAF Members Services Department and held at the Great Fosters, one of England's most distinguished country hotels in Egham, Surrey in 1984.

It was not surprising that it was really well attended and subjects included amongst other things development strategy, human resources, project management, planning of events and modern technology and communication.

In the evening, the bar was also well attended! Apparently, The Prince of Wales, before the war, danced here. Even Noel Coward gave Great Fosters a line in one of his plays and the hotel has welcomed guests as diverse and famous as the dancer Nijinsky, Bing Crosby, Orson Wells, Lawrence Olivier, Ava Gardner, Diana Dors and Charlie Chaplin. It is Charlie Chaplin who `gripped` the men at the bar when they were told by the senior barman at the time, he used to have a secret passageway leading to his bedroom so if he required the `services` of any lady, no one would know. It was always his favourite room and we were given permission to see it with our own eyes. So much so for the little man with a walking stick!

Great Fosters distinguished country hotel (Kind permission of Great Fosters)

Many of the experienced experts and consultants strived to further improve the training of coaches through the establishment of the IAAF Coaches Education and Certification System. They were asked to contribute to provide course materials and standard examinations for this system. Under this system, coaches who participated in IAAF courses in any country could be confident that they were receiving the best available training for their important work. As such, I was asked to prepare all the throwing material under Jim Alford's supervision and subsequently, further developed later on by Peter Thompson when he was working full time for the organisation.

There were two characters that I had met whilst undertaking this prestigious international coaching role on behalf of the International Amateur Athletics Federation which I would like to mention. The first one was Jozef Sir, the Head of the Athletics Development Department and former sprinter in his youth. Always friendly to me and when the opportunity arose he would always come into my class and listen to what I had to say to the young coaches. Afterwards, he would say, "Bill, fantastico" and leave. In the twenty times I had met him over the years, he would say, "Bill, fantastico". I do know from high authority at the time, he was very supportive of me and wanted me to work full-time for the IAAF Development Department team.

On the other hand, I never really liked the IAAF President Primo Nebiolo on the very few occasions that I spoke to him. He was most arrogant and probably did not like to speak to me as I stood 6ft 4in to his very small stature even when wearing his `built up` shoes. He remained a controversial figure in international athletics and was President of the IAAF for 18 years. He did lead in the expansion of athletics to his credit but had some murky business deals which made him unpopular and furthermore, under suspicion of having Mafia links.

My final major contribution to the word's governing body was to contribute writing research articles for IAAF in their publication entitled 'New Studies in Athletics'. It was a quarterly magazine dedicated to the technical and scientific development of athletics. A further aim was to act as a link between sports sciences and coaches with regards to the practice of the sport. New Studies in Athletics eventually constructed a worldwide team of top specialists whose knowledge could only benefit everyone connected with athletics.

I was very privileged to have two papers published in this scientific journal with brother Geoff entitled, 'An examination of the benefits of warm up: a review' (December 1995) and 'Physical exercise in the treatment of low back pain: guidelines for athletes' (January 2000).

For me working albeit in a voluntary and part-time basis these past 30 years has meant a lot to me. I have worked with interesting coaches from all over the globe, serious and funny administrators but the most satisfying, is giving my services freely and voluntarily to help to develop athletics along the right lines in the poorer countries of the world.

TEACHING AND COACHING WEIGHT TRAINING: THE BRITISH AMATEUR WEIGHTLIFTING ASSOCIATION (BAWLA) 1980-1990

I was first involved in weight training and lifting during my time as an athlete and progressed over the years due to all the practice needed by a strength athlete. I was always interested in performing various exercises to build up power, fitness endurance and muscle.

After qualifying as a weight training teacher, I attended further courses to upgrade to a senior coach at Bisham Abbey once the home of Henry VIII and Elizabeth I and now one of England`s National Sports Centres. This enabled me to conduct both Teachers and Leader courses, for both school teachers and for those working in the fitness industry. Soon after qualifying in 1980, I organised with BAWLA`s permission, courses at the famed Loughborough Summer Schools and the Blackpool Easter Schools for over 10 years helping people to gain awards.

BAWLA coaching badges.

240

Such success lead me with brother Geoff to take other institutions on board such as the Armed Forces personnel, Schools, Universities sports departments and the Police Forces around the UK. On one occasion, I went to Nicosia in Cyprus for one month to coach various sports clubs in promoting weight training and of its merits and correct application.

Even then and I maintain today, that force or strength is as important to the explosive event athlete as breath is to the runner. What is more, whilst runners and coaches may argue over the relative merits of various running-based training programmes to improve performance, no one can seriously doubt the absolute specific needs of weight training for a great majority of athletic events. Therefore it behoves any of us who are in any way concerned with the improvement in performance in sport to heed the research, the added knowledge, the guidelines that are reached in learned books and journals relating to training with weights and resistance machines.

On a lighter note, there were a few comical incidents concerned with running weight training courses which we all found amusing. One involved teaching a group, the overhead press with a light barbell. I went through the technical aspects of the lift to include breathing technique and then asked the class to practice. An older Irish man suddenly collapsed on to the floor, so we rushed to his aid and when he recovered said, "I am terribly sorry sir but I forgot to breathe after 12 repetitions!" Enough said.

The other involved a class lecture and at the end of a fairly strenuous morning I suggesting `tongue in cheek` that they should go and do some `Egyptian PT`. Unfortunately, a hand went up and said, "Sir, I am from Egypt and have never heard of this expression?" Slightly embarrassed I informed him that it was an Army joke for all those individuals who were lazy and meant going for a nap!

With my brother Geoff as a co-author, we wrote a book entitled 'Weight Training for Sport' published by Hodder and Stoughton in 1984 which sold very well as there were not many books published in the UK on weight training during that time.

However, we were asked by the publisher that for the cover of the book we needed to have both sexes and importantly, an Indian to make it international. We were stunned as no one on the course came from this country but surprisingly just when we were giving up an Indian on a bicycle came past the building! I immediately stopped him and asked if he had ever done weight training before to which he replied, "Never, Never". So I said would he mind appearing on the cover of the book and we would provide some basic training. He jumped at the chance, so with 5 minutes training and in borrowed training gear, he performed majestically for the cover photograph, with everyone appearing happy and content! (Hodder & Stoughton book below).

WEIGHT TRAINING
FOR SPORT

Bill Tancred and Geoff Tancred

All in all, I thoroughly enjoyed the weight training coaching experience and met so many different and interesting people during my time as a weight training senior coach and examiner. In addition, I presented papers at various conferences, wrote many articles on the subject and hopefully, contributed in helping sportsmen and women improve their sports performance who applied weight training programmes in their training. As an added bonus, I was involved as a strength and conditioning coach to the British Olympic Association`s 1992 Olympic Games preparation.

14.   THE UNIVERSITY OF SHEFFIELD 1980 - 1993

It was in late 1980, when I applied to the University of Sheffield for the position of Director of Physical Education and Recreation. I was successful in my application, so after five years at Trent Polytechnic it was time to move further up north to Sheffield, South Yorkshire.

After the interview, the Vice-Chancellor advised me to bring my wife through beautiful Derbyshire and not up the M1 and then through the Parkway into Sheffield, viewing Manor Top on a bleak day otherwise she would refuse to move from Loughborough!

As it turned out, we stayed in Loughborough for another four years before eventually moving to Sandygate, Sheffield close to the wonderful Peak district. Commuting first by car and then by train became the pattern for travel from home to work and return during the week.

My first task at the University was meeting the mother and son of `Sarge` Cofield who at one time was the University's Recreation Officer and had died very recently. As I was the new senior Physical Education Director at the University, I was asked to accompany his wife and son, say a few words and scatter his ashes over his beloved Bramley cricket pitch. I duly accepted this task but as it was windy, most of his ashes landed on my blazer! Anyhow, his wife did not mind and said, "Dr Tancred, my husband will always be looking over your shoulder now!"

It was reputed that Mr Bramley bowled a delivery on this exact pitch when he reached 100 years of age and by all accounts was quite eccentric but loved to watch and play cricket.

Very soon after carrying out this `University business`, I was approached by two old lecturers to ask me to lecture their students on education courses, as they thought I was enthusiastic. Immediately not being naive, I realised very quickly they were trying to `off load` their own lecture responsibilities. My post was not to lecture on education courses as my Department at the time, provided opportunities to both staff and students to take part in recreational and sporting activities but devoid of any academic courses.

The first year was spent working very closely with the Student Union and their Clubs and Societies to promote sport and physical activity. However, there was much unease in the autumn term of 1980, after Jacqueline Hill, a student of Leeds University, became the thirteenth victim of the Yorkshire Ripper. Although none of the attacks were committed in Sheffield many females were scared to go out and especially to walk around the red light district near Broomhall which was across the road from the Student Union. Occasionally porters in the Union organised an escort or lent taxi money to women going home after discos on Friday and Saturday nights. Precautions such as this were prescient because on the 2 January 1981, Peter Sutcliffe travelled to Havelock Square in Sheffield, picked up a woman and drove her to Melbourne Avenue, a short distance from the University. Two very alert duty policemen spotted the false number plates on his car and immediately arrested him. Subsequently, a few days later Sutcliffe confessed that he was indeed the Yorkshire Ripper.

During this period, I was also involved in Coaching on behalf of the British Amateur Athletics Board (BAAB) and the International Amateur Athletics Board (IAAF) including being a committee member, treasurer and finally, the last chairman of the International Athletes` Club (IAC) before the sport went `professional` around 1989.

The IAC was an independent body and was formed to help international athletes in their quest to be better athletes and `protect` them from officialdom matters, similar to a trades union. They also organised warm weather training opportunities, grand prix events and provided physiotherapy needs for injured athletes.

The committee mostly had retired international athletes serving and at the time had Derek Johnson, the co-founder `directing the ship`. He was the silver medallist in the 800m from the 1956 Melbourne Olympics, narrowly being beaten by Tom Courtney of the USA who needed medical attention from the sheer exertion needed to beat the very determined Johnson. Also, on the committee was an independent member Les Withers who was the Financial Accountant and Advisor. A most likeable man who always enthused athletics and had the interest of the club at heart.

On one particular Grand Prix event in Meadowbank, Scotland in 1987 we had to pay the expenses to some of the athletes which included a certain Michael Johnson from the USA. He was due his fee and had run the fourth fastest ever 200m on a cold evening and asked Les if he could have a bonus for achieving such a world class time? Les replied, "Certainly not!" Johnson politely left the room at The Caledonian hotel in Princes Street overlooking the grandeur of Edinburgh Castle. I told Les that his refusal to act on Johnson`s bonus request was hard and unfair. Les came back and said, "If he`s any good, he will have another opportunity!"

Well Michael Johnson went on to win four Olympic gold medals and was the world record holder for the 400m event until it was broken this year at the Rio Olympics. He had a stiff upright running position and very short steps with a knee lift which was not seen by coaching experts as how to run fast! Today, he is often seen as a BBC TV athletics commentator. Les was right Johnson certainly had further opportunities and proved to be an exceptional athlete and a knowledgeable voice in athletics commentary.

Having The Caledonian Hotel as the accommodation base for all athletes and officials, was a fantastic experience, as many international stars had also used this venue at certain times. These have included Charlie Chaplin, Elizabeth Taylor, Sean Connery and Lloyd Bridges. I spoke to the latter briefly in the lift and in the foyer of the hotel. He was there to see Scotland and watch the athletics match as he was a fan. He had always kept fit by training daily and found international fame as an underwater investigator in the TV series Sea Hunt.

In 1988 the IAC were in danger of losing its Grand Prix hosting event and the IAAF were sending some officials to observe that we could still attract top class athletes to such an event. I was responsible for looking after a Finnish sports administrator who apparently liked a drink or two. We entered the bar at the hotel at 11am and proceeded to drink as many pints as possible before the dinner and meeting scheduled for 3pm. We arrived for dinner at 2pm and sat down to order. Being polite, I asked him to order first. He mumbled and slurred every word to the astonishment of everyone and then raised his right hand to his mouth so as to inform her that `wanted another drink!` I ordered my starters and told my `slurring` guest that I was going to the toilet and would be back very shortly. On my return, I was totally shocked to see him carried out completely drunk by three smiling waiters!

We were worried that he would not give us the required permit but in his report the next day we were given 10 out of 10 and wanted to thank me most sincerely for being a fantastic and kindly host! However, the sport was changing and eventually the IAC were no longer required.

Sheffield University did have a number of sports fields mostly at Norton some distance from the main University Campus. At the time, cuts to university funds featured highly and suddenly income generation was at the forefront for many staff heads including myself.

As a result, I was in touch with the new manager of Sheffield United Ian Porterfield who is probably best remembered as the goal scorer of the winning goal for second division Sunderland against mighty Leeds United in the 1973 FA Cup final. We got on fine and managed to work together to the benefit of both Sheffield United and the University of Sheffield. Most football Managers don`t last long and eventually Porterfield was sacked.

On the academic front and a desire to get the `recreation` department some credibility, along with my deputy Mike Bracewell, we were given approval to offer a Post Graduate Certificate Course in Physical Education for teachers. We also offered a similar course for International students as these students were lucrative to the university coffers. All of these newly validated courses were a complete success and fully supported by the HM PE Inspector Danziel Flanagan from the then Department for Education and who at one time, played in the reserves for Ipswich Town FC.

ONE YEAR POSTGRADUATE CERTIFICATE COURSE IN PHYSICAL EDUCATION AND RECREATION FOR OVERSEAS STUDENTS

UNIVERSITY OF SHEFFIELD
PHYSICAL EDUCATION
SUPE

Department of Physical Education and Recreation
University of Sheffield, England

I was also busy writing my PhD thesis and on May 1981 went back to Morgantown, West Virginia to defend it in front of the five committee members and to the Graduate Faculty. After a two hour `grilling`, I came away with the title of Doctor Bill Tancred which was a great achievement in the eyes of my parents and myself having failed my 11 plus aged 10 all those years back. All my fellow students to include Rick Phulanus and Ken Sissons, were on hand to celebrate this award with me until the very early hours of the morning.

On my return to the Sheffield University, having such a title proved to be an advantage in trying to convince the Academic Board with my vision for the Department to introduce further courses in sports science and sports management.

On my daily rail commute from Loughborough to Sheffield, I met an interesting chap by the name of Alan Eastwood who was the Managing Director of the Midland bank at Griffin House, Sheffield. During one of our many conversations, I mentioned that Pukka Pies (based in Syston, Leicestershire and founded in 1963) were delivered to the Student bar and I could purchase some at the trades` price. He jumped at the chance by saying he and his adorable wife Barbara did much entertaining and having such pies would be splendid for such occasions. I ordered on his behalf 20 steak and kidney pies and another 20 chicken and mushrooms pies to be delivered at his work place.

On catching the 4.20pm train back to Loughborough from Sheffield, just before departure, I saw Alan struggling with a huge dispatch black box and just made the train with sweat pouring down his red face. Inside the box contained the 40 Pukka pies and he was so relieved to make his `get- away`, as he had told his staff, he was taking home some large files to read during the weekend!

On another occasion, on the train he seemed fed up with work and told everyone he had had a very bad day and wanted to retire early. He carried on by saying he would love to send his boss a telegram to this effect. He continued and said these are the words to be sent in the telegram: 'STICK JOB UP ARSE ABUSIVE LETTER TO FOLLOW'. We all had a laugh but he never sent such a telegram.

One of the irritating jobs I encountered at Sheffield University was answering complaint letters sent by the community residents about student behaviour over the weekend. One letter which was always delivered at my desk was from the chairperson Mrs Coe from the Marlborough Road Association who lived very close to the Goodwin Sports Centre where all the facilities existed. Generally it was about noise after 11pm but more often about the floodlights being too bright and left on too long. After 10 weekly letters going to and fro, I decided to speak to Mrs Coe and meet her in her house which was not far away from where my office stood.

On entering I noticed a few athletic pictures showing Seb Coe, one of Britain`s greatest athletes on the wall and I suddenly realised it was Seb`s mother Angela! Well, she also realised who I was and quickly called Seb`s father Peter to come and meet me. We discussed athletics the full morning with no mention of floodlights or student behaviour and shook hands on my departure. Interestingly, no further letters were exchanged by us, only the odd phone call.

What is sad is that I did not know at the time that she was an Anglo-Indian and with me being born and living in India for a short time, we could have discussed our experiences about this country. She died age 75 from Progressive supranuclear palsy, a rare brain disease.

Seb turned out to be a phenomenally successful athlete, politician and businessman and is now known as Lord Coe, having organised the most successful 2012 Olympic Games.

In 1982, Sheffield University appointed Dr John Padley as the Registrar and Secretary when he was only 39 but was experienced and highly respected. John was innovative, energetic and could quickly complete routine work and then be ready to entertain and make progress for the university. Furthermore, he thought the workings of University committees to be slow with a few to be ineffective. He much preferred action to be swift and decisions made to be realistic and progressive. If you had a good idea in John Padley`s office it was said that it would be implemented before you left! However, some of these ideas were inspirational and others sadly were not. Members of staff were motivated into action and firmly believed that improvement was possible, even at a time when University morale was extremely low. In fact, I thought he was the `face` of the University and it`s spokesperson as he was very effective in dealing with the media questions and answers.

I soon made friends with John and we seemed to have the same views on how to improve the university`s image and attract more students on courses that were relevant and up to date in a fast changing world.

He also had a sense of humour especially on April Fool`s Day. The University Newsletter dated 1 April 1988 indicated that a rift under the large Arts Tower in the centre of the campus had been found and therefore, the building would have to be moved to a safer place. The relocation was to take place for a weekend and was expected to attract a substantial number of tourists so as to increase the catering income. Also, the University`s television service had been granted exclusive rights to film this move from the world`s TV networks. What was so funny is that a dozen Professors wrote angrily to him stating that they were not asked to vote on this move!

In the 1989 issue on April Fool`s Day, John had indicated that the World`s first swimming female nudist championships were to take place at the swimming pool and all the windows were to be `blackened out` so as to keep it private. Surprisingly some members of staff complained to both John and I, that their swimming was more important than the nudist swimming event. It was also reported, that the male attendances outside the pool had increased substantially with most hoping to see the women arrive for the inaugural world championships. John was full of mischief.

During February 1983, we had the sad news that Angela's mother Eileen (Moore) had died at the relatively young age of 55. She was not too well but none of us expected the death. She never had the opportunity of seeing her grandchildren grow up or to travel and see the delights of our country.

With the 1984 Olympic Games approaching, I was asked by Ladybird Books Ltd. based in Loughborough if I could write a 60 page booklet to inspire primary age schoolchildren to be interested in sport and the Olympic movement. With my young daughter Andrea who was about 8 years of age we set about doing this with vigour and enthusiasm over a weekend. We just managed to do everything within the 60 pages limit and finished it late on Sunday night.

Such was the success of this book that it became the best seller for August in the UK and importantly, teachers used it for project work in the schools. I was paid just £500 for this best seller and did ask the then Director of Ladybird Books Ltd. for a bonus, to which he replied no, as he held the copyright! So a hard, expensive lesson learned from this encounter. Ladybird re-modelled the book in subsequent Olympic years and most annoyingly, did not involve me despite it being in the same format. In the 1988 Olympic year only, did I receive 5 complimentary copies!

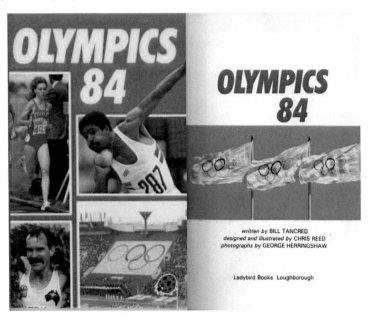

My department of Physical education was beginning to get noticed academically at the University and recruitment from overseas (International) students was good and we also had strong links with the British Council based in Leeds for financial support and advice.

RESEARCH

Furthermore, the first ever departmental research grant of £90,000 which was substantial in 1986 was awarded to me from The Health Promotion Research Trust for a research project entitled `Preparing Children for a Lifetime of Health and fitness`. It was a four year study and my research team consisted of Dr Mike Banks (research consultant), Nigel Gleeson (research officer) and Val Tibbenham (secretary). All of a sudden, the Department had credibility in the eyes of the University and was `applauded` by John Padley and the Vice Chancellor Geoffrey Sims.

The study involved secondary schools with catchment areas of comparable socio-economic composition in Sheffield, South Yorkshire. We provided an educational intervention programme (EIP) thereby equipping the students with the necessary information to make intelligent choices regarding health-related fitness behaviour and future lifestyles. This progressive approach to the teaching of health based physical education had been used extensively in the United States.

The EIP standardised core syllabus included health, fitness and active lifestyles, the nature of fitness, the importance of flexibility to health, the importance of cardio respiratory fitness to health, muscular endurance and strength and the importance of body composition and weight control.

After four years, improvements were made in health related behaviour by the pupils and importantly, many schools adopted a health related curriculum to the long term benefit of many Sheffield pupils. (Below photograph Sheffield University Newsletter).

Ken Howard, Myself and Stan Wardle Sheffield University Sports Personality Shield presented by the XXI Club

The Health Promotion Research Trust had two wonderful trustees who provided me with enormous encouragement and support during these four years which needs mentioning. The first one was Angela Buxton the former English tennis player. She won the women's doubles title at both the French championships and Wimbledon in 1956 with Althea Gibson who was the 1957/8 Wimbledon champion and professional golfer.

The other trustee was Lord Butterfield who was the Chair. He was also the former Master of Downing and Vice-Chancellor of Cambridge University and his research interests was the study of burns. He had also advised Margaret Thatcher when she worked on her NHS reforms and was passionate about sport. He had unstuffy approachability and loved me telling him a few jokes. The one that made tears come from his eyes stands out today:

'Here are five rules for men to follow for a happy life that John L Murphy had inscribed on his headstone in Tempe, Arizona. He died not knowing that he would someday win the 'Coolest Headstone' contest.

1. It's important to have a women who helps at home, cooks from time to time, cleans up and has a job.

2. It's important to have a women who can make you laugh.

3. It's important to have a women who you can trust and does not lie to you.

4. It's important to have a women who is good in bed and likes to be with you.

5. It's very, very important that these four women don't know each other or you could end up dead like me'.

During 1986 several conference papers were presented at the King's Fund in London, Arizona State University at Tempe, West Virginia University at Morgantown, North Dakota University at Grand Forks and at The American Alliance for Health, Physical Education, Recreation and Dance (AAHPERD) in Indianapolis.

The latter was an opportunity to meet up with former colleagues who were now lecturing in the States such as my former athletics weight training partner Jim Whitehead and to discuss research collaboration in health based physical activity.

On my return with John Padley's approval, I set up the Health and Fitness Unit open to the public as a business venture for the University and my Department. This new initiative provided adults with a comprehensive, scientifically based system of assessment, prescription and monitoring of all aspects of fitness and health for the individual.

Within one month, the University accumulated £3,000 so it was an inspired business venture and all were pleased. We even found people who thought that they were healthy to have high blood pressure which resulted in many of them to be referred to the University Medical School or to their general practitioners.

AN EVENTFUL YEAR 1987

1987 proved to be a successful year in that I managed to accomplish many things and meet some interesting people all round. The first was to attract another research grant of £25,000 for one year, from The Health Promotion Research Trust to study `Injuries and different playing surfaces`. I had the support of Emma Burnett, an Oxford University graduate who could quite easily read four to five books in a week and retain all what she had read! The project was a major advance in an area of study where there had been previously little conclusive research in the UK and it provided valuable information for local authorities and other bodies, when installing playing surfaces for tennis, football and other sports.

Also interestingly, footwear could have been the hidden component in sporting injuries. This concern with regard to the shoe and its determination of both safety and performance is certainly shared by the leading athletes in this field. There was a need at the time for proper education with regards to what constitutes safe footwear. We advocated six *steps to success* that should be followed closely:

1. Stability with regard to the way in which the shoe grips the foot,

2. Shock absorption,

3. Support,

4. Cost,

5. Quality and

6. Style.

The third book I wrote happened to be the first on this subject in the UK and published by Hodder and Stoughton entitled 'Health related Fitness' in early April of that year, was well received by the public and sold very well. This publication intended to help both adults and students on keeping fit and healthy and having active lifestyles.

It was also the year I managed to meet the newly appointed Manager of Sheffield United Football Club Dave Bassett in my office as he wanted his team to use the practice pitches at Norton playing fields and I, to earn some finance for the University in letting out these facilities. We got on famously and I thought highly of him as a motivator with a real sense of humour. Such was his influence that I became a fanatical *Blades* season ticket holder for nearly 30 years!

Former Sheffield United Football Club Manager Dave Bassett and Myself at a conference in 1990. (Sheffield University/Matt Dickenson)

Dave Bassett brought the good times back to Bramall Lane and in the team, had some influential players such as Brian (Deano) Deane who later earned three caps for England. My fondest memory with Dave at the helm is the 1990/91 season. The *Blades* failed to win any of their first 16 league games in that season and by the end of the year were bottom of the league. I am not sure what he said or did but the team came out `fighting` in the New Year and played brilliantly in the second half of the season to finish in 13th place in the final table. 3 April 1993 was a bad day for all Blades fans as we lost the to our city rivals Sheffield Wednesday 2-1 in extra time at Wembley in the FA cup semi-final, so it was another unhappy long journey home. I had better get used to this as there were going to be a few more heartaches to come following this football team!

Another major development in 1987 was trying to improve the standing of the

253

Army Physical Training Corps (APTC) in academic and sporting communities. With John Padley, Lt. Colonel`s Don Glynn and Phil Hargraves support and approval, I was able to get APTC officers for the first time accepted onto a diploma in a physical education course at a British University. The very first officer to enrol was Lt. Colonel Tom Steel, followed by Major David (Cass) Clay, Colonel Ian Horn, Major Jim Noble and Major Alan File. All of them turned out to be excellent `students` and a credit to the Corps. In fact, they fitted in the Sheffield University environment very quickly.

Major Cass Clay, Lt. Col. Tom Steele, Col. Ian Horn and Myself – these were the first officers of the Royal Army Physical Training Corps to attend a University on Postgraduate studies in 1987. (Sheffield University Newsletter)

Later on the Department from 1987-1991, organised annual seminars for all APTC personnel and were offered the very best of speakers on a range of subjects relating to sport and sports science and included one year (1988) when Sir Arthur Gold spoke on the topic of `Drugs in Sport`. It was tremendous having Sir Arthur speak at a conference such as this as many academics, interested members of the public which included coaches and athletes attended, thereby raising the profile of my small department both within the University and in the City itself.

Vice Chancellor Geoffrey Sims, Sir Arthur Gold, Myself and Lt. Col. Phil Hargraves at Sheffield University's conference on Sport and Wellbeing 1988 (Mark Dickenson)

Soon after Lt. Colonel Phil Hargraves, as the Assistant Commandant of the APTC (1986-1989) invited me to give two lectures to a Military Symposium to 100 APTC Instructors in Berlin in 1988 which provided me with the opportunity of viewing the magnificent 1936 Berlin Olympic stadium, a boyhood dream as the great Jesse Owens won four gold medals in the 100m, 200m, long jump and was a member of the winning 4 x 100m relay team. He was credited with destroying Hitler's myth of Aryon supremacy and his boast that Germany would dominate the Games. His long jump of 26ft 8in/7.81m stood for 25 years as the world record and is documented along with many other 1936 events in the wonderful film *Olympia* by Leni Riefenstahl in 1938. At the age of 66 he died of lung cancer and had he performed today, he would have not resorted in trying to make money racing against horses but to have lived with a comfort lifestyle. He was perhaps the world's first black star.

After the Symposium, my old friend John Jennings who was stationed near Berlin, took me around Berlin to see the various sights to include parts of the Berlin Wall, Reichstag building, Brandenburg Gate and the dreadful Plotzensee Memorial centre which had seen between 1933 and 1945, 2,891 executions handed down by the `Peoples Court`. A frightening thought.

The Physical Education Department was awarded another grant to improve the multi-gym facilities at the Goodwin Sports Centre and I was asked by the

University authorities, if I could find someone `famous` to open this new facility but no fee was available!. Luckily I knew local resident Emlyn Hughes who was happy to help out as I did him a similar favour a year back. Emyln had earned 62 caps for England and was nicknamed `Crazy horse` for his larger than life personality and captained Liverpool FC in the 1970`s. He also brought real enthusiasm and laughter to the TV quiz *A Question of Sport*`. Sadly, he died of a brain tumour aged only 57.

Also along with Emyln, Dave Bedford the former world record holder for the 10,000m attended saying, "Emlyn might need a hand!"

Interestingly, the Goodwin Sports Centre where my Department was based was named after Sir Stuart Goodwin, a steel and tool manufacturing millionaire at the time. In 1920 he was diagnosed as a diabetic and gave the Sheffield Royal Infirmary £10,000 as a gift. He was told to exercise although he played golf but as a matter of helping others to stay healthy, he gave the University a blank cheque to build the present Goodwin Sports Centre.

Emlyn Hughes (former captain of Liverpool FC and England) is pictured with (left to right) Myself, Dr John Padley, David Bedford (former world record holder for the 10,000m) and Vice Chancellor Geoffrey Sims on the opening of a new multi-gym facility at Sheffield University. (Kind Permission The Sheffield Star).

I was most fortunate to be invited to attend a Garden Party at Buckingham Palace in July and both Angela and I were thrilled to accept and attend. We dressed up, Angela looking lovely and were joined by hundreds of other smartly

256

dressed individuals all looking forward to the occasion. When her Her Majesty the Queen entered the Balcony, everyone wanted to be close enough to see her, so the crowd moved closer. I noticed that Captain Mark Phillips was standing on his own so I informed Angela we should introduce ourselves to him, as I trained him at Sandhurst many years before and he would recognise me.

As I approached him I muttered, "Good afternoon Sir" and straight away he replied, "Who the hell let you in?" We had a brief laugh and caught up with our news since leaving the British Army. It was a most memorable day for both of us and is still treasured today.

Shortly after this invitation, I had to perform some External Examining at both Leeds University and Manchester University for their degree/diploma courses in Sport, Physical Education and Teacher Training. I found this `work` stimulating and it provided me with the opportunity to meet some very talented students, including the hard working and dedicated staff.

I was also privileged to be asked by Professor Ted Wragg, Head of the Education Department at Exeter University to be the External Examiner to Neil Armstrong`s PhD submission and who subsequently, went on to become a Professor himself and the Director of 'The Children`s Health and Exercise Centre'. Neil was also a former President of the Physical Education Association of the UK and had played soccer as a part-time professional in his youth and was a former student colleague with me at Loughborough College and at the University.

Professor Wragg, a most ardent Sheffield Wednesday supporter who was born in Sheffield, was an outstanding educationalist who was a regular columnist in The Times Educational Supplement and to the Guardian Newspaper.

Due to the success of our research into Injuries and Different Playing Surfaces, an opportunity arose for me to act as a consultant to Balsam (UK) Limited under the direction of its Managing Director Roger Orton based in Melton Mowbray. I was able to offer a range of services to include design specification, injury prevention, sports technical markings and in visiting athletics tracks in the UK with progressive feedback to the Board of Directors.

One really eventful happening took place in Sheffield`s Town Hall where David Blunkett (the blind senior politician and now Lord Blunkett) was the Leader of the Sheffield City Council known at that time as *The Socialist Republic of South Yorkshire* by many Sheffield people, particularly from those living in the south west of the city.

I attended a meeting at the City Town Hall on behalf of the University as its representative because the main agenda was related to recreational facilities for Sheffield leading to the 1990`s and beyond. Somehow, I was asked to speak and during my answer, I used the word discipline. I was immediately informed by

David Blunkett that discipline was not a word spoken in these chambers and that I was not in the Army now. To put it mildly, I was not happy about this outburst by the leader, but I `bit my tongue` and stayed calm.

Years later when he was the Home Secretary, he was prepared to confront the Police about the changes to the Police Officers pay and conditions and reported to say that they needed some discipline! He stated on another occasion that school children in Sheffield lacked discipline. What a `U` turn! From that day onwards, I lost complete faith in most politicians.

During August, I had to travel to London by train for a meeting and at Leicester station a very large man asked if he could sit next to me. He must have bought all the various newspapers available and kindly asked if I wanted to read any special paper. I then recognised him to be Patrick Moore and was surprised how big he was both in height and weight. Soon the very kind man offered to buy me a coffee and we proceeded to talk on any subject that he brought up and by all accounts, he liked cricket and golf. He was a celebrated astronomer and author of over 60 books and furthermore, a self taught pianist and xylophone player.

Apparently, he liked to play jokes and the one that made me laugh was is that on an April Fools` Day spoof on BBC Radio 2, when Patrick Moore announced a once in a lifetime astronomical event that meant that if any listeners could jump at the exact moment, 9.47am, they would experience a temporary sensation of weightlessness. There were numerous phone calls made to the BBC stating that they indeed experienced the sensation!

Around 2004, I did meet Patrick Moore again at the Lyceum Theatre in Sheffield when he was conducting a `one man show` on his favourite subject Astronomy. I bought his book, asked him to sign it and mentioned that we had met up years ago and had been kind to buy me a coffee and read one of his papers. He replied, "I have never met you in my life" and gave a broad smile and a firm wave as he went back for the second half of his presentation.

John Padley sent me to California, USA in October to attract students to come to Sheffield on a Junior Year Abroad Scheme. I said to John at the time, "Leaving California to come to Sheffield will not be an option for the students. Anyhow, we don`t have wonderful sports facilities to attract them!" John replied, "Bill use your persuasive powers, they will listen to you as an Olympian". So reluctantly, I left his room and told Angela that I was off to the States to recruit students on an exchange scheme.

I landed in Los Angeles and made my way to the already booked hotel for the restful weekend before attending several recruitment fairs. On 16 October 1987, I was informed that Great Britain had been `severely damaged` by hurricane winds and had caused many casualties. I immediately phoned Angela to enquire if all was well and luckily she, the girls and the house were fine. Apparently, the

BBC`s weatherman Michael Fish stated that the hurricane was a false alarm and everything would be okay thereby celebrating a classic gaffe!

My hired car to go to the University California Los Angeles (UCLA) campus was a nightmare as there were so many lanes to travel in and no SatNav help. Anyhow, after much travelling I just made the first Student Recruitment Fair and met up with another lecturer Richard Hales from Leicester University, who was also pleased to see me as he too was on a similar assignment albeit learning English at a British University and not in any way connected with sport.

We then travelled to Long Beach, California and stayed two nights giving us the opportunity to see the majestic Queen Mary docked now as a hotel with a variety of restaurants, nightlife and special events on board. It is also purported to be *haunted* and there are many activities on board centred on ghostly themes. With regards to student recruitment, I managed to get several `most interested`, so this venue was uplifting to say the least.

After this, we drove the 112 miles to San Diego which was a most pleasing place to visit. Many of the housing had a Mexican influence, there were countless parks and gardens and some of the best beaches I had seen. The city also hosts the largest naval fleet in the world and I was in awe of seeing the largest aircraft carrier USS Midway which can have a crew of 4,500 personnel on deck. One word summed it for me `Awesome`.

Our meeting place was San Diego State University where I met up with Ed King who was an Associate Professor in the Department of Physical Education and an ex-pat. After the recruitment business had finished, Ed took me on a most scenic drive from San Diego to La Jolla, hugging the Pacific coast and seeing stunning coastal views and seaside villages. No wonder Ed made this place his permanent home!

I then left my Leicester University companion Richard to fly to San Francisco to attend a very large student Recruitment Fair. San Francisco had a lot to offer the visitor and as I had a day off university business, I decided to see and do as much as I could. My first call was to see Golden Gate Bridge which was used widely in the TV drama Streets of San Francisco (1972-1977) starring Karl Malden in the leading role and a young Michael Douglas as an inspector, who were trying to solve crimes in the city.

Then I was off to Chinatown, travelled on the tram and drove down the famous crooked Lombard Street. The highlight was to get the ferry to the former Alcatraz Federal Penitentiary, some 2km from San Francisco. This small island was developed with facilities for a lighthouse, a military fortification, a military prison and a federal prison from 1937 until 1963.

It has had some of America's most difficult and dangerous criminals sentenced there to include for example, Al 'Scarface' Capone, Robert 'birdman' Stroud, George 'Machine Gun' Kelly and Alvin 'Creepy Karpis' Karpowicz who was listed as *Public Enemy No 1* by the FBI in the 1930's. Apparently, not one inmate has ever successfully escaped from 'The Rock' as its prison is nicknamed.

Each prisoner had his own cell at Alcatraz and had only four rights namely food, clothing, shelter and medical care. Everything else was a privilege and had to be earned. To visit this 'scary' place was a total experience right from leaving the mainland by ferry and listening to the stories by both the inmates and custodians. One of the best films made about this place was *Escape from Alcatraz* (1979) based on a book by J. Campbell Bruce and starred Clint Eastwood playing the part of inmate Frank Morris and Patrick McGoohan (famed for his roles in Danger Man and The Prisoner) as the tough warden. It's a most gripping film. Today, some one million tourists visit Alcatraz each year.

Late afternoon I met Richard at the Ferry terminal as previously arranged and we continued to view the harbour for an hour when two police officers stopped us and asked to 'pay a fine' for looking at the local women. We were mystified and I refused to pay any dollars to the police officers, so they said, "You will be reported and subsequently sent home to the UK in disgrace".

Richard paid the $5 dollar fine so as not to cause any problems. Only later on in our hotel, were we told that there were a number of so called police officers who were charity collecting! It could only happen in San Francisco but in reality we did look at the girls albeit briefly.

After this experience both good and bad, we reported for 'duty' and worked tirelessly to recruit Californian students to attend both Sheffield and Leicester Universities. Richard and I departed and both made our separate long journeys home, with me flying for the last time viewing the Golden Gate Bridge of San Francisco.

Incidentally, ten students were recruited to attend Sheffield University so both I and the Institution thought the whole 'exercise' to be most successful and worthwhile.

The next major event for me happened in 1989 when I was awarded a prestigious Winston Churchill Fellowship, which to me and my family was an honour to receive, as more than 2,000 people applied for the Fellowship for the 108 Fellowships awarded in eleven areas of study, mine being in the Sports Science category.

Goodwin Athletics Centre showing the swimming pool and multi-gym facilities (Sheffield University)

15.   WINSTON CHURCHILL FELLOWSHIP 1989 - 1990

One of the ideals most firmly expressed by Sir Winston Churchill was that men and women from all walks of life should be able to travel overseas and learn about life, work and people from other countries. In this way, as a result of personal experience gained during their travels, they would make a more effective and valuable contribution to the life of this country and of their particular community. Those who are selected travel to all corners of the world as representatives of this country and in the name of Sir Winston Churchill.

In my opinion – Britain's greatest leader Sir Winston Churchill (WCMT)

With the recent announcement that Sheffield would host the 1991 World Student Games, an opportunity had arisen to develop an integrated programme of science in sport aimed at coaches, trainers, doctors, therapists and the practitioners of sport. There was a genuine need at the time for more contact between coaches and doctors at the highest level, in an attempt to understand better the injuries and illnesses which often had beleaguered our top stars. Although many of our top coaches had a great deal of experience in knowing how much work an athlete could endure, this should be complemented by the expertise from the medical profession.

By visiting both the USA and Australia, programmes could be observed and experienced which would strengthen the programmes being offered here at Sheffield and in the UK. Discussions and contacts with internationally renowned sports scientists would also foster a basis for long term international links between these countries and their centres. More importantly, with the growth in the Science in Sport, the information gained from such a travelling fellowship would give a more synthetic approach to presenting the Science, Medical and theoretical side for rapid absorption into practical coaching. It would undoubtedly go a long way towards bridging the gap between the various areas of performance support.

The project would be undertaken in two parts—USA in September 1989 and Australia in March 1990 with my findings and recommendations submitted to both 'The Winston Churchill Memorial Trust' and to 'The Minister for Sport'. Hopefully the report would be sent by the end of April in 1990, so as to receive my Churchill Medallion which would be presented by Her Majesty the Queen at the Guildhall on Friday 11 May 1990.

PART 1 - USA (SEPTEMBER 1989)

My first visit to the USA was to The University of Texas in Austin, meeting the internationally renowned Exercise Physiologist, Professor Jack Wilmore to gather information on the `Performance Team Concept for Elite women athletes`. This visit was extremely informative and interesting in that the University had a team of sports performance experts helping athletes to succeed, such as biomechanical analysts, physicians, an allergy and immunology doctor, psychologists, an anthropologist, nutritionist, pharmacology support, dentists, physiotherapists, strength training and conditioning including an obstetrics and gynaecologist! This team directory was exactly what I wanted to find because in 1989 no such programme existed in Britain let alone a University. Furthermore, the sports facilities were good enough to cater for Olympic standard athletes.

Jack was a quiet, studious man and thought before answering any questions in a most logical way. At home, he had a study room full of books, journals and certificates displayed all around his very large study. Apparently when he worked at home, no one was allowed to enter this study, so who needs a shed in retirement!

After leaving a very hot Austin, the next visitation was at Tempe, University of Arizona to see Professor Daniel Landers and his research team in the Exercise and Sports Research Institute which included a charismatic Dr James Skinner who was a health and exercise expert. We looked at the team concept for Archery given that on the staff was Rick Mckinney, the 1983 World champion. Much of the discussions focussed on various factors that might influence archery performance and the interface between the human performer and the equipment. It was important and a requirement, that archers, coaches and researchers worked and co-operated together to achieve a complete understanding of archery as possible. This contributed to the success of the USA Archery team during this period.

I was really looking forward in going to Colorado Springs, which was the home of The USA Olympic Training Centre and `shadow` Dr Jay Kearney, who was Head of the Sports Science Division and Sports Physiology Department at the Centre and was a former international rower.

The Colorado Springs complex at the time was home to 17 of the 48 National Governing Bodies and was in its 10th year of operation having moved from New York. It had fantastic sports facilities and backed up by medical staff. Its services were divided between two primary programmes namely, the Sports Medicine Programme and the Sports Science Programme. The Sports Medicine personnel handled overall medical, dental, vision care, drug testing education and nutrition services for elite athletes who trained at the Centre.

The Sports Science staff conducted sports-specific tests on teams training at the Olympic complex which included biomechanics, physiology, psychology and computer technology. They also had on-hand research facilities which included state of the art laboratories to test athletes` performances and training, so again, emphasizing the importance of integrated sports science partnership as the way forward in elite performance on the global stage.

It was interesting to hear from the Olympic Training Centre that Sue Campbell (now Baroness) had been there a week before I had arrived, presenting a paper on coach education. I knew her from my days at Loughborough as she was in her youth, a promising discus thrower and with Lord Coe, are presently, the current leading `lights` of British Sport.

Jay was a most co-operative host who looked after the `Churchill Fellow` extremely well and always invited me as a guest observer to all the technical meetings which all staff had to attend. We did have one day off which was spent driving from Colorado Springs to Cripple Creek, some 50 miles away and famed for the *Gold rush* in the 1890`s. Gold was discovered in 1890 by ranch hand-turned prospector Bob Womack and the district itself is reputed to have produced 35 millionaires. I had no such luck so I bought some `fool`s gold` for $1 dollar.

My next stop was to visit the University of Oregon in Eugene where the Head of the Physical Education and Sports Science department was a certain Mike Ellis, a former British 1960 Olympic Games hammer representative. A larger than life character who` opened all the doors` for me to see the various `sports experts` in his department, all being very cooperative. Again, a wealth of information was gained particularly on `Sports Psychology—injury and how athletes deal with it`. On the completion of my USA fact finding trip, it left me feeling that Britain lagged behind many countries in terms of providing the necessary facilities, sports science and sports medicine support and becoming more professional in its approach, to help our athletes compete on a `level playing field` if it were to compete successfully on the world stage.

Prior to my visit to Eugene to see Mike he had applied a few years back to be the new Head of the Loughborough University`s Department of Physical Education and Sports Science. On being selected he enquired, "Can we discuss the salary?" The Vice–Chancellor received advice and confirmation from the Director of Finance and gave Mike the salary details. Mike then asked, "Is that for the term?" The Vice-Chancellor embarrassingly replied, "No, it is for the year!" Needless to say, Mike turned the position down as his salary in the States was three-fold bigger.

Before we left Eugene, Mike and his lovely wife Margaret took us to see a very small part of the *Oregon Trail,* which dates from around 1843 and still shows some of the tracks and ruts used by the pioneering settlers driving their wagon trails in search of fertile land and a better life in Oregon. Once in Oregon (and California), settlers would start a new life and build farms or set off for the gold mines. Another fascinating look was seeking some of the tracks used by the *Pony Express* who employed riders travelling on horseback delivering mail during the summer and winter. They must have been tough, rugged and most adventurous pioneers.

There was another individual who I saw in connection with *Health Related Fitness* who was Professor Charles (Chuck) Corbin from the School of Nutrition and Health Promotion. He is internationally recognised as an expert in physical education, health and wellness promotion and youth physical fitness.

He stressed the importance of fitness education and fitness assessments within physical education as the way forward in helping schoolchildren and young adults to keep and stay healthy. It also provided us the opportunity to collaborate together and forge international links in Health Related Fitness and Youth Wellness promotion.

PART TWO AUSTRALIA (MARCH 1990)

I left Manchester Airport on a very windy day which did not help my nerves as I am not a calm flyer. I settled in my seat and thought of my first stop at Hong Kong, to stay at the Robert Black College and present a paper to the University where Mike Speak was heading the Physical Education Department. I knew Mike when he was working at the University of Lancaster and he had arranged this conference on Active Lifestyles.

He showed me around the excellent sports facilities that the University had and we visited the famed Kowloon Cricket club which was opened in 1904 and since then developed into one of Hong Kong's finest sports clubs in the world. There were also a number of various bars dotted about the club the most popular of these being the *Main bar* and *Lounge*, to some the heart of Kowloon Cricket Club. Naturally, Mike and I took advantage of this facility and remained here for most of the evening to simply unwind and catch up with our news.

Although not a gambling man we also visited the famous Stanley Market to do some shopping and visited The Royal Hong Kong Jockey Club which is a horse racing operator and Hong Kong's largest community benefactor, operating as a not-for-profit organisation. Membership of the club is 23,000 and to become a member one has to be nominated and elected.

Next stop was Perth, Western Australia to see Dr John Bloomfield and his team at the University to study the 'Effects of Overtraining in Athletes'. Weather on arrival was over 40 degrees and humid but I was happy to be In Australia after such a long flight from Hong Kong.

At the end of my meetings with various members of staff to include the knowledgeable Professor Brian Blanksby, the conclusions reached by all at the time was that the whole concept of overtraining needed serious scientific reappraisal. Differences in symptomatology, objective findings, stages of development, forms of overtraining, all needed further investigation.

However, John Bloomfield was the greatest influence and we thought on the 'same lines' about the future of Sports and the importance of establishing Institutes of Sport. He was a Sports and Human Movement academic and author of several books. In 1973 John was commissioned by the Australian Government to prepare a Sports Plan. His report *The Role, Scope and Development of Recreation in Australia* was based on studies of Sports Institutes in Europe and their success in developing elite athletes. Bloomfield suggested to the Federal government that it should establish a National Institute of Sport similar to those operating in European countries. As such, he played a significant role in the development of the Australian Sports Institute between 1978 and 1989 and was a former chairman of the Institute in 1985. I greatly admired the man who was innovative and effective in the sports world.

So in anticipation, I headed to Canberra and see for myself first-hand the successful Australian Institute of Sport and my guide was Merv Kemp, the throws coach at the Institute.

The Australian Sports Institute in Canberra (Image courtesy of the AIS)

The objective of The Australian Sports Institute (AIS) based in Canberra is to `Promote, Encourage and Develop Opportunities for Australians to Pursue and Achieve Excellence in Sport and Activities associated with Sport`. Its ambitions lay with the elite sportsmen and women in providing them with first class facilities, expert coaching and sports science support that would be the envy of the world.

It offered within its framework of intent the following:

1.   Facilities that were second to none in the world,

2.   The appointment of world ranking coaches with good salaries paid and having access to a budgeted coach development programme,

3.   Having realistic travel budgets that allowed coaches and athletes to travel regularly for domestic and overseas competitions,

4   Scholarships provision for selected students to attend the Institute which covered board and lodgings, an educational allowance, training and transport costs,

5   A permanent, on site sports science and medical back-up centre, with physiologists, biomechanics, doctors and physiotherapists working on a full time basis,

6   A resource centre with world wide access to research and publications on all aspects of coaching knowledge, including video and computer banks,

7   Provision of corporate business marketing programmes to supplement Government funding,

8   Administrative support to deal with everything from finding the right schools/colleges for its students, to booking team flights to competition venues both at home and abroad.

At the time, it offered all of the above support to talented youngsters in the following sports: basketball, gymnastics, netball, soccer, swimming, tennis, weightlifting and athletics. Outstanding graduates include Robert De Castella (athletics), Glenn McGrath and Ricky Ponting (cricket), Mark Viduka (football), Pat Cash and Leyton Hewitt (former Wimbledon tennis champions).

The outstanding coaches have included Bill Sweetenham (swimming), Charlie Walsh (cycling), Marty Clarke (basketball) and Wilma Shakespeare (netball) and backed up by Sports Medicine specialists Dr`s Dick Telford, Peter Fricker and Bruce Mason.

When I turned my thoughts to Britain, I could identify a strong pyramid in most sports. National Governing Sports Bodies had, on the whole, established strong coach development schemes and direction, squads were set up regionally and nationally to bring together talented youngsters.

Perhaps I figured strongly, that if a British Institute of Sport (based on the Australian model) were to be in Sheffield, as the City were to host the World Student Games in 1991 with fantastic new facilities being built, it would have even greater success that the Australian model. Geographically such an Institute would be less isolated and would experience a closer proximity to international competition with all its attendant benefits.

In 1990, if you mentioned a concept like `a university of sport` to a long suffering British athlete you would probably get a reaction of laughter or envy. Those who laughed at the idea of having so many high-profile sports on one university complex, along in conjunction with the top sporting brains, excellent training facilities and the medical back-up second to none, including having a major stadium seemed then, little more than a fantasy in a country where the government was only just starting to view sport as an important political tool. Also, in this change of philosophy that would be required to sanction it, funds from the Treasury would have to be extracted or some form of Lottery be introduced.

There would also be envy as it was common knowledge that elsewhere around the globe, some of the finest athletes the world had seen such as those coming from Eastern Europe, the United States and now Australia, had prepared and carefully tuned their sportsmen and women to `whip` the world.

To me it was time that a British Institute of Sport was set up as it would give British sport such an impetus to perform well against the more `professional` funded nations. Naturally, there would be arguments about its location and disagreements about who was going to fund it. However, if Britain wanted to become a `super sports power` this was the time to invest and plan for future Olympics.

It was interesting to see an injured Jonathon Ridgeon (then 1988 110m Hurdles Olympian) being treated at the Institute as no medical facility existed in the UK at the time. Speaking to him in Canberra about my plans was fully supported by him including other young British hopefuls training at this brilliant sports complex.

Other places visited included Adelaide`s South Australian College of Advanced Education studying the `Clinical implications of children and young adults participation in sports`. Alan Launder a successful throws and pole vault coach from Norfolk, who I knew from my junior days living in Suffolk and now resident in Adelaide, was most helpful in guiding me to see the various specialists at the College.

This visit also gave me the opportunity to visit my uncle Will who emigrated here many years before and worked in the Department for Correctional Services in Adelaide. The Centre was established to give prisoners various programmes to facilitate their gradual release into the community.

In our discussions on sport he mentioned that he had `looked after` a certain Reg Spiers who said that he knew me when we were javelin throwers in 1964 at various London athletics tracks. I indicated that I did meet him briefly when he was trying to qualify for the 1964 Australian Olympic team.

Reg Spiers was a former leading athlete and had finished 5th in the 1962 Commonwealth Games javelin event with a throw of 228ft8in/69.70m. He went to England in 1964 in the hope of achieving the Olympic standard and in addition, competed against John McSorely and John Greasley who at the time were the best javelin throwers in Britain. However, he was unsuccessful in his bid to make the team and at the end of the season was penniless. He wanted to go back to Australia and enlisted the help of John McSorley, who was working part-time at Heathrow airport. John helped him build a man sized wooden box in which Reg then air-freighted himself back to Australia and nearly dehydrated himself on the Mumbia runway. Eventually he made it back to his homeland. Many years later, he was sentenced to death for drug smuggling on the 2 June 1987 and subsequently reprieved on appeal.

On leaving Adelaide I headed to Melbourne to see some of the Sports Scientists and practitioners of sport in the training environment. It was also a good time to go to Melbourne as they were gearing to bid to host the 1996 Olympic Games in the City but unfortunately losing out to Atlanta, USA. My friend Peter Cook the Suffolk hammer thrower who had emigrated to Melbourne, kindly gave me a tour of the sites and surprisingly to Captain Cook's Cottage (no relation to Peter) which was located in the Fitzroy Gardens in Melbourne itself. The cottage was constructed in 1755 in the Great Ayton, North Yorkshire where he lived. Eventually, it was sent to Melbourne, brick by brick and re-erected. Today, it is a popular tourist attraction.

My last Australian city visit was to The Queensland University in Brisbane which provided more information on the successes that could be obtained by working in partnership between athlete, physician, trainer and coach.

On my return to the UK, I made a number of recommendations which included the following:

1. Setting up British Institute of Sport to be based in Sheffield,

2. Sports Medicine in the UK needed to get its act together,

3. A number of Performance Team Co-ordinator posts should be appointed by The Sports Council,

4. There should be a screening and monitoring service performed on a regular basis linked to the medical profession (Sports Medicine) and

5. There should be a National Sports research programme co-ordinated through National research co-ordinators.

Further seminars to include articles, were given to support my intentions in recommending the setting up of a British Institute of Sport in Sheffield to the Annual Conference for The Army Physical Training Corps at Sheffield University (8-11 April 8 1990), Sheffield Chamber of Commerce at the Don Valley Stadium (October 1991), Newspaper articles to include the Sheffield's Star (4 October 1991) and by word of mouth to interested parties throughout 1992.

Let's all get started on the right track!

week in The Star

WHEN Sheffield played host to the World Student Games one man in the crowd looked on with envy.

The magnificent facilities available to young athletes was a great source of pride for Dr Bill Tancred, Director of Physical Education and Recreation at the University of Sheffield.

But Bill was not just looking at the facilities from an academic point of view.

As a former Commonwealth Games discus silver medalist, Bill coveted a place in the spectacle Sheffield had staged before the rest of the world.

With a life-time in sport, Bill has seen athletics tracks and stadia all over the world and he is impressed and proud that Sheffield now has facilities comparable with other countries.

His main concern now that the Games are over is keeping the momentum going by encouraging local people, especially youngsters to use the purpose-built stadia.

By Debbie Smith

But he fears that with the reduction in physical education in schools youngsters will not take advantage of the sports centres and pools which have sprung up throughout South Yorkshire.

Reaped rewards

As someone who has reaped the rewards from sport – despite athletes being very much an amateur event in his competitive days – Bill believes young people ought to be encouraged to take part in more sport.

He has travelled the world, studied in America and has made lifelong friends through his interest in sport.

One vision he has is to set up a national sports institute and have it based in Sheffield.

With the world-class facilities built for the Games, Bill would bring national team coaches to the city and use the medical back up from the city's hospitals to forge a winning team.

He would also like to see sports

scholarships offered to talented young sports people, as they do in America but he appreciates financial constraints have stopped such schemes in the past.

"It's such a shame that these young people have to go and train in America because most of them would prefer to stay at home.

"People like Daley Thompson only go abroad for warm weather training. They do most of their work over here and still become world champions.

Avoided

"We have got the talent but we have got to nurture it from an early age. My father was very dogmatic and made sure I did my training and I'm glad he was that parents go too far and I think that is something which should be avoided.

"Sport has got to be fun and young people have got to enjoy it or there is no point," he said.

With his 50th birthday next year, Bill is determined to keep fit himself, despite back problems from a sporting injury, and still jogs,

works out with weights and swims regularly.

But his interest in sport has not been taken up by any of his three daughters.

"Young people know exercise is good for them but we should make sure they put what they know into practice," he said.

Sport has become big business and sports courses have developed to cater for the change in lifestyle.

Responsible

With sports science and sports management the leisure industry is starting to be taken seriously.

Bill said that, particularly in the 1980s, a lot of 'cowboys' opened up gymnasiums and aerobic classes without any proper training and were responsible for a great number of injuries.

"If this was America there would be all sorts of litigation by people claiming compensation.

"But with the courses now available there is an awareness of training and the need to keep one step ahead," he said. *The Fitness Factor – P4

My recommendation printed in The Sheffield Star on 4 October 1991 to set up a National Institute of Sport to be based in Sheffield (kind permission, The Sheffield Star)

As I mentioned earlier as soon as I received my Winston Churchill Memorial Trust medallion from HM The Queen, I sent copies of the full report to the Winston Churchill Memorial Trust and to The Minister of Sport (Robert Key) under Prime Minister John Major at the time in London.

An acknowledgement was given by the wonderful Director General of The Winston Churchill Memorial Trust Sir Richard Vickers (former Lieutenant – General in the Army), who wrote back a lengthy report and `the need for consistent quality performance demands scientific research into each sport, as well as the physical, mental and psychological selection, preparation, maintenance and rehabilitation of the athlete. It also demands a team approach by athlete, trainer, coach and doctor all of whom must be experts. And on top of it all there should be a National Body, perhaps as you suggest most strongly, a National Institute of Sport`.

On the other hand, not a single word or acknowledgement came back from the Department of Sport which was extremely disappointing to say the least. The Minister for Sport at the time was Robert Key (1992-1993) but Ian Sproat took over this position in 1993 and surprisingly went on a fact finding visit to the Australian Institute of Sport with colleagues from his Department, who on their return, recommended that an Institute of Sport should be set up and based in Sheffield, some 5 years after my recommendation! At least someone in Prime Minister John Major`s Goverment thought it a good idea! Following this, some people received public recognition and even a knighthood in the Minister's Department for implementing such an innovative Sports Institution for elite sportsmen and women in Britain. I lost further respect for these politicians who seem to pick ideas from the public and then say it was their idea in the first place.

The British Institute for Sport was based in Sheffield in 1996 but after a few years was 'split' up to go to other parts of England to accommodate National Governing Bodies of Sport needs and requests, although there is today (2016), the very successful English Institute of Sport based in Sheffield.

16.   WORLD STUDENT GAMES SHEFFIELD 1991

The City of Sheffield with the announcement by the Executive Committee of the Student Body (FISU) that the World Student Games were coming to Sheffield in 1991 was overjoyed. The World Student Games promised to be one of the largest sporting events in the world, hence the initial celebrations.

Members of Sheffield University had been actively involved in many aspects of the Sheffield bid right from the start from consultancy to lobbying with contributions   made at all levels. The University acted quickly through the Registrar and Secretary John Padley, to establish working groups to develop policies and activities in areas such as academic development, student accommodation, commercial sales and marketing, including physical facilities and the environment.

A University World Student Games Directorate Office was to be established in Firth Court, in the Main University Building. The office would be staffed by me as President of the Office, Allan Barnes becoming the Chief Executive and Linda Newbould, the Director of Administration.

I acted as one of the sports and technical consultants to the bid team and was quoted to say,   "This is fantastic news. The Games will be the biggest sporting event since the 1948 Wembley Olympics. The Games will leave Sheffield with the finest facilities in the country and we will be firmly on the map".

1991 University World Student Games Directorate Office at Sheffield University, from left to right, myself as President, Chief Executive Alan Barnes and Director of Administration, Linda Newbould. (Sheffield University)

With the attendance of many of the world`s future leaders in July 1991 at Sheffield could only lead to greater international goodwill and cooperation. In addition, many local students would be involved with the Universiade Festival of Youth. Their task would be to work with universities and colleges throughout the world to bring together a festival of student artistic talent.

The economic development in the City would prove to be tremendous and Sheffield would attract so many visitors and also place the University and Polytechnic on the World student stage. Having one of the largest sports events in the world such as the World Student Games covering such a variety of sporting activities, would obviously involve a massive multi-million pound programme of new building in the City. As such, new purpose built sports facilities included the following:

- A multi-swimming pool complex at Pond Forge in the City Centre, accommodating 2,000 spectators which included an Olympic standard pool.

- A world championship diving pool which would be the only one in the UK at Hillsborough.

- An Events Arena in the newly created East End Park to stage the gymnastic events and the finals of volleyball and basketball.

- Two large volleyball sports halls with one being built close to the Games Village.

- 20 grass tennis courts.

- An international standard Athletics Centre (Don Valley), with an all-weather, eight-lane track and grandstand for 25,000 spectators. (Sadly, this stadium was demolished in May 2014).

However, the World Student Games was not just about sporting activities as they were also the only International Games which included a cultural programme. As such, delegations from all over the world would be bringing cultural teams with them to the City of Sheffield in 1991.

Sheffield famed as the `largest village in England` was in my opinion a great venue to illustrate the `fun aspects of sport` and a celebration of youth involvement.

Having to accommodate so many cultural events, additional building and restoration was taking place in Sheffield. The wonderful Lyceum Theatre in Tudor Square, a beautiful example of old Victorian theatre design, was being restored to its famous past. By doing this restoration work it presented a unique opportunity to create a National Theatre of the North and in addition, with the close proximity to the internationally renowned Crucible Theatre and the renowned Ruskin Galley, be also a catalyst in having something similar as Covent Garden in Tudor Square.

The cost of the Games, unfortunately despite high optimism, was not covered either by the sponsorship or by the television rights, since both the BBC and ITV decided that the Games would only have very limited showing. Bitter rows about the cost to the local council taxpayer (eventually a £10 million deficit plus the annual interest on loans for buildings costing £140 million) formed a backdrop to the event and resulted to be the main item of interest to the eager media. To me and a few other committed `disciples` of youth sport, found these rows disappointing to say the least.

Peter Burns, Chief Executive of World Student Games attempting the seated press!
(Sheffield University)

There were also problems shortly after Peter Burns was appointed as the Chief Executive to `run the World Student Games`, so he resigned his position along with the Finance Director. Eventually, within two years, nearly 55 staff left the Organisation that appeared worse than a World War II bombing raid! It was an utter shambles before the Games had even commenced. I thought Peter to be a wise choice due to the fact that he was charismatic, a genuine sports enthusiast and a team player but politics and sport do not mix.

Even the Opening Ceremony on 14 July 1991 got off to an embarrassing start when the first British astronaut Helen Sharman, who had recently returned from a trip to the Mir space station, dropped the torch and extinguished the flame in the process. In this case it was not Houston but Sheffield who had the problem! Thereafter, the ceremony proceeded wonderfully and was spectacular.

The Games were in my view a complete success in terms of organisation and sports performances which included four gold medals for the British team. Many contacts were made in seeking collaboration work with other universities and credit should be given to the volunteers from the City which included our daughter Andrea who was spellbound by the Event.

Before the Games had commenced, I was involved with the World Student Games Conference Organising Committee which in 1991 in conjunction with the July Games, many academic papers were delivered by University world academics on subjects ranging from sport performance to wellness and health.

To take advantage of these Games, the wonderful sports facilities built and the success of my Winston Churchill Fellowship in recommending that an Institute of Sport be implemented in Sheffield, I proposed with full support from the University's Registrar and Secretary John Padley, to plan the first UK post-graduate Master's degree programme in Sports Management linked with the Management School, including the Master's degree in Sport Coaching linked to the Medical School, again being the first University to have such a sports and sports medicine partnership. After these two post-graduate courses were validated, they proved to be very attractive in terms of applications from around the world and on the MBA (Sports Management programme), many influential students attended to include Sir David Brailsford of British cycling fame.

In conclusion, the Sheffield World Student Games of 1991 provided me with a wonderful opportunity to showcase the benefits of sport and physical activity in the UK simultaneously promoting my small Physical Education Department to the academic world.

17. TANCRED FAMILY HOLIDAYS

As a family, we regularly visited our respective parents. In Bridport where Angela's father was a dairy farmer, the girls had an extremely pleasant time on the farm and in Ipswich at my parent's home, we spent the summer at the seaside. Like most families at the time, we tried to make most of it and see our parents as we both lived far away from them.

Our first family trip abroad in 1985 was to Larnaca in Cyprus which was magical as we spent three weeks swimming, eating delightful food outdoors and visiting tavernas in the evening with our Cypriot friends and their families, which included Mike Elia from our Loughborough College days.

La Pola in Spain in 1986 was the first camping holiday which was also great fun. As a result, all the girls now wanted overseas holidays, so the next few years we travelled to Corfu, Spain (Calella de Parafrugell) which was spent with our former next door neighbours in Loughborough John and Helen Beetham and their three children who were the same age as our girls.

In 1989 we spent 2 glorious weeks in delightful Menorca (Cala en Forcat), including France (Antibes) where I thought of becoming a millionaire after seeing so many expensive yachting boats docked in the harbour! We explored the Antibes' old town and had a trip to Juan-Le-Pins. It brought back memories to me as Peter Sarstedt sang the 1969 number one hit *Where do you go my lovely* and continues *When you go on your summer vacation, you go to Juan-Le-Pins.* This was a great song.

Majorca (C'an Picafort) in 1990, followed in 1991 by a British holiday in Looe, Cornwall which was really a wonderful break after the World Student Games and as a family, we explored the beautiful Cornish and Devon coast by enjoying long distance family walking.

1992 was quite eventful as we visited Rhodes (Ialyssos) as a family for the last time due to a factor that all fathers would understand if they had adult girls. After a few days visiting Lindos where the view from walking up to the acropolis is magnificent, the girls asked to go to Faliraki, famed for its night life which Angela and I had no objections. The next morning, I went on my early morning jog near the coast to see a taxi heading my way with what appeared to be three heads at the back of the car. I stopped, turned round and noticed that only the driver could be seen! I immediately went back to our apartment to check that the girls were safely `tucked up` in bed and on entering their room saw them lying asleep in their respective beds but unfortunately for them, they still had their shoes on! I informed them at breakfast soon after, "It is the last time that I as their father would be paying for their holidays to attend night clubs and coming home at 6am!"

So in future years we did go abroad and the UK but not as a `complete` family and have visited Australia three times, Guernsey, the Isles of Scilly, Crete, Isle of Wight, Zante, Kafalonia, the Canary Islands, Madeira, Croatia, Italy, Santorini, Lefkas, Malta, Ibiza, Turkey, the USA, Tunisia, Hungary, Sardinia, Mykonos, Slovakia, Austria, Portugal, Poland including the Lake District, Scotland, Wales and several English counties.

As a family, the girls were to attend University and marriages were taking place so it was evident, that family holidays together had past but looking back it was most rewarding to have `quality time` together as a family.

MILITARY HISTORY TRIPS

Angela and I have always been interested in military history and have `jumped at the chance` to go on super Leger excursions, accompanied by very knowledgeable military historians who were our guides. Walking the Ypres Salient was our first experience to the haunting battlefields of Flanders where more than 250,000 British soldiers fell during World War I.

Another reason to go on this trip was to visit The Tyne Cot Memorial one of the four memorials to the missing in Belgian Flanders where my Great uncle Arthur Donovan (on my mother`s side.) whose name, who amongst 35,000 other officers and men is displayed in memory of him. He was married to my grandmother Elsie and had he not been killed on Thursday, 1 November 1917, I would not have been born! Elsie later on, married his brother William who was my grandfather.

Next stop was to visit Dunkirk where in May 1940, during the battle of France the 'British Expeditionary Forces' in France aiding the French was cut off by the German advance. Winston Churchill ordered any ship large or small be available to pick up the stranded soldiers and as a result, 338,226 men were rescued in the codenamed 'Operation Dynamo'. The bravery of all those people involved in saving the lives of these trapped soldiers absolutely showed the `bull-dog spirit` and the spirit to keep going when things are against you.

Again, with the help of our historian Dave Warren, we went to the Boulogne Eastern Cemetery to pay our respects to my great uncle Thomas Donovan who was killed on Sunday, 8 November 1914 age 21. It was a very moving experience for me as I was the first member at the time to see his grave.

My Grandmother Elsie with her first husband Arthur, who was my Great Uncle

On the left is The Tyne Cot Memorial to the missing. I am pointing to the name of my Great Uncle Arthur who was killed on 1 November 1917. On the right is the Boulogne Eastern Cemetery. I am above the grave of my Great Uncle Thomas who was killed on 8 November 1914 aged just 21. Ironically, if my Great Uncle Arthur had not been killed I would not have been born as my grandmother went on to marry his younger brother William, who was my grandfather

"If I should die,

think only this of me

That there`s some

Corner of a foreign field

That is forever England ...."

Rupert Brooke, the young soldier poet who wrote those moving lines in 1914, died a year later, a victim of World War I.

World War I battle scene at Ypres in 1917 (kind permission IWM)

Another very moving experience was the visit to the dreadful and frightening Auschwitz concentration and extermination camp in Poland. It was the major site of the 'Nazi Final Solution' to the Jewish question. From 1942 until late 1944, transport trains full of Jews arrived to the camp gas chambers from all over German Occupied Europe. Most were given the pesticide 'Zyklon B'. At least 1.1 million prisoners died in the camp, most of them being Jews. Many of those not killed in the gas chambers died of starvation, forced labour, infectious diseases, individual executions and from dreadful medical experimentations.

The camp staffed over 7,000 German Schutzstaffel (SS) and around 15% of them were later tried for War Crimes. Many of them were executed including the Camp Commandant Rudolf Hoss.

We took another interesting military trip journey across northern Europe, visiting the 'Mohne and Eder dams' in the Ruhr Valley, scene of the famous `Dambuster` raids by the 617 Squadron under Wing Commander Guy Gibson who was awarded a VC for the success of this operation codenamed Operation Chastise. From here, we travelled to 'Colditz' the infamous `bad boys camp` and scene of many ingenious escape bids. Perched above a sleepy town of the same name, 'Colditz' has a varied history, although we concentrated on its use as an internment camp for Allied prisoners during World War II. Interesting that today, it is a hotel for guests to pay to enter yet during the war years, inmates tried to escape from it!

We also stayed in Dresden to uncover the tumultuous history of this great city. As the seat of the Saxon royalty, Dresden became arguably Germany's most beautiful city. During World War II, it suffered almost complete destruction, however, it's has since been painstakingly restored to resemble its former glory.

Leaving Dresden we crossed the border into Poland to visit Zagan, the camp where 'The Great Escape' was planned. This audacious plan for a mass escape in early 1943 by the man who became known as 'Big X', otherwise Squadron Leader Roger Bushell of the RAF. His plan was to dig three tunnels known as Tom, Dick and Harry at the same time, so that 200 could escape and was aimed to give an advantage to the escapee. If one tunnel was discovered by the Germans, it was felt that the Germans would not believe that another two would be in progress.

One of the most surprising aspects of the whole escape plan was how friendly the guards were who co-operated in supplying railway time tables, maps and even a large number of official papers that were used to create forgeries! This did not happen in those black and white films.

Group one of 100 was called the 'serial offenders' and were virtually guaranteed a place and included competent German speakers or had a history of escape attempts plus those who were considered to have put the most graft into the effort in order to escape.

The other 100 in group two, were called 'hard arses' and thought to have little chance of success so they had to draw lots to determine inclusion. Furthermore, they would be required to travel by night as they spoke no German and were equipped with the most basic fake papers and equipment.

From the onset, they were beset with many problems such as falling snow and one of the tunnels coming out short, so just 76 RAF men escaped. However, 73 were captured and on Hitler's orders 50 were shot singly or in pairs, leaving just 3 to make it to Britain. In Zagan, there is a memorial for these very brave men which is very moving to see.

Three other visits included the site where Violette Szabo the British secret agent was captured near Limoges in France and was executed by the Gestapo at Ravensbruck, France during 1945. She was dramatised in the film 'Carve Her Name with Pride' starring the delightful Virginia McKenna and the fine actor Paul Schofield. Today there is a Violette Szabo museum at Wormelow, Herefordshire.

The second one was codenamed Operation Frankton (1942) dramatised with the film 'Cockleshell Heroes' starring Trevor Howard and Jose Ferrer and took place near the site of the raid in France beside the River Gironde leading up to the Bordeaux (in the Bay of Biscay). From the 7 to 12 December 1942 with full size `Cockle` mark 2 and its crew in their low silhouette mode, The Royal Marine boom patrol detachment were dropped off from a submarine and then paddled up the River Gironde Estuary to Bordeaux harbour and set limpet mines against six enemy ships.

They then paddled away quickly and swiftly. As with all operations a plan is only good as when it starts. Of the original ten men launched from the deck of HMS Tuna, two died from hypothermia at sea, six men were captured and executed, but Major Hasler and Marine Sparks escaped to the North of Bordeaux and eventually made their way back to the UK via the Pyrenees and Spain using the `Marie-Claire Escape Line`, which was set up by Mary Liddell.

The third included a visit to Arnhem and the story about the failure of Operation Market Garden during World War II. The operation was intended to allow the Allies to break through the German lines and seize several bridges in occupied Netherlands including the Arnhem Bridge. It ended in disaster and the intended expectations of finishing the war by Christmas 1944 did not materialise. Eighty one soldiers mostly paratroopers died defending the Arnhem Bridge. A film was made of this operation in 1977 called A Bridge Too Far and Directed by Richard Attenborough.

All of this seems ironic to me because both Angela and I had visited the D-Day Normandy Beaches a few years earlier, we were on holiday in Lake Garda when on 6 June 2004, 60 years after the event that will be forever written large in the Annuls of human endeavour and sacrifice, tens of thousands of Allied troops crossed the Channel in a bid to liberate mainland Europe and deliver a final crushing blow to the Nazis (Operation Overload). We were walking high in the hills overlooking the Lake, talking and laughing with a group that included Germans, Italians and British! This fellowship is recommended in today`s uncertain world.

1992 - 1993

After the success of the World Student Games my Department became very busy and although we recruited two additional academic staff, the student intake was so successful that more staff appointments was required. We were promised that in 1993, help would be forthcoming, so patiently we carried on.

The New Year started with me being awarded an MBE in recognition of my services to athletics in the New Years Honours List. It was a great honour and meeting the Queen at Buckingham Palace was a very unreal experience. She said, "I believe you have been given the MBE for your services to athletics and we have met some years earlier. " I said, "Yes, ma`am" but then I don`t know what she said next because I was thinking that the last time we shook hands, I had sticky resin on my hands hence her white gloves! Also at the Investiture were the former Beirut hostages Terry Waite the Church of England envoy, John

McCarthy and Brian Keenan awarded CBE`s including Gary Lineker, the soccer player and now BBC Sports pundit receiving the OBE.

Myself with HRH the Queen after receiving an MBE for services to athletics in March 1992. (BCA Ltd).

Left to right with Joanna, Angela and Andrea at Buckingham Palace (BCA Ltd./Sheffield University)

Anyhow, afterwards we had a small family celebration at a restaurant in London, which was wonderful followed by a show 'Me and My Girl' at the Adelphi Theatre starring Les Dennis.

Brother Geoff and I had another book published by Hodder and Stoughton entitled `Leisure Management` which provided an account of some basic concepts in leisure management and of the professional competencies required by today`s leisure practitioners and this book sold really well.

Further conference papers were presented at Morgantown, West Virginia University, USA and at Grand Forks, North Dakota University on themes relating to Active Lifestyles and Wellness. At Grand Forks, we met up with my old Loughborough College training companion and hammer thrower and now Professor at the University, Jim Whitehead. He took Angela and me to see the very large American bison roaming in the fields. The animal`s temperament is often unpredictable. They usually appear peaceful, unconcerned, even lazy, yet they may attack anything, often without warning or apparent reason. They can also move at speeds up to 35mph and cover long distances. As a result, we did not get too close and in our amusement, had a `bison dung` discus competition to see who could throw them the furthest. Winning this contest gave me enormous pleasure!

Jim with physical education colleagues, took Angela and I wind surfing and to our surprise Angela `picked it up` very quickly and surfed straight across the large lake. We noticed that she was having trouble to turn round, so a group quickly went to her rescue otherwise, I might have lost her or did she plan that? It all ended in a happy and splendid reunion.

Soon after returning to the UK, we headed to Australia with my sister Maureen and her husband Bill and firstly, stopped at Bangkok, the capital of Thailand for two nights in a comfortable hotel. Bangkok had some wonderful temples, palaces and busy market places to visit. All of us loved the Tuk Tuk, which proved to be the best way to explore the capital by whizzing around the streets in one of these iconic three wheeled vehicles. We also bought ourselves a watch each and even today, it still works—what a bargain!

Next stop was Hong Kong again for two nights at the Robert Black College. Bill my brother in law had never been to Hong Kong and had heard that good suits could be made within 24 hours and made to measure. Eager to get one made, he thought two would last him several years, so off he went to get measured up and looked forward to the next day to collect them. On collection, we returned to the College so that he could try them on and `model for us`. Well without laughing out loud, he looked like Groucho Marx, the American comedian and film star who had a distinctive appearance with an overgrown suit. Well Bill was even funnier because the suit was big enough for a 6ft 10in giant and certainly not for his stature of 5ft 10in. Bill was looking at us without a smile! He got the point later on and said when we return to Britain, he would see a tailor to re-measure him. The two suits were not cheap in the slightest as the Hong Kong suit makers had `cottoned on` to the tourist market.

From here, we travelled to Adelaide and a presentation was made at the Adelaide College of Advanced Education and then a sight-seeing excursion to the cricket ground at the Adelaide Oval, which was amazing to see. We set off to Cairns to see one of the `wonders of the world`, the *Great Barrier Reef* which contains an abundance of marine life and many species of tropical fish. Australia is most fortunate to have such a breathtaking beauty of the world's largest coral reef. We were not disappointed and felt very thrilled to have experienced this trip.

Furthermore, we hired a car for the day and I was asked my surname by the car hire agent and replied it was Tancred. "Are you any relation to the meat baron?" I said, "No, where does he live, so I can see if there is a family connection". " He's somewhere in Queensland mate". I thanked him and off we went to explore the vicinity and before long stopped sharply at some mango trees, where the fruits had fallen down. We helped ourselves by eating a number and packed several more in the car for future eating. The mangoes were delicious to say the least.

When we returned the car, the rental car agent said he had further information on the meat baron Tancred. Henry Tancred who stood over 6 feet and weighed 15 stone was an international rugby player and an entrepreneurial businessman in both wholesaling and exporting meat and with his brothers, built the Tancred industries to become one of Australia's largest wholesale butchering firms. He loved horse racing and after his death in 1961, the Tancred Cup is an annual racing event in Sydney. Very interesting to all the British Tancred's but he sadly was no relation!

We departed and set off to Singapore, where I had a coaching commitment for the IAAF and after two days, Angela, Bill and Maureen left to go to Britain. I followed them after two weeks coaching.

It was also a time that after nearly 13 years as Director of Physical Education and Recreation at the University of Sheffield, I felt I had achieved all that was possible and needed a 'fresh' challenge and in March 1993, a post which attracted me came to be advertised and as a result, an application was sent, an interview followed and subsequently, I was appointed as Principal Lecturer at Buckinghamshire Chiltern University College.

18. BUCKINGHAMSHIRE CHILTERN UNIVERSITY COLLEGE 1993 - 2001

Angela and I made the decision to stay in Sheffield as the children were settled preparing for their studies to enable them to attend a University of their choice. I was to commute by train to High Wycombe in Buckinghamshire, famous for furniture manufacturing in particular the 'Windsor chairs'.

My accommodation initially was at a guest house near the railway station and the Mason Arms pub. This `arrangement` suited me for a few months and it was strange to be living on my own in a small room compared to my own detached home in Sheffield. The Landlord and Landlady were a strange mix of personalities, he being `shifty looking` and she rather `flirty` to all the men.

On one occasion, a rather well–spoken and `dapper dressed` second hand car salesman type arrived for a week and after seeing him for breakfast, I knew trouble was `afoot`. Returning to my lodgings on the Sunday night, I was informed by both the Landlord and Landlady that the `car salesman` had left without paying the bill and furthermore, taken all the blankets, pillows, TV, and kettle with him.

Then, some three weeks later, I was confronted by the weeping landlord who muttered, "She has bloody well run off with that smooth talking salesman". I did not know whether to laugh or cry but told him, "These things do happen occasionally"!

At the University College, I took on the role of Principal Lecturer responsible for both academic studies and research development. So it turned out to be a demanding position, `juggling` with so many balls in the air. Furthermore, it involved many hours of lecturing in areas of Health and Fitness, Sport Management and Sports Coaching.

It soon became apparent that having such a workload was not helping my health so I made an appointment to see the Chief Executive Bryan Mogford, who was a very competent and an engaging leader at the Institution. After a lengthy meeting in which he indicated, "Bill, I thought you were superman!" I replied, "Not at my stage of life Sir." I left his office with the knowledge that some changes would be made to accommodate my work worries.

Soon there were three lecturers promoted to the position of Principal Lecturer, so my responsibility was lessened but I remained `in charge` of guiding the Faculty of Leisure and Tourism course developments and continued in being its Director of Research. It proved that they had taken advantage of me, my energy and considerable experience.

As course leader of the new degree in Leisure and Sport, the Faculty were now making good strides both within the institution and in the community and as a result, some very capable staff being appointed. Furthermore, the Faculty were moving to a bigger site at a former school called Wellesbourne, which was a couple of miles away from the main Campus in High Wycombe. After this successful degree course launch, further courses were developed by my team in conjunction with the sports and leisure industry which enabled the Faculty to be large and attractive for student applications.

An invitation from the International University Sports Federation (F.I.S.U.), plus the Japanese University Board and the Organizing Committee for the World University 1995 Games in Fukuoka arrived for me to present a paper in 24 August 1995.

I was granted leave but the small financial support meant that I had to fly to Japan, sleep, present the paper and fly back to the UK straight away in a space of about 36 hours. So it was a long way to go for this presentation! However, it was successful in that the presentation went well. I travelled very briefly on the `bullet train` during my short leisure break which was an incredible experience. I had a four hour stop on my return home to visit Hong Kong again, especially Aberdeen Harbour and the Stanley market for some retail shopping.

Further academic papers were delivered to the Leisure Studies Association (UK) Conference in September at Brighton, my theme being `Youth Sport: Motivational Approaches for Coaches` and athletics seminars in various Institutions around the country.

The IAAF (1996) also required my services with regards to the `Techniques of Teaching the Throws ` for their Level I coaches and in updating the `Coaching Theory for the Throws` syllabus. All of these technical updates were required by Professor Helmut Diegel, a leading member of the IAAF Council, as a matter of urgency and in his words to me," The show must go on".

A surprising honour bestowed on me and my family (Tancred) by being a Great Grandson of Henry Thomas Cook, was the Freeman of the Borough of Ipswich on the 30 May 1995.

There are a number of prominent people who were granted the Freeman of the Borough of Ipswich, including his Grace the Duke of Grafton, who was presented with his Freeman 21 November 1709, also His Grace the Duke of Marlborough on the same day. In addition, Lord Nelson on the 11 October, 1798, after winning his famous battles and The Most Honourable the Marquis of Wellington, 8th September, 1812 after his victories over the French. So it is a treasured certificate.

Certificate of Admission
as a Freeman
of the Borough of Ipswich

No. _95/2_ Name _Dr William Raymond Tancred, MBE_

Address _59 Sandygate Park, Sandygate, Sheffield, S10 5TZ_

Admitted by virtue of _Birth_

Nature of Claim _Great Grandson of Henry Thomas Cook_

I hereby certify that
the person named herein
was admitted as
Freeman of the
Borough of Ipswich

Signed _AW Grant_
Mayor

Dated _30 May 1995_

Back in High Wycombe, in research there were two of us (Dr Barbara Humberstone and I) who submitted research papers for the 1996 Research Assessment Exercise and after the panel consideration, we obtained a 2 star grade, which enabled us to get some funding from the Government to conduct research activities. This was a great result which established a research culture from scratch to one which has a substantial research profile today at the University.

Due to the success of the new Faculty, I was promoted to Professor of Sports Studies fulfilling an ambition especially after failing my 11 plus all those years ago. Having such a title, gave some status not only to myself but to the whole sports team.

I was very fortunate to meet two outstanding young men at High Wycombe. John Harris, my first successful PhD (Doctorate) student, wrote eloquently and was `bright as a button`. He went on to teach at Kent State University in the USA and is currently a Reader at Glasgow Caledonian University. Author of books, he also served on the editorial board of the Journal of Sport and Tourism. The only downside is that he is a passionate supporter of Welsh rugby!

The other talented man was Tim Snaith who was a popular lecturer on campus and went on to gain his doctorate and is currently, Chief Research Officer for OnePoint Global Ltd. He also happened to be my landlord for a time and was good fun to be with. However, there was one near fatal event in his terraced house. At the time, a `criminal` was renting the place to the left of his property, who had parked his lorry opposite Tim`s house.

We had both been away for the weekend, me to Sheffield to see my family and Tim to see some friends away from High Wycombe. On returning, we found the lorry burnt leaving just the chassis and Tim`s terraced house partly burnt that it would need some rebuilding. Luckily, someone had phoned the Fire Service and Police otherwise the property would have been completely destroyed.

It appeared to the Police that someone had a grudge with the `criminal` who was involved with drugs and wanted to `give him a lesson` and thought he was living in Tim`s property because the lorry was parked opposite Tim`s front door! We laugh about it now but it could have been a different story had we both slept there that fateful night!

Soon after this incident, I found another place to stay, close to the railway station, with another lecturer Nigel North, a former Cambridge University graduate and a member of the CAMRA club (campaign for real Ale) and a passionate theatre attendee. He could tell you what real ale drinks were available in the country, as he had visited virtually all pubs that were advertised in the CAMRA large booklet. He was also very fond of Belgian beer which included amber ales, golden ales, Flemish red, Lambic beer and champagne, most of them brought back to his house from his many frequent trips to Brussels.

After lecturing, he could not be seen on the campus because he was either off to Brussels by Eurostar or the Chiltern train, to be at the *Shakespear`s Globe* in London or the Royal Shakespeare Theatre in Stratford upon Avon to see various theatre productions. He was particularly fond of the Globe and would mention that it stood only a few hundred yards from the original site. The rebuilding of the iconic building stemmed from the founding of the Shakespeare Globe Trust by the pioneering American actor and director Sam Wanamaker.

I was still supporting Sheffield United but due to working in High Wycombe, I could not attend Tuesday fixtures but in 1997 the team did well and reached the Championship Play-Off Finals at Wembley against Crystal Palace. Now under manager Howard Kendall who had also managed Everton F.C. in the 1980`s, the greatest era of success in the team`s history finishing the close neighbour Liverpool F.C. stronghold exerted on the domestic game for ten years. All Blades supporters thought they were going to win it this time. It was a hot afternoon and just as full time loomed, the team were on top so if it reached extra time, then we would be favoured. However, a mistake by a defender let Crystal Palace score in injury time and that was the end of the dream followed by a lonely, depressive journey up the motorway to Sheffield. No sooner after this defeat, Kendall left the club.

A further sadder day took place when my father died in February 1998 at the age of 81 and by all accounts he was not well for a period, as he suffered from a few health problems such as diabetes and cancer. He had had a good life and was indeed an inspiration to me. My lasting memory of him some weeks earlier on meeting him was for him to say he was changing his surname to Mustafa and was wearing a Taliban hat in the process! I asked him why and he replied quite forcibly, "I will be better looked after in this country by having that surname, so I am sorry to disappoint you!" He had a point.

In 1999, I was feeling very tired, thirsty, losing weight and had no energy left to keep fit so something was obviously wrong. I made an appointment to see Doctor Taylor at the local surgery in Sheffield and exercised before the appointment. He gave me a urine test which indicated no diabetes, so we both assumed it was stress at work and the commuting which was taking its toll on my health and well-being. At Christmas, my girls thought I had lost too much weight and prescribed their own medicine—Mars bars, Quality sweets and slices of my favourite Christmas cake to put on weight! This certainly was not the answer, so another appointment in the New Year 2000 was made to have a blood test for blood glucose control (HbAlc) by the excellent and most professional Dr David Savage.

An HbAlc test (also known as glycated haemoglobin or Alc) gives you a picture of your average blood glucose control for the past 2 to 3 months. My average test result showed 28 which far exceeded the norm of 6 (today, an HbAlc level of 6.5% or above, indicates Type 2 diabetes). Commonly, but not always, this is associated with being overweight and obese. I was neither overweight or obese but fit and healthy for my age, so had to `thank` my father and grandfather from my mother`s side for the dreadful condition as it looked to be heredity.

Naturally, I was upset and thought `poor me` for a few weeks and then started to live with it by exercising after every meal and watched what I ate daily. For the past 16 years, one glicazide tablet, healthy eating and exercise has meant that

I have continued to function in a very normal way. So the message to anyone reading this book is that if you have some of the symptoms that I had, please see the doctor as an emergency because failing to do so could have catastrophic consequences for you and your family.

In 2001, many things in my life were changing and with my diabetes, extensive travelling and job disaffection, I decided to take early retirement to work as a Sports Consultant and more importantly, `master` better diabetes control which was now a priority. The year involved a slower paced life, catching up with friends and family and visiting Wales for a spell of walking on the Pembrokeshire Coast.

In December, Angela and I attended a Winston Churchill dinner at the Houses of Parliament, which was delightful and included a guided tour of both the Houses of Parliament and the House of Lords, the `Great heart of British Politics`. It was absolutely fascinating and a fabulous way to finish the year. Our guide provided a most interesting overview on the history of Parliament and told us a story of a young politician who was preparing to give a speech in the House asking Winston Churchill for some advice, "How can I put some fire into my speech?" Winston Churchill replied, "The best thing is to put the speech in the fire!" A great end to what was a most enjoyable visit.

19. WALKING, NATIONAL TRUST AND OTHER INTERESTS

WALKING

One never knows when two people get married, that new interests together start to appear which are lifelong. Angela and I have always enjoyed coastal path walking especially along the coastal paths of Cornwall, Devon and Wales. A Christmas present from Joanna, our youngest daughter, enriched our interests further by giving us membership to the wonderful National Trust many years ago.

Membership of the National Trust gave us free entry to most Stately Homes, including special places in Scotland, Wales, Australia, Canada and New Zealand. There is also free car parking to access glorious countryside and coastal paths.

Today, we can say we have walked nearly all of the Cornish coast and back (because we have to collect our parked car), most of Devon and virtually all the beautiful coastline of Wales. In fact, looking back, we have been lucky to have walked in some of Britain's most beautiful countryside to include the National Parks of England (Dartmoor, Exmoor, Lake District, Yorkshire Dales, South Downs, New Forest and the Peak District). Then there were the National Parks of Wales (Snowdonia and the Brecon Beacons) including the National Parks of Scotland (Lochmond and the Trossocks).

So if you really are into walking as a leisure pursuit, as we are, then there are also the National Trails to walk on (Cleveland Way, Peddar's Way, Pennine Way, the Thames Path, the Ridgeway and the South West Coast Path- all of these have been so rewarding and enjoyable, especially when you finish up for some 'liquid' refreshments or two! We have also completed the Suffolk coast in stages and stopped at the various towns along the way including Southwold, Aldeburgh, Orford and Lowestoft.

My only regret has been my failure to do much of the Wainwright Walk which involved walking coast to coast and is 192 miles. It was devised by Alfred Wainwright and it passes three contrasting national parks, the Lake District, the Yorkshire Dales and the North York Moors. He also recommended that walkers dip their booted feet in the Irish Sea at St. Bees and at the end of the walk, in the North Sea at Robin Hoods Bay. Still, hopefully there is some time left to tackle this long walk done in stages.

We have also been interested in social history so visiting Stately Houses have given us an insight into the experiences of people living in the past and a history of great men and women in bygone years. We have indeed been fortunate and seen many of the National Trust Properties far too many to mention but I would like to share a few with you.

Arlington Court near Barnstable, home to eleven generations of the Chichester family had a collection of antique furniture and an eclectic collection of family memorabilia. Related to the family was the pioneering yachtsman Sir Francis Chichester (1901-1972) who in his Gypsy Moth IV single –handily sailed around the world by the clipper route. Along with brother Geoff we met him at the Loughborough railway station when he was proceeding to give a lecture at the University in the late 60`s. We remarked how small he was and therefore his achievement was more than remarkable.

The Cotehele house near Saltash had some family connection and was of great interest to me and Angela. The Edgcumbes built this rambling granite and state-stoned home high above the River Tamar. At the time of our visit, it was managed by my great uncle from my mother`s side Lt. Colonel Fred Donovan OBE (for services during the 1948/9 Berlin Airlift) and his wife Kay. They `ran it` like a military organisation but the staff enjoyed working for them as they were fair and warm during their Management. My mother and Aunty Joy did stay there for a holiday and enjoyed their company. We missed seeing them because we arrived late at Cotehele and failed to knock on their house door so as not to intrude-a sad missed family opportunity as they passed away shortly afterwards.

Greenway the holiday home near Brixham of the much loved author Agatha Christie was a delight to visit. A family of collectors the house filled with diverse artefacts, archaeology and her murder mystery books. I am a great fan of her film thrillers and theatre productions and it appears that she has many more. It`s amazing that her 'Whodunit' play the Mousetrap has been running for over 60 years making it the world`s longest on record.

Lanhydrock in Bodmin, home to the Victorian Agar-Roberts family has many rooms to see and plenty to discover across the estate. There is a room and suitcase dedicated to their loss of their beloved son Tommy, a reminder of the dreadful World War I, which had a devastating impact on many families at the time, including my mother`s family who lost Arthur and another Tommy.

Nuffield Place near Oxford was the home of William Morris who at one time was the richest man in the world. He was the founder of Morris Motor Cars and one of Britain`s greatest philanthropists and influencers of the 20th Century. This place excited me because our first car was the delightful Morris Minor pre-1955 with the split- windscreen and my placing of` chewing gum` around the windows to prevent the rain coming in!

William Morris was my hall of residence at Loughborough College so it was fitting to go to Red House in Bexleyheath, the home of William Morris, founder of the Arts and Crafts Movement. The building had extraordinary architectural and social significance and was described by Edward Burne-Jones as `the most beautiful place on earth`.

Brought up in East Anglia, Flatford near East Bergholt was an attraction and more so, because it was the home of the very famous painter John Constable whose landscape paintings are known throughout the world, particularly the Dedham Vale of 1802 and the Hay Wain of 1821. Although his paintings are now the most popular and valuable British art, he was never financially successful and surprisingly, did not get elected to the Royal Academy until the age of 52. Furthermore, he sold more paintings in France than in his native country.

Born in India and familiar with the positions of Viceroys, Kedleston Hall near Derby provided an additional insight as it belonged to the Curzon family. Lord Curzon at one time, the Viceroy of India from 1899 -1905 and was an enormously talented and energetic man who worked hard on behalf of British Imperialism. For example, he extended the railways to a great extent making communications that much better. However, he quarrelled endlessly and his arrogance including being inflexible made more enemies. There is an area dedicated to his time as Viceroy with all his regalia.

My father`s interest in photography stemmed from living in India and he pursued this hobby with vigour. So when we visited The Hardman`s House in Liverpool which had just opened, some years ago, they wanted any visitor to tell them why the bath was in the cellar and what was it for? Interestingly, my father used the family bath upstairs in our Ipswich house for his` film developing` apparatus. He would remove the film in complete darkness and place it in the bathtub, full with chemicals and after a period, hang the photographs to dry by using mother`s clothes pegs. No one was ever allowed to go in this room even for having a bath that day or two! I informed them straight away that the bath was for developing photographs in the darkness of the cellar. They were delighted with this information but it brought a few tears to my eyes remembering my father and his passionate hobby.

Chambre Hardman spent 4 years in the Gurkha Rifles in India and found time for photography with his Eastman Kodak No 3 special camera and processed his own rolls of film (as did my father). During this time he met Captain Burrell and they made firm friends with each other and on leaving the Army, established a photography business in Liverpool before `branching` out with his wife.

As someone who has commuted most of his working life then visiting George Stephenson`s Birthplace was a must. The railway pioneer birthplace was a simple cottage with it`s pretty garden and amazing to think that in this small place, the great innovator lived and what an engineering legacy left for the world to use.

Little Joshua and Thomas our grandsons love steam trains and Joshua who often misses certain letters says his favourite train is, "The Iffing Otsman" (Flying Scotsman). On another occasion we saw a very young youth smoking and Joshua remarked, "He is like a steam train with smoke coming from his head!" We try not to laugh in front of him, but we all think it hilarious.

Hadrian's Wall and Housesteads Fort near Hexham is one of the Roman Empire's best maintained outposts in northern Europe and is 100 miles long overlooking breathtaking views when out walking. The fort provides a real insight into the life of a Roman soldier and standing guard would have been miserable due to the cold and wind. Luckily, my infantry soldier's life was easier, although no one likes to perform guard duties.

People come from all over the world to Nostell Priory near Wakefield to see a clock made in 1717 by John Harrison who was born on the estate to a carpenter father. Today he is remembered as the man who came up with the first reliable way of establishing longitude at sea. Sailors in the 18th century travelling east to west had no way of determining where they were with any accuracy and this had terrible consequences. While others looked at the stars for an answer to the longitude problem, Harrison realised the solution lay in creating a timepiece that would provide precise time anywhere in the world. Sailors knew that for every 15 degrees travelled eastward, the local time moves forward one hour. While they could measure local time by observing the sun, they also needed to know the time at a reference point such as Greenwich to calculate longitude and pendulum clocks could not cope with the movement of ships at sea. John Harrison spent most of his life developing special mechanisms designed to overcome these problems.

What was remarkable is that he produced a timekeeper no larger than a pocket watch which when tested, loss only five seconds over six months duration. This was the maritime Chronometer now known as H4 made in 1762. Furthermore, he had to fight for his promised prize of £20,000 by the Board of Longitude and it needed King George III intervention, for it to be paid to him when he was 79 years of age.

We were delighted to see one of his chronometer's in the Clock Museum in London and the others in the Greenwich Observatory.

You might ask why I have mentioned this great inventor in some detail, the reason being is that from my father's side of the family, his mother was a Harrison and by all accounts, John Harrison has been traced back in the family tree as a relative. Sadly, I do not have any of his genes or talents and I am `pretty` useless in any engineering mechanics, so I specialised in throwing things instead!

My last Stately home to be mentioned is not owned by the National Trust but has a story is Burghley House near Stamford. Built by Sir William Cecil, later Baron Burghley was Lord High Treasurer to Queen Elizabeth I between 1558 and 1587 and modelled on the Privy lodgings of Richmond Palace. At this Grand and splendid Stately Home a corridor was devoted for all the sporting memorabilia of the Marquess of Exeter, former 1928 Olympic 400m hurdles gold medallist and a former President of the IAAF (a position that Lord Coe holds today).

At a brief meeting in 1976 between myself, Sir Arthur Gold Chairman of the British Amateur Athletics Board and the Marquess of Exeter, discussing Amateur versus Professional Athletics, the Marquess stated emphatically that professionalism had no place in athletics today! After this brief episode, I informed Sir Arthur, "That response was fine coming from him, after all he lives in a Stately Home and I, in only a mortgaged semi –detached property". Sir Arthur nodded his head and we all went our separate ways. Lord Burghley went down the Amateur trail, Athletics went down the Professional trail and Sir Arthur sat on the fence!

OTHER INTERESTS

There are so many other interests that we have shared together during our 46 years as a married couple going to the Theatre, Viewing Art Galleries and Museums, attending `Pop` Concerts, English Heritage Membership, and going to the Cinema. All of them entertaining and enjoyable to see and attend.

With regards to the English Heritage membership, we have viewed many properties in England and Scotland for many years. Recently we visited Eltham Palace, Edinburgh Castle, Broadsworth Hall and Bolsover Castle. Bolsover Castle was most interesting, because our eldest daughter Nicola is interested in horses so the visit was truly meaningful. Sir William Cavendish used Bolsover as his showpiece party palace in the 17th Century and used horses to put on dazzling and high quality displays in the Riding House. We were thrilled to see the exhibition and this inspired us to go to Austria later on to see the Spanish Riding School performances in Vienna. The amazing acrobatics of the Lipizzan horses and their riders are an absolute must for any equestrians or horse lovers.

Although Angela and I had always enjoyed viewing art and did some amateur water colour painting ourselves, it was only when we visited the Fitzwilliam Museum in Cambridge in December 2009 which was showing an exhibition of three painters that we were `hooked`.

The three painters were Sargent, Sickert and Spencer. Sargent (1856 - 1925) an American based in Europe, was one of the leading portraitists of his day, whose suave society paintings appeared in sharp contrast to the darker social realism of his contemporary, the German–born `London Impressionist` Sickert (1860-1942) and ever further from the naive visions of Spencer`s (1891 - 1959) native Berkshire. Yet the exhibition showed their lives and careers were intersected in a number of ways.

Sickert as a matter of interest painted an informal portrait of Winston Churchill around 1927 and it was Clementine (Winston Churchill's wife) who introduced him to Sickert, who had been a friend of her family for many years. Apparently, the two men got on so well because Churchill's hobby was painting. Churchill was reputed to say that Sickert had given him a new lease of life with regards to painting.

Also, Sickert's sister was Helen Swanwick, a feminist and pacifist active in the Women's Suffrage Movement.

After this 'introduction', there was no holding us back as we then visited a multitude of art galleries for example, the National Portrait, Guildhall Art, Leeds Art, Perth Art, Dulwich Picture, Courtauld, National and abroad, the D'Orsay, Uffizi, Belvedere Palace, Predo Art and the Art Thyssen.

It has been pleasing to see the talents of the great painters such as Picasso, Leonardo da Vinci, Cezanne, Klimt, Rembrant, Monet, Caravaggio, Turner, Goya, Van Gogh, Matisse, Raphael, Rubins, Sisley, Hockney, Sorolla, Vermeer, Seurat, Lowry and the Suffolk painters, Constable and Gainsborough and not forgetting the Pre-Raphaelites.

There have been so many Museums visited but space and time prevents me to list them all. They have all had something of interest to accommodate everyone and as most are 'free' to enter, what better place to go and wander? For example, Fitzwilliam Museum in Cambridge is worthy of a visit as it has a vast art gallery and has various exhibitions and displays in the museum. It also gives a chance for the visitor to see the Cambridge University Colleges including the splendid architecture. If Cambridge is not your University City, there is always it's academic rival Oxford which also has wonderful Colleges buildings and architecture to include the Museum.

The Ashmolean Museum (Oxford) is the oldest museum in the UK and probably, one of the oldest in the world. It also houses the University's extensive collections of Art and antiquities ranging back over 4 millennia. Other fantastically interesting museums that 'spring' to mind are the Churchill War Museum, The Imperial War Museum, Maritime Museum, British Museum, Science Museum and the Victoria and Albert Museum.

The one museum abroad that I would like to share with you is the one in Hong Kong. It has a number of galleries that are informative and well presented to include the natural environment, pre-history Hong Kong, Folk culture, the Dynasties from Han to Qing, the Opium wars, Birth and Early growth of the City, the Japanese occupation, the Modern Metropolis and the return to China. Also, since 1975, the Museum has staged more than 100 special exhibitions which have covered a wide range of topics such as the 150 years postal service in Hong Kong—fascinating!

Sheffield is a great City for its theatre productions and shows, so while living there we took full advantage of the Lyceum Theatre and the Crucible Studio.

We have seen most of the shows including some of the very famous actors and actresses such as Kenneth Branagh, Timothy West, Edward Fox, Prunella Scales, David Suchet to include the lovely Francesca Annis and Raquel Welch, the latter who starred in the production Millionairess by George Bernard Shaw. The critics were not kind to her and the show flopped later on but to all the male audience, she could do no wrong. She was stunning for her age and as far as the men were concerned, could act brilliantly!

Her son Damon Welch married Rebecca Trueman, daughter of Fred Truman the Test cricketer who is acknowledged to have been one of the greatest fast bowlers in Test Cricket. He was nicknamed `Fiery Fred` and was the first bowler to take 300 wickets in a Test career. The marriage between the pair was short-lived as they divorced after two years with Fred declaring, "My Run-Up lasted longer!"

When we were really young the opportunity to attend `Pop` Concerts was limited due in my case to a shortage of cash. However, we have made up for those lost opportunities and seen many of the stars in the City Hall, the Arena and at the former Don Valley, all of these venues in Sheffield. Other venues have included the Regent in Ipswich and in London. It was a great time to be young in the 60`s and what fabulous stars Britain had at the time. So in middle and older age, we have admired the stars and their songs with youthful gusto.

Some of the groups seen are the `ageless` Rolling Stones, The Drifters, Amen Corner, Beach Boys, The Yardbirds, the Hollies, Cliff Richards and the Shadows, Status Quo, Marty Wilde and his Wildcats and not forgetting the fabulous Four Tops. Solo artists seen include Shirley Bassey, Neil Diamond, Cher, Rod Stewart, Paul McCartney, Tom Jones, Joe Brown, Neil Sedaka, Diana Ross, Kylie Minogue, Joe Cocker and Lulu. Every concert attended has been wonderful and music has been an important part of my life.

If asked what were my top twenty pop songs, I think I would have trouble to answer as there were so many good ones. However, to be pressed for an answer, here goes:-

1. I Can`t Help Myself by The Four Tops,

2. Start Me Up by The Rolling Stones,

3. Moody Blues by Elvis Presley,

4. More Than This by Bryan Ferry,

5. Hold Back The Night by The Trammps,

6. Get it On by T. Rex,

7. Great Balls of Fire by Jerry Lee Lewis,

8. It`s The Same Old Song by The Four Tops,

9. What do You Want to Make those Eyes at Me For by Emile Ford and the Checkmates,

10. The Sun Ain`t Going To Shine Anymore by The Walker Brothers,

11. Everybody`s Talkin by Harry Nilsson,

12. Brown Sugar by The Rolling Stones,

13. Saturday Night`s Alright by Elton John,

14. Walk Right Back by the Everly Brothers,

15. A Kind of Magic by Queen,

16. You`re so Good to Me by the Beach Boys,

17. Long Cool Woman in a Black Dress by The Hollies,

18. Stoned Love by The Supremes,

19. Cockney Rebel by Steve Harley,

20. My Way by Frank Sinatra.

I have always been interested in watching films in the cinema or `flicks` as it was known in the 50`s and 60`s, especially the black and white ones. My favourite films as a young man were for example, 'The Cruel Sea' starring Jack Hawkins and Donald Sinden, about World War II adventures of a British Convoy escort ship and its officers. Another film starring Stanley Baker and Sean Connery in the 1957 'Hell Drivers' was tense and exciting at the time which involved a haulage firm where drivers could earn bonuses for speeding along poorly maintained country roads.

Other films often short in time (half hour thrillers), were the excellent Scotland Yard series about crime drama and introduced by the celebrated writer and criminologist Edgar Lustgarten. Murder cases included for example, The Missing Man, The Blazing Caravan, The Silent Witness, Evidence in Concrete and the Last train. They were all based on real- life from the vaults of London`s Metropolitan Police headquarters and were a successful regular feature in cinemas over nearly a decade from the 1950` s onwards.

Many other war films in colour were attractive to me like 'The Bridge on the River Kwai' (1957) directed by David Lean and starred William Holden and Alec Guinness. It was about the construction of the Burma Bridge in 1942-3 by Prisoners- of –War at a Japanese prison camp. 'The Man Who Never Was' (1956) was the true story of the British attempt to trick the enemy into weakening Sicily`s defences before the 1943 attack, using a dead man with faked papers and starred Clifton Webb and Gloria Grahame.

As long as the films were of war stories, crime drama, mystery thrillers then I was a real fan. With Angela, I now tend to go and see period dramas and historical productions and a few well produced war epics. Recently we managed to go to the local cinema and see more films together than we had done in the 30 plus years of living in Sheffield. For example, we saw The Revenant, Joy, Spotlight, Bridge of Spies and Spectre.

There is also the role of playing with our grandchildren which is fun but now we are older, more tiring. Meeting with our own children is very valued along with other family members and friends. It`s a busy life with much still to do such as reading books, especially autobiographies and World War dramas. Looking at all the books that we have accumulated, we will need another life to read them!

20. THE RETIREMENT YEARS 2002 – PRESENT (2016)

2002 - 2004

Retirement certainly gave us time to travel together and we went to Paris on Eurostar, a case of me back on the railways again. This journey through France was more enjoyable and we arrived in Paris with the enthusiasm of young `sweethearts`. We did most of the sights including the Eiffel tower, Notre-Dame, Arch de Triomphe, Moulin Rouge, the illuminations of the Champs-Elysees and a very pleasant river cruise on the Seine.

We also attended several Army Physical Training Corp reunions in Bristol, Blackpool, Scarborough and Bury St. Edmunds. Plenty of talking about `all war wounds` and on how good we were as young men not forgetting the many anecdotal stories and incidents of past Army life. Related to the Army, we visited the excellent Eden Camp near Malton, North Yorkshire. It is one of the largest and most comprehensive museums covering British Military and social history from 1914 onwards. It occupies a former World War II prisoner of war camp of 33 huts.

On the left Tony O'Neill and Dave Bayes in the centre, my old friends from the Army. On the right my Sandhurst Colleague Jim Fox (team member of the 1976 modern pentathlon Olympic champions)

Other visits included many beautiful islands such as Crete, Zante, Sardinia, Scilly Isles, Malta and the Isle of Wight which illustrates our penchant for islands.

It was wonderful to go to Manchester to see part of the 2002 Commonwealth Games especially the discus event. I was impressed by the winner South African Frantz Kruger who threw 217ft 10in/66.39m for a Games record beating the previous best set by my old and now deceased rival Robin Tait of New Zealand. He threw wearing `expensive` looking sun glasses so maybe that`s what I should have done all those years ago in the 1974 Christchurch Games? Bob Weir who had broken my long standing British discus record of 25 years came 3rd with 194ft 3in/59.24m.

It was also pleasing to see many other athletes who competed with me during the 60`s and 70`s such as gold medallists Mary Peters, Lynn Davies and David Hemery. From all accounts, the Games were a complete success and augured well if London bid to host the 2012 Olympic Games. The only downside was the `slow` sprinting of a `streaker` on the track in front of the many spectators including Sophie, the Countess of Wessex!

Dave Otley (javelin), myself and Robbie Brightwell (Olympic Team Captain 1964)

Former athletics champions, left to right Chris Black (hammer), myself (discus), Barry Williams (hammer), Peter Gabbett (decathlon), Paul Dickinson (hammer) and Dave Travis (javelin)

The year ended with the wedding of Joanna to Keith (Palmer) at the end of September. The wedding was a wonderful, enjoyable and memorable event As they say, it`s a chance for all the family and long standing friends to meet up on such an occasion and this wedding was no exception. As father of the bride, I thought Keith was a very lucky man as she looked beautiful.

As father of the bride, you want everything to be well organised and work like clockwork so naturally like all fathers, I wanted to relax as soon as my speech was over. With the dinner over, my opportunity arose and gave my speech which went down very well and I want to share one of my jokes with you all again from that afternoon which had everyone laughing apart from a few old Grannies!

THE GIFT

`The young man wished to purchase a gift for his fiancée`s birthday and wanted to give her a surprise present. After careful consideration, he decided a pair of gloves would strike the right note.

Romantic, but not too personal.

Accompanied by his fiancée`s younger sister, he went into Marks and Spencer and bought a pair of white gloves. The younger sister purchased a pair of panties for herself. During the wrapping, the assistant mixed up the items and the sister got the gloves and the fiancée got the panties. Without checking the contents, he sealed the package and mailed it to his fiancée along with a note:

My lovely darling,

I chose this because I noticed you are not in the habit of wearing any when we go out in the evening. If it had not been for your sister, I would have chosen the long ones with buttons, but she wears short ones that are easy to remove. These are a delicate shade but the lady I bought them from showed me the pair she had been wearing for three weeks and they are hardly even soiled. I had her try on yours for me and she looked very smart. I wish I was there to put them on you for the first time, as no doubt other hands will come in contact with them before I have a chance to see you again. When you take them off, remember to blow in them before putting them away, as they will naturally be a little damp from wearing them. I hope you will wear them for me on Friday night.

All my fondest love xxxx

PS The latest style is to wear them folded down with a little fur showing.'

Father of the Bride – my beautiful youngest daughter Joanna—lucky Keith!

2003 was an interesting and eventful year and started with a holiday in Australia with no coaching and lecturing commitments, so as to fully explore and saviour the beauty and culture that is offered. Hong Kong was the stop over again as I have always enjoyed the colony with its sky- scrapers and peoples` bustling lifestyles. I felt a change this time and items were more expensive and people not as friendly. Of course on the 1 July 1997, the transfer of Sovereignty of Hong Kong from the UK to the People`s Republic of China took place, thereby officially marking the end of Hong Kong`s 156 years under British Colonial governance, so this event might have been a factor when I arrived? Anyhow, it still holds fascination and my memories of my youth flooded back again remembering that

I nearly became an Inspector in the Hong Kong Police in my late teens and not to serve in the British Army.

It was from here that we travelled to Melbourne to see my old friend from Ipswich, Peter (the hammer thrower) and Jane Cook for a few days. They were wonderful hosts and arranged for us to have a number of trips to include the famous scenic Great Ocean Road by bus. Built by nearly 3,000 returning soldiers from World War I between 1919 and 1932 and dedicated to soldiers killed in that conflict. It`s a must for anyone visiting Melbourne. We also walked parts of the River Yarra and saw Flinders Station, Federation Square and the Cricket Ground, which has hosted memorable events such as the Olympic Games, Test cricket and Australian Football.

Peter also took us to Portsea in Victoria and informed us of the disappearance of Prime Minister Harold Holt while swimming at Cheviot beach near Portsea in December 1967. At the time he supposedly had a recurrence of an old shoulder injury, which caused him considerable pain and resulting in taking painkillers, so perhaps he should not have gone swimming. His body was never recovered. As Prime Minister, he was responsible for the relaxation of the *White Australian Policy*. It was the name given to laws that stopped non-Europeans from coming to live in Australia.

Leaving Melbourne was sad because we was saying `goodbye` to two lovely and kind people but it was time to fly to Adelaide and see an unwell Uncle Will who was suffering from cancer and his partner Christine. We took both of them to places of their choice and had a few days together talking of our youth and enjoyed walking the coast albeit not too far. Then it was Cairns to see the Rain forests and the Great Barrier Reef again. We then flew onwards to Sydney, my favourite city.

The first British settlers arrived in 1788 to found Sydney as a Penal colony and now it`s a fantastic destination for thousands of tourists. In fact Graeme Frost who was Angela`s relation by marriage took great pride that his ancestor was one of the first to be sent to Australia on the first Fleet and he has the certificate placed on the wall of his study to show everyone, no shame today but fame!

We saw most of the City landmarks to include the Harbour, Harbour Bridge, the Royal Botanical Gardens, Bondi Beach which was over- rated, the Opera House and The Rocks to include the Sydney Cricket Ground.

The cricket ground is a wonderful venue which has a seen so much history for the cricket enthusiast. For example the great Don Bradman scored the highest ever first-class innings of 452 runs at the Ground for New South Wales against Queensland in 1928. The record was beaten by Hanif Mohammad (Pakistan) who managed 499 runs only for it to be surpassed again, by Brian Lara`s (West Indies) 501 runs in 1994 representing Warwickshire against Durham.

On returning to the UK, it was time to give full support to Sheffield United and they were having a most successful season under manager Neil Warnock. He had enjoyed a long career in football and played for Chesterfield, Scunthorpe, and Barnsley but was in my view, one of the best managers who could get the best out of his team with limited funds. However successful the team were in 2003, it ended in utter disappointment because he led his team to two semi-finals and the play-off finals and lost all three. At the time under Neil Warnock it was a good time to support the team as Bramall Lane at home games, as it had such a fantastic and uplifting atmosphere.

The 2004 season ended in disaster when the club was relegated on one goal difference when David Unsworth, ex-Sheffield United, took the penalty for Wigan and scored. The Blades nearly scored at the end when Danny Webber went clean through, lifted his shot over the goalkeeper, hitting the post and rebounding away to safety. It had been a season full of controversy with the West Ham United player Carlos Tevez playing most of the season while ineligible and Manchester United fielding a weak team with no Ferdinand, no Vidic, no Scholes, no Giggs and no Ronaldo against West Ham in a crucial relegation battle! This gave the Blades a `kick in the teeth` and not fair in many people`s eyes.

This was not the end because after the game against Wigan and with the Blades relegated by the smallest of margins, apparently Sean Bean the avid Blades supporter and Board Director burst into a room where Warnock`s wife and young son were waiting for Neil to return after giving a press statement. Bean started swearing and was reported to have said," Your f...... wanker husband has got us relegated". So much for teamwork and trying to `stick together`, no matter what! Shortly after this episode, Neil Warnock left as Manager of Sheffield United Football Club and hundreds of letters were sent to his office including one from me, to say how sorry to hear that he was leaving and had been a great Manager for the Club. Interesting, since he left, the Club has spiralled downwards and now struggling playing in League I.

Further holidays took place in Crete, Santorini, and visiting the Normandy Beaches to include the Pegasus Bridge which acquired celebrity status due to the D-Day film, produced by Darryl Zanuck, *The Longest Day* in 1961. On June 26th 1944, the Caen Canal Bridge was name changed to Pegasus as a tribute to the British Airborne Forces. Pegasus, the winged horse, was the badge worn on the sleeves of the men of the Airborne Division. The insignia was picked by the author Daphne de Maurier who was the wife of General Sir Frederick Browning, the wartime commander of the British Airborne Division.

2005 - 2010

Like most retired folk, we do not like the winters particularly January and February, so Angela and I headed to Tenerife in January 2005 which has wonderful walking trails up and around Mount Teide and in February, visited the volcanic island of

Lanzarote. Later on during April, it was the delightful island of Malta which has an incredible naval history and famed for its stance in World War II. In fact, on 15 April 1942, King George VI awarded the George Cross which is the highest civilian award for gallantry to the island and its brave people.

The highlight in May (20) 2005 was the arrival of our first grandson Oliver (Palmer) who was an absolute delight but being a grandfather made me feel old for the first time. Still he was fun to be with and seemed a very happy boy which he still is today plus having an engaging personality.

Another military tour this time to see Fortress Europe `Blitzkrieg` and the `V` Weapons in France and Belgium. Our first day began with the attendance of the moving *Last Post Ceremony* at the magnificent Menin Gate in Ypres, Belgium. This was followed in day two examining the huge guns and missiles designed primarily to fire directly across at Britain seeing sites at Sangatte, Cap Blanc Nez, cap Gris Nez, the museum at Todt Battery with its immense railway Gun and the V3 London Cannon site at Mimoyeques.

The V3`s were very special missiles which resembled small rockets. They could be projected at a speed of 1500 metres per second and a rate of 600 per hour, in other words, one every six seconds. Luckily allied bombing made it impossible to ever use the `cannon` from Mimoyecques.

We then went to the massacre site of Wormount to see the site of the mass murder of 80 British and French Prisoners of War in a barn on the 28 May 1940 by the *Waffen-SS* soldiers. They were ordered to throw stick-grenades into the barn killing most of them. Due to the bravery of two non- commissioned officers Moore and Jennings from the Royal Warwicks who jumped on top of the grenades to suppress the force of the blast so as to protect their comrades, all would have been killed. The survivors from the grenades were then led out and shot. Miraculously still alive, Bert Evans who took refuge in a nearby pond survived the massacre. This was a very moving experience for me and everyone else hearing about this terrible and tragic story.

The last interesting trip extended to Ostend where the *Atlantic Wall* Museum summarised the strength of the Fortress Europe. The Atlantic Wall was an extensive system of coastal defence and fortification built by Nazi Germany between 1942 and 1944 along the coast of Europe and Scandinavia as a military defence against any anticipated allied invasion during World War II.

Further holiday destinations abroad in 2006 had walking themes and the beautiful Islands of Madeira and Crete provided these trails in abundance. Maderia had the interesting Levadas open canal systems developed to distribute water from the rainfall heavy and wet regions on the north of the island to the drier south). The Levada walks were through beautiful scenic countryside, filled with laurel forests and if you wanted harder walks, then there were the walks over the peaks, through tunnels and under waterfalls. One favourite walk is the tortuous Pico do Ariero walk which was a hike over a rugged terrain along part of the central mountain chain that runs across the island with the views being truly spectacular.

Crete has so many walks that it is a walker's paradise. Two Gorges which I fondly remember as a walking accomplishment is the Samaria gorge walk which takes between 5 and 7 hours depending on one's fitness and is 16km long albeit downhill, starting at an altitude of 1230m and finishing at Agia Roumeli near the Libyian Sea. There is a narrow passage near the end of the Gorge called 'The Iron Gates' and the walk itself is only opened to the public from May as the weather is more settled. Interestingly, the next morning both Angela and I were so stiff, we could hardly walk as a result of using different leg muscles walking downhill!

Zakros Gorge known as 'The Valley of the Dead' because of the Minoan Cave burials which were found there, is another fantastic walk through a rugged terrain and is challenging.

Other highlights included the island of Mykonos, a River Rhine cruise, Gran Canaria and Halkadiki in Greece. There was of course, walks in beautiful Britain which we really love to do especially when the weather is favourable, such as the North Downs and the Three Shires Head and back walk. This latter route remains within Cheshire throughout but follows the county boundary with Derbyshire and then Staffordshire near the Three Shires Head. Technically, you could stand one foot in Cheshire, the other foot in Derbyshire and a hand in Staffordshire. You don't need to be flexible to do it!

Two further exciting events that took place this year was an invitation to attend another Royal Garden Party at Buckingham Palace on the 20 July 2006 which as far as I can remember was an extremely hot day with gallons of drinking water being ordered to accommodate the thirsty invited guests. As always, I admired the lovely hats and dresses worn by the ladies including my lovely wife Angela.

The other exciting news was the arrival of another grandson on the 18 November Luke (Palmer), who would be a delightful companion to his brother Oliver with his family living in Cheadle near Manchester. He is now a fanatical Manchester City supporter and a talented footballer himself.

Myself and my lovely girls on my 65th birthday - from left to right Joanna, Andrea and Nicola (What a proud father)

The following year I was Inducted into the West Virginia University College of Physical Activity and Sports Sciences Hall of Fame for my contribution to my profession. Apparently, in the thirty year history of the College`s Hall of Fame, I was the first international recipient to have been honoured in such a way. This was a tremendous honour for me especially to be recognised by another major University in the States. The whole ceremony was brilliantly organised and celebrated.

After leaving Morgantown, West Virginia we travelled to Salt Lake City in Utah for a day`s rest and the following day, hired a car to travel through Utah and Arizona to see the world wonder Grand Canyon. We were not disappointed as it had stunning views and is simply magnificent to see. It is 277 miles (446km) long and 18 miles wide (29km) with a depth of over 1 mile (1,857m) and we were in awe in seeing it. Luckily, we also saw a number of broad winged soaring Condors which are the largest flying land birds in the Western hemisphere. This visit should be on every ones `bucket list`.

After the USA induction ceremony and Grand Canyon excursion, we still managed to visit La Palma, Fuerteventura and wonderful Barcelona, the enchanting seaside city with boundless culture, fabled architecture and botanical gardens. We had a wonderful Barcelona city break exploring Gaudi`s architectural genius and Picasso`s art work and museum including seeing the football stadium Camp

Nou which holds a capacity of 110.000 spectators. Also, as mentioned previously I conducted an athletics course in Indonesia on behalf of the IAAF as well, so lots of travelling was entailed.

After all these activities, I decided to implement a number of initiatives to improve the quality of life for young people starting at primary school age in Suffolk. At West Virginia University, a very successful programme called *Choosey Kids* (Standing for Choose Healthy Options Often and Start Young) under Dr. Linda Carson created a fun learning experience for young children to develop good motor skills.

So with that in mind, I proposed to have a `cartoon character` to enable primary school children in Suffolk to engage with it and have fun with exercise and learn about good eating habits. This was published (October 2007) in the Ipswich Evening Star and The East Anglian Daily Times by the excellent Sports reporter Stuart Watson. Some schools adopted the idea with success so I wrote to the Health and Well-being Division under the Department for Children, Schools and Families and yes, no acknowledgements given by this government section.

Later on, I wrote to the Medical Correspondent at The Daily Telegraph who wrote back at the end of February 2008 to quote `I understand the government is looking at a cartoon character much you described`. I thought not again and my trust with government officials was at a very low point at this stage. Eventually, after writing to the Rt Hon Ed Balls MP, I received a letter dated 12 June 2008 from Kevin Brennan MP informing me that both The Department for Children, Schools and Families and the Department for Health had funded the piloting of HENRY (Health, Exercise and Nutrition for the really Young) and includes cartoon characters called The Glugs, who engage pre-school children with messages about healthy eating and exercise. He then went on to thank me for my ongoing commitment in this field. So instead of `Choosey`, it was `Henry`! Yet again someone else picked up my idea and subsequently got the credit for it!

Extract from the East Anglian Daily Times on 29 October 2007 (Archant)

The Government named their project Henry in June 2008 which includes a cartoon character! (The Daily Telegraph)

Another initiative of mine was to use a sports bus, similar to the mobile libraries that serve many communities across the country which would go out to Suffolk's more rural communities and try to engage pre-school children with fun exercise. I emphasised that, 'This bus would be providing help to those that actually need it. It is the socially disadvantaged, those cut off from the facilities in big towns and cities, that need someone to come to them' (December 2007). Eighteen months later, a bus did arrive but no mention of the instigator!

Extract from Ipswich Star on 17 December 2007 (Archant)

Sadly my mother died in a Nursing home in Ipswich (during February 2008) which was her 'home' for 6 years but she was gradually suffering from dementia and as time went on, she did not recognise me, which was upsetting. She was knocked over by a car several years earlier which was detrimental to her health and probably led to slow decline and death.

During May I set off to the United States again to give a few public lectures as a Visiting Professor to both West Virginia University in Morgantown and Kent State University in Kent, Ohio. It was always very pleasing to do this as firstly, I enjoy lecturing young students and secondly, catching up with former friends and colleagues in the Sports and PE profession.

Further ceremony attendance took place at Trinity Park, Ipswich in October 2008 as I was awarded an Honorary Doctorate by University Campus Suffolk (now the University of Suffolk, August 2016) in recognition for my contribution to Sports

Education and Sports Development, so again a very special honour as it was my home town and I started my academic journey at Ipswich Civic College in 1957, all those years ago.

Honorary Doctorate awarded by the University Campus Suffolk in 2008 with my lovely Andrea and Angela (UCS).

I was now getting involved with a number of Sports Bodies and also at the University Campus Suffolk in Ipswich. So in 2008, I was a committee member of The Olympians (a club of former Olympic Sportsmen and Sportswomen), Healthy Ambitions Suffolk (a committee in helping Suffolk being the healthiest by 2028), Felixstowe & District Sports Council, Suffolk AAA, UK Athletics Mentor for Throws, Council member for England Athletics (East) and finally, Chairman of Suffolk Sport (2008-2014).

On top of this, I went back to work part-time at University Campus Suffolk as Professor of Sport under Dr Peter Funnell, who was fully supportive in Sports Development at this new Institution. Later on at this University, I planned and instigated the first ever Sports Scholarship Scheme for talented sports students which was implemented in 2014.

I enjoyed my voluntary role as Chair of Suffolk Sport which is one of 45 County Sports Partnerships across England. Its aim is to make Suffolk a physically active and a successful sporting county. Working at University Campus Suffolk gave me an opportunity to mentor young staff, provide guidance to the young sports students and support the Student Union, all of which I found very satisfying.

It was pleasing for both Angela and I to receive Honorary Bachelor degrees from Loughborough University, which gave us enormous pleasure in seeing past students after 40 years or so. Some looked really well, while sadly with the passing of time some looked slightly older than their years.

We did manage to travel in what has now become a very busy life and stayed in beautiful Sorrento along the Amalfi Coast. Pompeii and Herculaneum were extremely interesting to see and are located in the shadow of Mount Versuvius, which erupted in 79 AD and was buried in volcanic ash and debris. The Isle of Capri was also worth the short boat ride. Dame Gracie Fields, star of both cinema and music hall had a villa on the island.

Originally from Rochdale in Lancashire, she became famous for singing her song *Sally* but never forgot her `roots` even when she moved away to warmer climes and reputed to have helped Rochdale FC in the 1930`s when they were struggling to pay fees and in buying sports equipment.

2010 TO THE PRESENT (2016)

The year 2010 started with my appointment as Director of Sport at University Campus Suffolk which from 1 August 2016 will be known as The University of Suffolk. In addition, I was appointed a Visiting Professor in Sport and Sports Science. I took these roles very seriously and travelled by car from Sheffield to Ipswich every week so as to `develop sport` as I had previously done working at Sheffield University and Buckinghamshire Chilterns University College. With this experience, I soon made my mark and the Sport and Physical Activity profile within the University was raised considerably. I had the support of the Provost and Chief Executive Professor Mike Saks and the Dean of Health, Sciences and Technology Professor Brendon Noble to expand the sports portfolio at the Institution. We managed to offer Sports Scholarship in 2014, improved considerably the students experiences in sports provision and physical activity with good coaching support provided by Suffolk Sport. With student numbers being increased in the sports sciences there was a genuine need for a sports facility as none existed at the time.

With the University hierarchy`s full support I was asked to develop a sports facility adjacent to the main campus on the Ipswich Waterfront to cater for the needs of students, staff and the community. So with much energy and time , I along with Terry McEntee of Suffolk Sport, set about applying to Sport England`s Inspired Facilities Fund for a grant of £100,000 to develop an outdoor multi-purpose sports facility next to the James Hehir building at the University Campus Suffolk. In addition, we had the full support of the Police, Waterfront Businesses, the Residents Association and other interested parties.

Sport England approved the proposal and this facility would also have had the London 2012 Inspire mark, celebrating the link to the Olympic Games. When completed, the facilities would have provided an accessible space for students, staff and the local community to participate in recreational sport and physical activity, as well as becoming a hub for UCS sports clubs and teams.

Terry and I were absolutely delighted to receive this investment on behalf of the University as it would also create a lasting sporting legacy for Ipswich, the University and help towards making Suffolk the most Active County in England.

Even local MP, Ben Gummer said, "This is a great addition to an increasingly busy Waterfront. Now as well as cafes, restaurants, bars and shops, there will be a sports facility. This is a brilliant new asset for the University and for the Town. Well done to UCS and Sport England for their joint contribution to it". (Archant).

Both Terry`s and my excitement to have secured this sum of money to build a multi-sports facility soon evaporated as we learnt (after so many assurances from the important decision makers that everything was well) that planning application was turned down from the appropriate personnel.

Under these circumstances, the £100,000 had to be returned to Sport England and even to this day, no one has told either Terry or I, the truth of the matter and the area in question is still derelict. I was totally dismayed by all of these political webs as no one had the decency to tell the truth.

It`s a shame as so much of my retirement years and time was wasted and importantly, it would have helped Ipswich`s two linked issues of ill-health and deprivation.

A holiday is always good either before a wedding or certainly after one but in our case both! Tunisia, a place that I was not too keen to visit due to my military service in Aden, went better than expected. The hotel was first rate and the weather perfect with the very occasional trip outside and in our case, a visit to the El Djem amphitheatre. It was built by the Romans under proconsul Gordian, who was acclaimed Emperor at Thysdrus around 238AD and was mainly used for gladiator fights and chariot races. There was also an interesting museum nearby showing some Roman ruins and wonderful and colourful Mosiacs.

The hotel ran daily `Strictly Come Dancing` classes and we rapidly improved from being non-dancers to be fairly accomplished. Sadly on our return to the UK we did not practice and all the `nimble footwork` was lost. It`s a big regret to both of us.

It was time for the wedding of middle daughter Andrea and Mark (Fulcher) at Bury St. Edmunds with a three day Reception and stay at the delightful Gawthorpe Hall near Fakenham, Norfolk. After the ceremony in the Registry Office at Bury St. Edmunds the Registrar mistakenly said, "Oliver and Mark are now married," instead of Andrea and Mark! As quick as a flash young Oliver (6 years) their nephew raced to Mark and gave him a kiss and said, "Mark, are we now married?" The Registrar realising her mistake, corrected the names amid laughter from the guests and the happy couple.

The church blessing held the next day with Andrea looking really lovely I thought, `lucky` Fulcher! He promised me before they got married he would be my `best son-in-law`! Today, I am still watchful as he his sadly an ardent Norwich City fan!

At speech time for the father of the bride, one of my jokes to the wedding guests related to the BBQ rules which many of them were planning after this lovely wedding.

`New standard operating procedures have just been announced today so please learn the BBQ RULES as we are about to enter the BBQ season. It is important therefore, to refresh your memory on the etiquette of this sublime outdoor cooking activity.

When a man volunteers to do the BBQ the following chain of events are put into motion:-

The Routine....

1. *The woman buys the food.*

2. *The woman makes the salad, prepares the vegetables, and makes the desserts....*

3. *The woman prepares the meat for cooking, places it on a tray along with the necessary cooking utensils and sauces, and takes it to the man who is lounging beside the grill with a beer in his hand.*

4. *The woman remains outside the compulsory three metre exclusion zone where the exuberance of testosterone and other manly bonding activities can take place without interference of the woman. Here comes the important part:-*

5. *THE MAN PLACES THE MEAT ON THE GRILL.*

    More routine....

6. *The woman goes inside to organise the plates and cutlery.*

7. *The woman comes out to tell the man that the meat is looking great.*

He thanks her and asks if she will bring another beer while he flips the meat.

IMPORTANT AGAIN.

8. *THE MAN TAKES THE MEAT OFF THE GRILL AND HANDS IT TO THE WOMAN.*

More Routine.........

9. *The woman prepares the plates, salad, bread, utensils, napkins, sauces, and brings them to the table.*

10. *After eating, the woman clears the table and does the dishes.....*

11. *Everyone PRAISES the MAN and THANKS HIM for his cooking efforts.*

12. *The man asks the woman how she enjoyed `her night off` and upon seeing her annoyed reaction, concludes that there`s just no pleasing some women`.*

All the family at Mark's and Andrea's wedding, Bury St Edmunds in Suffolk

After this most enjoyable wedding amongst long term friends and guests, we attended the Army Physical Training Corps (now Royal) 150 years of existence celebrations at Aldershot. Formed in 1860 as the Army Gymnastics Staff, the RAPTC is responsible for the physical training and development of the British Army. Well organised as you would expect, a thoroughly enjoyable three days. I am indeed very grateful to have served in this Corps albeit briefly but the training I had from them has been priceless in both my sporting and education career.

It is worth visiting their Museum which has a large archive and photographic collection, including personal documents and historical papers relating to physical training in the British Army.

Angela and myself at Fox Gymnasium, Aldershot (APTC)

After Aldershot it was time to head off to Sardinia, a most sophisticated Italian island with beautiful beaches, turquoise sea and fascinating rock formations. It also has an array of splendid walking trails and `pit stops` for lovely ice creams.

We also managed to visit Bonifacio in Corsica some 12km north of Sardinia by boat. Bonifacio perched on a limestone pedestal is one of the most spectacular towns on the French island. The ancient houses appear to rise seamlessly out of sheer cliffs and just to see this was worth the boat trip. Incidentally, Napoleon was born on the island in 1769 and his ancestral home Maison Bonaparte, is today used as a museum.

A visit to Sicily certainly has as one of its highlights the famous and glorious mosaics in the Cappella and in Monreale Cathedral. Indeed the fact that Roger Tancred (of the French de Hauteville family) conquered Sicily and his son, another Roger, became King Roger I of Sicily in 1130. These historical facts were an obvious draw having the family surname Tancred. Impossible to trace a blood line to myself, but incredibly exciting, to find such famous people with my surname. This instigated our visit and I must say that the mosaics and cathedrals a wonder to behold. King Roger`s grandson Guglielmo I (William) ordered many of the mosaics to be installed in a number of cathedrals including Monreale.

Another interesting fact is that in 1096 another Tancred, again from the de Hauteville family, joined the *First Crusade* as one of the Norman leaders. He was famed for taking Antioch becoming Prince of Galilee and Regent of the Principality of Antioch. The pinnacle of his achievement in the *Crusade* was to be the first Crusader along with Gaston IV of Bearn to enter the city of Jerusalem on 15 July 1099.

I am in awe of King William Tancred and his father King Roger. Amazingly, the works of art are stunning even today nearly 1000 years later!

On our return a fascinating excursion to Bletchley Park in Buckinghamshire to read about the clever and most secretive code breakers of World War II really was inspirational as well. I was impressed by all these very clever men and women whose work helped enormously shortened the war and saved many lives in the process. All their secret work was not known until the 1970`s. Of particular interest was of Alan Turring, the brilliant mathematician who had studied both at Cambridge and Princeton Universities, the later in the States for his Doctorate.

He worked in Hut 8 to try and decipher military codes used by Germany and its allies. The main focus of Turring`s work was to crack the `Enigma Code` which was a type of enciphering machine used by the German forces to send messages securely. Alan Turring and Gordon Welchman invented the Bombe machine which helped to reduce the work of the code breakers.

Alan Turring was awarded an OBE for his war time work but in 1952 was arrested for homosexuality which was illegal then and was found guilty. Instead of prison, he accepted chemical castration but in 1954 committed suicide by taking cyanide. He was given a posthumous Royal Pardon in 2013.

It is not widely known that the `Founder of Computer Science` Alan Turring was also an accomplished runner who finished 5th in the 1947 AAA marathon in Loughborough in his attempt to make the 1948 Olympic Games team in the following year.

The Olympic year of 2012 will not be forgotten as it was a most memorable one. Both Angela and I had a break in glorious Dorset, seeing friends and family including the delights of Portland Bill, Swanage, Stonehenge and Avebury on the way down. Stonehenge, a pre-historic site in Wiltshire and believed to be constructed from 3000 BC to 2000 BC. It could have also been a burial ground as archaeologists have found many cremated bones whilst pursuing their research. Avebury, not too far away, is argued to be the most impressive of all the remaining earthworks in Europe.

Soon after this we changed direction and headed to Scotland to catch it at its best as we were given two weeks of summer weather. We walked around the Isle of Arran and up small parts of Ben Nevis the highest mountain in the British Isles. A few distilleries were visited and we tasted a `few drams` of scotch whiskey notably Johnnie Walker, one of the world`s best-selling products. The next day we were off to Stirling Castle, including the Trossacks both being interesting but the saddest moment was seeing the site of the Lockerbie bombing disaster. On the 21st December 1988 a Pan Am jumbo jet with 259 passengers on board died when a bomb exploded on the plane and also killing 11 people on the ground.

Libyan Abdelbaset al-Megrahi was jailed for life after being guilty of murder in connection with the Lockerbie bombing. Subsequently in 2009, he was released by the Scottish government on compassionate grounds after being diagnosed with prostate cancer.

With the excitement building up for the 2012 London Olympic Games many events were held throughout Suffolk which was pleasant to witness and to be involved. It appeared that everyone supported the Games 100% after some initial doubts from some quarters.

Many towns were involved in the Olympics Torch Relay and in Ipswich, my brothers Geoff and Peter, my sister Maureen plus Angela watched the arrival of the torch on the Waterfront in front of thousands of spectators blessed with glorious sunshine.

The Olympics torch Relay ran from the 19 May until 27 July and although a fantastic showcase for the Olympic Movement sadly I was not selected to carry the torch in my home towns of either Felixstowe or Ipswich, although being former double Olympian. The nearest I got to hold one, was at Bury St Edmunds when I managed to have a picture taken holding it at a Suffolk Schools Athletics Championships.

The Olympic torch at Bury St Edmunds, Suffolk. (T. Bush).

During the excitement of Olympic period Andrea gave birth to her first son on the 20 July and our third grandson named Joshua Tancred Fulcher. He was a lovely looking baby, who looked `cute` in his Olympic tunic in preparation for the impending global sports event! He had fierce competition to be the star of the show as it was `Super Saturday` when great Britain won three gold medals in athletics.

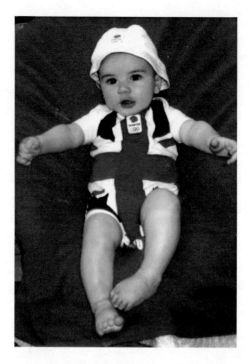

Handsome Joshua already a fan of the Olympics! Come on Team GB!

The Games received widespread acclaim for the organisation, with the volunteers (Games Makers), the Military personnel and the adoring public enthusiastically praising the spectacle very highly. Seb Coe and his team delivered perhaps the most successful Olympic Games on record.

I managed to have Andrea's ticket for the first day at the start of the athletics at the majestic Olympic Park and witness first-hand the excitement from the 80,000 spectators at a qualifying day. In my `old` days in seeing and competing in a qualifying event(s), the crowds would have just been a third of London's attendance. Furthermore, every British athlete was cheered when his or her name was called out which made the `hairs on my back stand rigid`! The atmosphere was really fantastic.

Jessica Ennis from Sheffield set the stadium alight with the first event of the heptathlon, the 100m hurdles with a new British record of 12.54 sec and gaining II95 points in the process. To be back to the Olympics Games held in our own country was exciting for me and thousands of other fanatical supporters. Some of us may not be young any more but the Games made us feel young again. Never before has any sports event so captured the imagination of the British public with such fevered intensity.

On the 4 August as mentioned above, the family met up and watched the Olympic Games from home. It turned out to be the greatest day`s performance by a host country in athletics to win three gold medals by Mo Farah (10,000m in a time of 27mins 30.42 sec), Greg Rutherford (8.31m in the long jump) and Jessica Ennis (6955 points in the Heptathlon). Britain was on a roll and it was a `Super Saturday`.

My 70th birthday 6 August was spent at the Olympic Park watching the athletics with Angela. We watched David Rudisha (Kenya) looking majestic in the 800m who later on, ran a world record of 1min 40.91secs for the gold medal. Lawrence Okoye threw well in the discus qualifying to reach the final which was won by the athletic German Robert Harting with a throw of 224ft 0in/68.27m.

With Nicola my eldest daughter and the generosity of boyfriend Chris Stirland with boxing tickets at the Excel venue, we managed to see a number of finals that included the gold medal performances of Super heavyweight Anthony Joshua and Bantamweight, Luke Campbell. Joshua won his contest by a jury`s decision over the former Olympic champion Cammarelle, as it was so close. I was very fortunate to witness seeing some of the best Gold medal Olympic heavyweight boxers in one place at this venue namely, Lenox Lewis (Canada, 1988), Wladimir Kiltschko (Ukraine, 1996), Audley Harrison (Britain, 2000), Robert Cammarelle (Italy, 2008) and Anthony Joshua (Britain, 2012). Also seen were Amir Khan the lightweight silver medallist when aged just 17 at the 2004 Olympics and Dick McTaggart, the 1960 lightweight gold medallist who retired as an amateur winning 610 out of 634 contests and now an official at these Games. I had not seen McTaggart since his win for Great Britain against the United States at Empire Pool in 1961. This was a wonderful opportunity for me in seeing the boxing greats in one place.

Michael Phelps (Swimming) became the most decorated Olympic athlete of all time winning 22 medals, a phenomenal feat.

Angela and I stayed at the Olympic Park all day and looked at all the other sports facilities including the Aquatics Centre, the Velopark and seeing the unusual designed Arcelor Mittal Orbit. It appeared that everyone was doing the same as it was crowded all day.

Team GB had their preparations for the Games at Loughborough University and was the best prepared and best team supported by The British Olympic delegation in history. Doctors, physiotherapists, nutritionists and coaches made sure that everything was perfect with no stones left unturned, so that they could perform to the best of their abilities. Interestingly, this `partnership` approach, was recommended in my Winston Churchill Integrated Sports Science Partnership to the Government in 1992! It proved to be a good one.

Britain had a most successful Games in winning 19 gold, 17 silver and 19 bronze medals and there is no doubt that without considerable funding, the results would never have reached the level that they did. Funding had allowed many members of Team GB to train full-time, under the guidance of highly qualified coaches, exercise physiologists, nutritionists, psychologists as well as sports medicine support. Furthermore, the benefit of competing on home soil was a huge advantage and incentive.

From 29 August until 9 September 2012, The Paralympics Games were held at the same venue and again, Britain's had considerable success with record crowds, participating nations and a fantastic haul of medals- 34 gold, 43 silver and 43 bronze. Four gold medals each were won by Sarah Storey in the cycling events and David Weir in athletics.

I look back fondly of two people I worked with at Nottingham College of Education who were partly responsible for creating an interest and the necessary motivation in developing disability sport in Britain in the late 70's and early 80's. Had Colin Rains MBE and Fred Abbott been alive today, they would have equally been impressed by the success of these athletes and the Games.

To round off a phenomenal summer of sport, 700 London 2012 Olympic and Paralympic athletes, including nearly all the medal winners, took part in Our Greatest Team Parade on 10 Monday September. Over a million people came out to cheer the team and celebrate the success of Team GB, Paralympics GB and the London 2012 Olympic Games.

After the Olympics it was going to be difficult to emulate the sports excitement in the following year and soon it was off to do other things in 2013 like travelling to Wales and climbing by train to the peak of Snowdonia, the highest mountain in Wales (3,560 ft/1,085m) boasting vast areas of natural beauty and unique scenery. On our decent, we met a number of Pakistani's who wanted to know, "Why are you all walking up a hill?" So we mentioned politely that Snowdonia was a great mountain to walk up and down as it was a challenge with beautiful scenery. "Is it far to walk?" We left them to decide.

The other highlight of the year (November) was the arrival of another grandson Thomas to keep Joshua company, if need be. We would soon have a football team with four grandsons, all new territory for us as we had three daughters. He appears to be good long distance runner as he runs everywhere since the age of two.

Grandsons Luke, Oliver, Joshua and Thomas

Recent addition lovely and very precious Granddaughter Lillia at 1 week old

Other voluntary work included being a Patron for Suffolk SportsAid Foundation which had been very successful leading up to the 2012 London Olympic Games by providing grants to young and up and coming athletes.

In February Angela`s father Jack (Moore) died at the age of 90 and he too like my mother had been in a nursing Home for several years and was not well near the end of his life. What is remarkable is that both Angela and I lost our parents during the month of February!

After 6 years as Chairman of Suffolk Sport, I stood down to concentrate on my voluntary role as Visiting Professor in Sport and Exercise Science which keeps me in touch with degree students in sports science including sports matters. For my contribution to Suffolk Sport I was given a Life –President's role for them, so I still keep in touch with Board members and attend the odd sports functions and events.

As a supporter of Sheffield United you know very well there will be disappointments along the way. Now under Nigel Clough, (Brian's son) the team had a good start under him and in 2014 made headlines again to reach the semi-finals of both the Capital One and FA Cup. Full of anticipation of reaching at least one Final resulted in defeats again, this time to Tottenham Hotspur in the Capital One Semi-Final and on 14 March to Hull in the FA cup semi-final. It appears that a Final is not possible to attain at the club but as they keep saying, "there is always next year."

One family holiday involved Joanna, Keith and grandsons Oliver and Luke to Disney Paris in April. We were fortunate to have fine weather which made the family holiday so much better. From thrill rides to family adventures, there's plenty to explore, all of this an unforgettable experience. We all summed it up by saying it's a magical place not only for the young but also for the old alike. Oliver and Luke loved the photographs with Mickey Mouse but now prefer Lionel Messi, the Barcelona great football star, so with the next grandchildren we hope to do the same before they are too old or in our case, we get older and cannot move.

In September, we decided to move not to a different house in Sheffield but to Felixstowe, Suffolk where I grew up. We had discussed this move for several years but it was a question of Now or Never, as we had been residents in Sheffield for over 30 years. The house sold to the first person viewing it, so we had to quickly search in Felixstowe for a similar property but close to the sea. After some viewing, just as we were giving up, we saw the house we liked and after some upheaval, settled in very quickly. 'The Wheel is come full circle', *I am here* to quote Shakespeare's King Lear Act 5, scene 3, 171-175.

The move to Felixstowe has given me and Angela the opportunity of socialising more with friends such as Mick and Ann (Ware) but also playing with grandsons Joshua and Thomas who live in Norwich but on visits to see us, love to go to the seafront and so far, this has indeed been a treasured contact to see them grow and bond with us. They can be funny and naughty with a `turn of a switch` and by the end of the day entertaining them leaves us exhausted. I remember fondly of speaking to Andrea in Norwich and asked if I could speak to Joshua? Andrea asked him, "Grandad wants to speak to you". To which he replied as a three year old, "Tell him that I am too busy to speak!" Lovely!

Last year (2015) to mark the Winston Churchill Memorial Trust's 50th anniversary, a number of events were organised by the Association of Churchill Fellows. One particular event organised by the East Anglian Association was to visit the Stanford Training Area or STANTA in Norfolk, offering a rare view into the training area established at the outbreak of World War II.

It was a great opportunity to see first- hand what actually lies within the 30,000 acre expanse of land where in the mid-1940's, Villagers were ordered out of their homes (similar to Tyneham in Dorset) when the Army needed a training area as planning began for the invasion of Europe.

There were a number of churches to be seen as well including West Tofts church which was restored in the 1850's by Pugin who was at the time a leading figure in the revival of the Gothic Style replacing Classical Styles of Architecture. It boasts what is reported to be the most impressive Pugin Screen in the UK and is regularly visited by members of the Pugin Society.

The year's highlight was the invitation to Buckingham Palace in March for a selection of Fellows to be introduced to the Queen. Her Majesty The Queen who is patron of The Winston Churchill Memorial Trust and hosted the reception to mark its 50th anniversary of Sir Winston's living legacy.

Since 1965, over 5,000 British citizens have been awarded Churchill Fellowships, from over 100,000 applicants, to travel overseas to study areas of topical and personal interest. The knowledge and innovative ideas they bring back are shared, for the benefit of their profession, their community and in many cases, the nation. For many people, a Churchill Fellowship proves transformational and they go on to achieve great things to make positive changes within society.

In my case, this Fellowship gained in 1989/90, helped me enormously in developing new post graduate degree programmes at Sheffield University in sports management and sports coaching and in the recommendation to the government at the time, to set- up a British Institute of Sport.

A great honour and pleasure to be introduced once again to Her Majesty The Queen who on shaking hands said, "Nice to see you again", which will always be remembered by me for as long as I live. It was also a pleasure to speak a few words to the His Royal Highness The Duke of Edinburgh and HRH Prince Michael of Kent leaving me to have a few minutes conversation to the delightful HRH Princess Michael of Kent. She was really interested in my project and thought sport and physical activity to be extremely important for young people and in healthy aging.

HRH the Queen at a reception for the WCMT Fellows – March 2015 (BCA Ltd)

The last invitation on behalf of The Winston Churchill Memorial Trust was from the Chairman The Rt Hon the Lord Fellowes, who at one time was the Private Secretary to Her Majesty, to have Afternoon Tea in the Cholmondeley Room and Terrace at the House of Lords in June. Many Fellows attended the function and the setting overlooking the River Thames was magical.

Following this we managed to see Florence for a short break which was interesting and enjoyable especially seeing the Ponte Vecchio, the art gallery Uffizi and other tourist sites with an excursion to Siena to view the fine piazza and magnificent cathedral and the `tilting` Pisa. Croatia was another destination and we were based in Porec which turned out well for Angela and I as it had splendid walking trails through pine forests and along the coast. Pula an hour or so away possessed one of the best remaining Roman amphitheatres in the world which today is used for concerts. Some of the performers have included Pavarotti, Tom Jones, Elton John and Sinead O`Connor. It was also interesting and a surprise to meet my brother Geoff and his wife Jane there, so it turned out to be a very special day.

Travelling abroad was not finished as with a quick decision we set of to go to Carcassonne (France) with its most impressive medieval fortress and now a UNESCO World Heritage Site. From here we travelled through the Pyrenees to Collioure which at one time thrived with artistic activity with artists such as Henri Matisse, Pablo Picasso and Charles Rennie Mackintosh being based there. Mackintosh was an accomplished Scottish architect, designer and painter who made his name in Glasgow. He then moved to Walberswick on the coast of Suffolk in 1914 where he was accused of being a German spy due, to his unfamiliar Scottish accent and briefly arrested! In 1923 he moved to Port-Vedres not too far from Collioure. The English novelist Patrick O`Brian also lived in the town.

After leaving Collouire, Narbonne was the next destination to see it`s Cathedral and the first Roman road to be built in Gaul, finishing with a trip on the Canal du Midi which is 240km long and has a great number of locks and bridges. It is an engineering wonder.

Terry Baxter the Chief Executive of the Education and Sports Charity 'Inspire Suffolk' asked me to be one of its Patrons which I gladly accepted and believe passionately that sport and education is a combination for success in young people. 'Inspire Suffolk' is an Independent charity which uses sport to engage, motivate and educate young people in Suffolk.

For the second time in my life (after back surgery in 1979), I have been plagued with both shoulders restricting any movements above shoulder level and having severe chronic pain at night when trying to sleep, resulting initially with pain killers and some physiotherapy treatment. After numerous medical appointments to find out the cause, an MRI scan revealed a `pinched` nerve in the neck which had caused the problem. I am very lucky that no surgery is required and at long last, with exercise and being careful, dramatic improvements have been made, so we can`t blame it all on old age! Most top class sports people suffer some kind of injury in later life due to the severe intensity of their training in their youth. Running or jogging has not been possible for a long time due to the back injury.

So with the health improvement and the diabetes under control, we have managed to have a number of City breaks abroad that have included Oporto, Lisbon, Valencia, Madrid, Vienna, Bratislava and Budapest. The latter was quite nostalgic as memories flooded back to when I had competed against the Hungarians and in the European Championships of 1966. It also a pleasure to visit and taste some delightful port and wine at Sandeman`s House in Oporto. George Sandeman founded the company in 1770 and the famous trademark the `Don`, was painted by George Massiot Brown in 1928. The mysterious Don, in his black cape, wide –brimmed black hat and glass of port in hand was based on the Portuguese student`s black cape and a Spanish Caballero hat. It was also the first wine company to use a logo as part of their branding.

London Olympics 2012 – Angela and myself at the Olympic Stadium (top), with Nicola at the Excel Arena (bottom).

As Angela is the one with `green fingers`, we had an amazing day at the Chelsea Flower Show with my sister Maureen. It was also an opportunity to speak to a number of very smartly dressed Chelsea Pensioners about Army life and their wonderful accommodation at the Royal Hospital Chelsea Home. I did know from an Army source that an ex-Army Physical Training Corps Instructor by the name of Bert Twitchen was now a Chelsea Pensioner and therefore asked them did they know him? One said, "Is he a relation of yours?" I replied, "No, but I met him in Aldershot when I too was in the PT Corps". "That`s good, because he`s a bloody big-head!" We all had a laugh and wished each other all the best.

We are very proud of our daughters Nicola, Andrea and Joanna. Nicola has made a very successful career in accountancy and has held many senior positions in her field. On top of this, she has a tremendous adventurous spirit having also travelled the world, sky and scuba- dived combined with a great sense of humour. She is undoubtedly the career girl of the family.

Andrea is extremely kind and considerate and is a wonderful mother to her children. She is fantastically creative in interior design and there is no doubt in my mind had she pursued this over time, would have been very successful. Before her marriage she worked in Insurance and was my fellow supporter of Sheffield United football club during many seasons at Bramall Lane. She knew more of the off-side trap than some of the men, much to their embarrassment!

Joanna excelled at Manchester University by achieving a first class honours degree despite having ME during her final year. This indicated to me her determination to succeed despite having a serious health problem. She has always worked in marketing and has excelled as a mother to her two boys despite having such a busy life. I have always admired her quick and excellent cooking skills and her sense of humour.

All three daughters have exhibited extraordinary energy and enthusiasm, wonderful work ethics with engaging personalities and looks. To their immense credit they have been fully supportive to us and we are delighted, blessed and honoured to have them as our daughters.

All the girls at my 70th birthday celebration in Loughborough – August 2012

We have become grandparents again when in June (2016) Andrea gave birth to our first lovely granddaughter Lillia, our little princess who has broken the trend of having just grandsons. To have another girl in the family has been just wonderful and we as grandparents are truly blessed.

In July, I along with Angela visited the O2 Arena to see the Muhammad Ali boxing exhibition which showed all his boxing contests and life as a boxing great. Everyone said the visit would take 90 minutes but we stayed for 3 hours taking note of all his achievements and accomplishments during his life. He was the greatest athlete of all time in my eyes. A three time world heavyweight boxing champion who was also known for his public stance against the Vietnam War and his long time battle with Parkinson`s disease. He was also full of eternal optimism. I was very sad to hear of his death in June this year aged 74.

In September, we flew across the Atlantic to visit mesmerising New York, the wonderful Niagara Falls, the sparkling Toronto waterfront, romantic Ottawa, sophisticated Montreal, historic Quebec City overlooking the mighty St. Lawrence river, elegant Boston, Cape Cod and finally, to Newport, Rhode Island. The latter destination is The East Coast`s premier resort town for America`s wealthiest families and for a few days we joined them! This was certainly a trip of a lifetime for both Angela and I. We still love to travel together and see the beautiful parts of the world. There is still so much to do with time running short.

I would like to have the opportunity to acknowledge the wonderful support and encouragement that my lovely wife has given to me for over 46 years towards my sport and education endeavours. Most certainly, without her help many of my dreams and achievements would not have been accomplished. There is the saying that behind every good man there is a good woman. This is very true in my case.

It would go amiss if I did not mention about my brothers and sisters on how they feared in later life. Maureen is still the happy girl from her youth and looks extremely well considering she is now 71 years old. Generous and kind and now a great grandmother herself, she has been a wonderful sister to me. Geoff now 70 years has continued to be interested in all sports and in his youth represented England juniors in the hammer event and also served in the Army Physical Training Corps as a remedial gymnast (physiotherapist branch). Peter 67 years old followed me as an international discus thrower and competed in the 1976 Montreal Olympic Games. He was a former physical education teacher and is now retired. Anita much younger at 54 years of age is now a grandmother and has three children herself. Life seems to go by so swiftly these days. One minute you are young, the next you are old. So you have to make most of it every day while you can!

Myself with my lovely sister Maureen and brothers Geoff and Peter celebrating Maureen's 70th birthday.

We all meet up occasionally and reminisce our days of active athletics and of the places visited and personalities met, some sadly no longer with us. The Tancred's have done well in life through hard work and having exceptional energy even if we did not start on a level playing field in our youth.

All things considered, it has been a wonderful life, there have been lows, as you have read, but there have been fantastic highs as well. An early life in magical India, living on the coast in Felixstowe as a boy, a former regular Army soldier with the Royal Army Physical Training Corps, Loughborough University and West Virginia University graduate, University Professor and an Ordinary Double Olympian but what a life.

Team GB have also come a long way from when I first recommended establishing a British Institute of Sport after seeing the 1991 World Student Games in Sheffield and by visiting the wonderful sports set-ups in both the Australian Institute of Sport and the USA Olympic Training Centre in Colorado.

The Rio 2016 Olympic Games success has been due to 20 years of investment, having great national federations, brilliant technical coaches, fantastic medical/ sports science support and of course, having supreme athletes who desire to be the best. To finish with a medal haul of 27 gold, 23 silvers and 17 bronze is truly magnificent and Britain today is indeed a sporting super power. Roll on Tokyo in 2020!

I hope in some ways that I have been an inspiration and actually encouraged young people to take up sport and be physically active throughout their lives. Everyone needs support and encouragement and if that is given, then with hard work and determination, anything is possible.

For me the two things that have helped me in shaping my life are Sport and Education. Without it, I would not have been the person I am today.

In conclusion, many people walk in and out of your life but only true friends leave footprints in your heart. To you all a very big thank you.

Finally, `There are two ways to live your life. One is as though nothing is a miracle. The other is as though everything is a miracle`. Albert Einstein.